Praise for *Primary Heads*

Bill Laar has spent a lifetime enchanting primary heads their pupils. He weaves magic and here you will find out this energised and with renewed determination for the ye

Sir Tim Brighouse, Visiting Pr[ɔ] ... [ɛ]ducation

This is a timely, well-written account of the challenges and joys of being a primary head teacher during a very challenging time in English education. He has given a voice to a diverse range of heads, who all have a clear belief and a passion about their role.

Bill Laar has always made sure his knowledge is up-to-date and relevant and throughout this book his love of children and those who teach them is evident.

Pat Morrissey, former head teacher,
St George's Catholic Primary School, Harrow

Bill Laar sets out the framework for leadership of primary schools as we see them today and charts the way the role has changed over time. He then tells the story of a series of heads as they describe their passions, philosophies and working practices. He draws out what matters in headship with incisive analysis. The book has that lovely balance between the theoretical, the practical and the persona – just like a good primary school.

Mick Waters, Professor of Education, Wolverhampton University

There are many books on school leadership, but few which speak through the voice of the primary school leaders themselves. In rectifying that gap in the literature, this book provides a most welcome service, deserving a prominent place in every head teacher's study. The highly experienced Bill Laar reproduces the interviews he has had with head teachers of many schools which are recognised for their successes and high quality. The schools represent a wide range in terms of location, intake and religious status, and the questions and their answers address the many problems which head teachers have to face. As the book points out, there is now a dearth of teachers responding to the need for school leadership. This book confronts the reasons why that might be, but also shows how potential but doubting recruits might see how they too might become good 'Primary Heads'.

Professor Richard Pring, University of Oxford

Bill Laar brings his characteristic insights and passions to this highly readable collection of leadership stories. His own significant experiences as head teacher, inspector and leading local authorities underpin his sharp, carefully crafted analysis of what great primary school leaders do for the communities they serve. Each head he has interviewed has a distinctive journey to share, both personally and professionally. There will be few primary heads in the country who will not want to turn and turn again to the wisdom and inspiration in these pages.

Roy Blatchford, Director, National Education Trust

In this veritable Pandora's Box of methods and experiences, one gains insight into modern headship of a calibre never before seen. For intending headship candidates, or indeed anyone contemplating middle management, this is a fountain of knowledge and practical common sense. It must take pride of place in any establishment worthy of its name. Investment in people to provide the wherewithal for a superb educational experience for all children is a paramount requisite. Human resources are the most costly element of any school budget. This highly illuminating book is a beacon of success.

**Cliff Jones, head teacher. Ofsted inspector, School Improvement Partner,
Secretary of South West Primary Heads group**

Primary Heads reveals the secrets of eleven exceptional heads, who together encompass a great breadth of experience and a wide range of primary school contexts. Bill Laar has always been a gifted story-teller: here he writes engagingly about different approaches to headship. All of the vignettes demonstrate the importance of a clear vision and the courage to pursue it in the face of resistance. The heads provide honest descriptions of the difficulties they have confronted and how they overcame them. There are no easy answers here, but this book is an amazing resource for anyone who would like to learn more about what distinguishes outstanding leadership of primary schools.

**Dr Linet Arthur, Senior Lecturer: Educational Leadership and Management,
Oxford Brookes University**

Bill Laar's book, *Primary Heads,* shines a bright light on the real life stories of eleven heads who have had transformational success as primary school leaders. Their stories are mapped against accepted qualities of leadership, revealing how successful heads significantly surpass these qualities. Laar tracks the teachers' journeys, tracing their beliefs back to childhood, revealing ways in which beliefs and early experiences are manifested in practice, and exploring how their practice has changed and transformed others. The stories are inspiring and complex, revealing the struggles and costs as well as the rewards of realising their visions. Examples of extraordinary practice are shared: we see teachers at their very best, functioning at the peak of their skill in spite of constraints, challenges and blocks. The book is an inspiration to any teacher questioning the value of their work, any enquirer wondering what 'success' might look like in a primary school, and how it can be achieved; it is a mantra against the defeatist. Primary heads such as these answer our search for role models: they assure us that, whatever the onslaughts from the outside world, our education is in safe hands and that it is its best leaders and practitioners we should be listening to. This book, from an author with decades of insider experience, gives us the opportunity to do so.

Jane Spiro, Reader in Education and TESOL, National Teaching Fellow,
Oxford Brookes School of Education

In 524 words in his Introduction, augmented by his Overview chapter, Bill Laar describes the essence of what works in education. His long and impressive experience has taught him about the realities of learning beyond the narrow current confines of selective attainment. He reminds us that education is about life and living and at a time of imminent and radical changes in education it is essential we focus on the truths of the processes.

The focus on headship very properly explains and acknowledges the considerable research evidence showing that leadership is central to quality. Individual teachers can display leadership. Many will be good teachers. The effective school is one that recognises such strengths alongside the capacity to improve and the central binding element that shapes real success is leadership. Bill deals with key elements – continuous professional development, succession planning, monitoring and evaluation – very clearly.

Mervyn Benford, former teacher, head teacher, Local Authority adviser/inspector,
Ofsted Registered Inspector and quality consultant

This is a great read for many teachers who feel they would like to take on a school but feel they are not courageous or good enough – it will inspire many who can find similarities in the character of one or more of these Heads to understand that they can do it too. (One size doesn't fit all!)

Every story is engrossing and shows the many difficult issues Heads have to face – but do so by thinking and planning in creative and lateral thinking ways. They communicate their vision and plans in a way that involves everyone. I enjoyed each and every account because although heads are surrounded by people, it can be a very lonely job for those who are afraid to share problems. A problem shared is a problem solved and this will be an invaluable read for aspiring head teachers.

Dame Anna Hassan, education consultant
and Chair of OCAT Oak Community Academy Trust

PRIMARY
HEADS

EXCEPTIONAL LEADERSHIP IN THE PRIMARY SCHOOL

BILL LAAR

Crown House Publishing Limited
www.crownhouse.co.uk
www.crownhousepublishing.com

First published by
Crown House Publishing Ltd
Crown Buildings, Bancyfelin, Carmarthen, Wales, SA33 5ND, UK
www.crownhouse.co.uk

and

Crown House Publishing Company LLC
6 Trowbridge Drive, Suite 5, Bethel, CT 06801, USA
www.crownhousepublishing.com

British Library of Cataloguing-in-Publication Data
A catalogue entry for this book is available
from the British Library.

Print ISBN: 978-184590890-4
Mobi ISBN: 978-184590913-0
ePub ISBN: 978-184590914-7
ePDF ISBN: 978-184590915-4

LCCN 2014931137

Printed and bound in the UK by
TJ International, Padstow, Cornwall

This book is dedicated to Jackie and Alex Laar, and the many outstanding head teachers and teachers with whom I have been privileged to work.

CONTENTS

ACKNOWLEDGEMENTS

I would like to thank Marion McNaught and Jackie Holderness for their patient typing and editing of the manuscript.

INTRODUCTION

This book examines the concepts of effective primary leadership and headship. It seeks to establish how far the concepts are exemplified in the practice of eleven successful head teachers, and the extent to which their work, and the performance of their schools, reflect currently accepted views of educational excellence, and the qualities deemed essential to exceptional leadership.

Each chapter, devoted to a head teacher, provides evidence of notable qualities of leadership. These leadership qualities are articulated in their professional narratives in/by:

- the shaping of inspiring vision;

- the professional development of individuals;

- the establishment of effective teams, committed to a common, aspirational purpose;

- the efficient management of systems and organisations, an unrelenting insistence on refining the quality of teaching and learning;

- an emphasis on distributed leadership; and

- the forging of productive links with parents, carers and the wider community in the interest of children's education.

The schools described in chapters 2–12 differ from each other in various aspects, sometimes significantly so. The differences relate to:

- Status e.g. state or faith school

- Location and socio-economic make-up of the catchment area

- Size, ethnic diversity and mobility of pupil population

- The professional experience of the head teacher and senior staff and the experience and capacity of all staff

- The nature and quality of the building and the immediate school environment

- Access to funding resources beyond the legislated minimum

- The nature of the governing body and the support it affords

1

- The context of the contributory school community, its perception of the school and its historic relationship with it

I have written about head teachers whose schools are widely acknowledged to be outstanding in terms of the transforming educational experience they provide. Such judgements are based on rigorous criteria and national standardised tests in which pupils consistently attain high standards.

Apart from these benchmarks there are other significant quality indicators that characterise the schools and their head teachers.

- These schools are commissioned by local authorities, national institutions and bodies such as the NCSL and the DfE as training grounds for other schools and their staff.

- Their teaching staff are regularly promoted to leadership and senior positions in other schools.

- The schools develop rich and creative environments that contribute significantly to pupils' learning and to the enlarging of their cultural experience and understanding.

- They use advanced and innovative educational technology to enhance the pupils' learning across the whole curriculum.

- Without exception, they provide an education based on strong, moral, ethical and spiritual principles. These are reflected in the unfailing care and support for children and the commitment to serving the rights and needs of every individual.

- Their reputation for excellence often extends beyond their immediate community, in some cases attaining a national status.

Finally, I took account of the criteria for effective headship/leadership based on academic research and literature devoted to the subject (see Bibliography), and how the head teachers matched up to them. These head teachers do the following:

- Build vision and set direction

- Redesign and restructure an organisation as required

- Manage teaching and learning programmes

- Respond effectively to the contexts in which they find themselves

- Effectively distribute school leadership

- Improve teaching and learning through their influence on staff

- Motivate staff, maintain morale, exploit capacity, and provide high quality working conditions

- Have high expectations of learning, achievement and attainment for all pupils and staff

Each head teacher inspires outstanding practice through highly effective leadership. Each works in his or her particular way; the schools are distinctly different in their characteristics. What they have in common is high quality leadership and demonstrable achievement.

There are three important and illuminating elements:

- Their home life and early formative (largely primary) years. These clearly influence their professional philosophy and practice. Consequently, they believe that schools need to make enduring partnerships with parents in a shared commitment to their children's education.

- Their vision for the school in terms of its potential to instil in children a positive concept of themselves and a belief in their ability to flourish in the world.

- Their professional experience and their progression to senior management and headship. Such experience underpins their understanding of the essence of good leadership.

The book is organised in the following way:

Chapter 1 – A brief review of contemporary theories and precepts about headship and leadership.

Chapters 2–12 – Each chapter gives a detailed account of the work and leadership of an individual head teacher, the life of their school, and the qualities and attributes that make them outstanding.

Chapter 13 – An overview of the work and practice of a group of head teachers, the leadership and management of their schools, and the education provided within them. There is reference throughout to the beliefs and intentions that inspire their work.

Conclusion – A brief reminder of what effective headship/leadership means, according to the accounts of the work and achievements of the individual head teachers, and articulated in the beliefs that inspire them. There are strengths and qualities that lie outside the canon of attributes generally regarded as prerequisites of effective leadership. These influence many of the head teachers, and contribute to any discussion of school management.

Finally, how context affects the ultimate fate of schools and the success or otherwise of those who lead them.

There is disquiet, at present, about what is seen as a growing and serious crisis due to a national failure to recruit head teachers.

The claim is that teachers – eligible in terms of experience, seniority and performance – are reluctant to make themselves available for these positions, for the following reasons:

- It is claimed that achieving an acceptable work/life balance as a head is virtually impossible

- The pay differential for the headship of a small school – which would be the appointment most likely to be secured by a first-time head – is not enough to tempt or compensate for the huge increase in responsibility

- Head teachers have suffered ill health as a result of the amount of stress they are under, due to inspection/accountability

- Head teachers are trapped between the requirement to follow statutory policy and the expectation to be creative and innovative

My hope for this book is that head teachers, and teachers eligible for headship but intimidated by the challenges associated with it, will find it offers inspiring and encouraging insights into the unique professional, personal, and even spiritual rewards that the position and experience can bring.

CHAPTER 1

TALKING HEADS

EXCEPTIONAL LEADERSHIP IN THE PRIMARY SCHOOL

Since the Education Reform Act, schools have come a long way in response to an unremitting stream of government legislation and demand. In the process they have made large advances in institutional management, curriculum development, teaching and learning, self regulation and accountability, staff development and the creative use of enhanced finance and resources.

As a result, primary schools today are, in significant respects, unrecognisable from their counterparts of a couple of decades ago. They are more suited to purpose in terms of organisation; more self-critical, rigorous and clear-sighted in relation to aims, intentions, planning and outcomes; more informed and coherent about teaching and learning; more effective and dynamic in practice; and managed with clarity and assurance inherent in forms of leadership radically different from former styles and models.

The nature and quality of leadership is now generally accepted as the critical factor affecting the quality and effectiveness of schools. In a 2003 report, 'Leadership and Management', Ofsted cited evidence from inspections and HMI surveys that asserted the importance of 'strong leadership and management' in:

- Addressing low achievement
- Providing for a broad, balanced and appropriate curriculum
- Ensuring high quality teaching
- Improving monitoring and evaluation strategies in relation to performance in teaching and learning

An insight into the changing views of headship/leadership over the last three decades is provided by a comparison of the first Ofsted Framework (1992), which sets out the detailed schedule for the newly inaugurated inspection process, with the most recent frameworks.

The first handbook is explicit in its expectations for primary education, thereby effectively ending divisive ideology and practice post-Plowden. It deals relatively briefly with the issue of leadership under the category of Management and Administration.

The 'well-managed school' – clear in its objectives and focused on pupils' needs and the promotion of effective learning – is driven by 'positive leadership' on the part of an 'accessible and approachable head and senior staff'. The roles and responsibilities of staff, 'aware of their part in the running of the school, are clearly defined and there is appropriate delegation.'

So, at first sight, there seems to be no great difference here from current expectations of leadership. But despite a sense of the importance of collegiality and corporate engagement, the unmistakable suggestion seems to be that the essential business of the school will be delivered and have its nature determined by, at most, a handful of senior staff.

There is a single reference to positive leadership but no attempt to explore in detail what that means. While the head teacher and senior staff are 'accessible and approachable', there is a hint at operational structures that create a divide; a divide in which a majority of staff, however secure and professionally supported they may feel, are largely dependent on a minority for direction, purpose, action and initiative. In the phrase, 'approachable and accessible', there is a sense of detachment, of senior leaders standing separate from the teachers they 'manage'.

Subsequently, successive inspection schedules have focused more on the influence of leadership on the success of schools as institutions of learning, and on the quality of education they provide. They have become more explicit about the nature of that leadership, with a particular emphasis on being inclusive, engaging all staff in the process at levels appropriate to their professional development and areas of responsibility. Leaders and managers are charged with being proactive, with 'communicating an ambitious vision for the school, with driving improvement and securing support from others'.

Inspections now evaluate the effectiveness of leaders and managers, at all levels, in conveying their vision for the school's continuing improvement, driving and securing that improvement, inspiring the school community, promoting improved teaching as judged within the context of the school, and enabling pupils to overcome specific barriers to learning.

Inspections now assess the impact of all leaders in relation to:

- The extent to which they secure sustained school improvement through the development of high quality teaching and capacity for leadership.

- Their evaluation of school strengths and weaknesses as a means to the promotion of general improvement.

- Their provision of a broad and balanced curriculum, meeting the needs of all pupils.

- Their implementation of systems for the safety and welfare of pupils, and for their spiritual, moral, and social development and behaviour.

- Their effectiveness in securing parents' engagement in supporting their children's achievement.

It is clear that in the period since the inspection system was first established by Ofsted, there has been a sea change in its perception of what is meant by the effective direction of schools. Effective management and organisation are still held to be prerequisites of a good and successful school. But there is now a growing emphasis on the concept of leadership, even an inclination to treat it as the more vital element in the crucial amalgam with management.

It is self-evident that head teachers are inseparable from the schools they lead. Therefore, before we consider headship and leadership in detail, we need to reflect on the nature of effective and outstanding primary schools, and the factors and constituents that make them so.

OUTSTANDING PRIMARY SCHOOLS

Ofsted frameworks identify key features for inspection in determining the quality of schools. They are:

- Achievement of pupils

- Quality of teaching

- Quality of leadership and management

- Behaviour and safety of pupils

- Pupils' spiritual, moral, social and cultural development

There is a growing consensus that some, if not all, of the following features will be common in such schools:

- A guiding vision, shared by all staff, generating aims, intentions and goals that are translated into policies and courses of action for curriculum, teaching and learning, assessment and evaluation of performance, staff development, and community partnership, all designed to bring about high achievement and improvement.

- A curriculum that provides the richest, most extensive and relevant education possible for all its pupils, and a quality of teaching and learning that offers a genuine experience of scholarship and high academic achievement and attainment.

- A commitment to collegiality, to staff working and maturing professionally together for positive change, development and improvement in the whole institution.

- Informed and ordered application of proven monitoring and evaluation strategies that enable secure judgements to be made about the school's effectiveness in providing for all pupils' success, attainment and improvement.

- Professional networking and collaboration – a readiness to share and learn from the experience, practice and innovation of others, through creating productive links with schools and educational institutions and agencies, including higher education.

- Inclusivity – a commitment to the provision of equal opportunity for all pupils, whatever their background, heritage, achievement, faith or ethnicity.

- Helping pupils to become 'internationally minded in a global and inter-connected world'.

- A commitment to the professional development, and the personal welfare, well-being and self-esteem of all staff.

THE LEADERSHIP OF PRIMARY SCHOOLS

Clearly headship/leadership of an institution as complex and sophisticated as the model set out above can be no commonplace or nominal role.

It has become an article of faith for educational academics, theorists and practitioners, that effective leadership is crucial to the life of every school. Its nature and quality ultimately determine, more than any other single factor, the kind of school it will be, and its success in the pupils' education.

These perceptions of the centrality of headship, not merely to the effectiveness of schools, but to the realisation of large-scale educational reform, are reflected in important steps taken by successive governments.

- The establishment of the Teacher Training Agency which, in consultation with teachers, head teachers, professional and subject associations, teacher trainers in schools, local education authorities, and higher education institutions, created *The National Standards for Headteachers*. These were subsequently revised by the National College. The Standards were articulated in the National Professional Qualification for Headship as 'a first map of the basic landscape of headship'. The publication, *The National Standards for Headteachers*, should no longer be considered to reflect DfE policy or guidance.

▦ Perhaps the most influential step, the establishment (in 2002) of the National College for School Leadership (NCSL),[1] with a remit to ensure that current and future school leaders develop the skills, capability and capacity to lead and transform what exists into 'a world-class education system'.

▦ The publication in 2004 by the then DfES of revised *National Standards for Headteachers* that 'recognise the key role that head teachers play in engaging in the development and delivery of government policy and in raising and maintaining levels of attainment in schools in order to meet the needs of every child.'

The critical importance of headship therefore seems to have been established beyond argument. But the question that inevitably follows is: what exactly is good, effective headship? We are not short of commentary or advice on the matter. In recent times, few areas of education have attracted so much attention, or indeed generated so much public interest, even excitement. In some cases head teachers have gained a kind of celebrity status, officially honoured for their achievements as leaders, being identified as National Head Teacher Leaders. These teachers are 'parachuted in' to rescue failing schools, occasionally assuming the direction and management of federations of two or three institutions. So much is written about headship/leadership that the body of literature could be described as a 'swamp'.

The official bodies referred to above have put forward the following as among the characteristics/prerequisites inseparable from effective headship:

▦ Effective management of the organisation

▦ The leadership of teaching and learning

▦ The building of 'capacity' through the development of the school as a learning community

▦ The securing and establishment of accountability

---

[1]   On 1 April 2013, the National College merged with the Teaching Agency (previously the TTA) to become the National College for Teaching and Leadership.

The insights and judgements drawn from academic research and theory about headship/ leadership – that 'swamp of leadership literature' – can be said to be broadly compatible with the views of the official bodies referred to above; they have almost certainly influenced such bodies in significant respects.

They suggest that almost all successful leaders draw on the same repertoire of basic leadership practices:

- Building vision and setting directions

- Understanding and developing people

- Redesigning the organisation

- Managing the teaching and learning programmes, and providing professional leadership through involvement in the curriculum, visiting classrooms and being generally involved in classroom activity

A recurring emphasis is placed on the theory of distributed leadership, marking a transformational move away from a long-established view of leadership identified with and invested in a single figure.

This concept of distributed or shared leadership has become a predominant belief among educationists, consistently advocated and accepted without reservation.

DISTRIBUTED LEADERSHIP

The whole staff share, to varying degrees – dependent on particular roles, competences, experience, skills and dispositions – responsibility for the learning achieved by both pupils and staff. Distributed leadership becomes the function of individuals, groups or teams who not only lead on the implementation of education policy, but are a source of guidance, advice, counsel, instruction, coaching and practical support for colleagues.

However peer-based and democratic it may seem, distributed leadership probably has a hierarchical configuration. There will be leadership from a senior perspective, comprising the head teacher and senior staff, who will assume main responsibility for such instructional leadership by virtue of their particular experience, knowledge and skill, as distinct from any formal role.

There are a number of styles of distributed leadership, influenced by the particular contexts and circumstances in which head teachers operate. Two predominant forms are transactional and transformational, which have many commonalities but differ significantly in respect of their core rationale. Transactional leadership aims to manage a school well and achieve efficiency, while transformational leadership, as its name implies, seeks to add a dimension that will move the school forward educationally, in line with major social developments.

TRANSACTIONAL LEADERSHIP

This is essentially about the effective management of a school. It is characterised by:

- The creation of a supportive and well-organised environment in which teaching and learning can be successfully carried out

- The assured provision of essential and appropriate teaching and learning resources

- The appointment and retention of high quality staff and provision for their professional development and pastoral care

- The maintenance of effective relationships with governors, parents, external agencies, the local authority and the DfE

Heads and senior leaders adopting this transactional style of leadership play a less active part in providing learning instruction. Their predominant concern is to establish the systems and conditions, and the maintenance of the school and its routines, to ensure the effective delivery of teaching and learning.

Consequently, this form of leadership has become equated with management: keeping the school running efficiently. This is in contrast to transformational or learning-centred leadership, which aims to move the school forward educationally. In reality, the distinction is probably not that significant. Transformational leadership, and the learning-centred and instructional emphasis that characterises it, are largely dependent on the contexts and circumstances created by transactional leadership. No educational ideals would flourish in institutions deficient in order, organisation or management. Therefore, it is more useful to see transactional leadership as a critical component of the transformational style.

TRANSFORMATIONAL LEADERSHIP

This is based on the belief that leadership is about moving an institution forward to be the best it can be, in terms of fully serving the interests of pupils. It is inspired by a conviction that schools can be transformed only through the actions of individuals who are themselves being advanced in their professional competence, awareness, and the readiness and capacity to work with others in the corporate interest. It is a belief that success lies in shared, not isolated, endeavour. It seeks to create a commonwealth, where the views and offerings of others are encouraged and taken into account. It welcomes intellectual and professional debate, constructive criticism and evaluation; it creates a climate of reflection, celebrates individual and collective achievement, and treats setbacks as momentum for fresh endeavour.

LEADERSHIP – VISION AND CONTEXT

VISION

All educationists hold that an essential attribute of effective leadership is the capacity to create, articulate and engage others in a guiding vision.

Vision might be described as a profoundly considered, wisely informed and inspirational view of the purpose and mission of a school in relation to the education of its children. The head teacher of a school must define and articulate that vision and inspire staff to uphold it.

It seems highly likely there will be more similarities than differences between the guiding visions of diverse schools, especially in relation to educational issues. After all, in almost all circumstances the vision of primary schools will be shaped, to a considerable extent, by: the broad principles that underpinned Every Child Matters[2] agenda; the aims and goals of the inclusive school; the national commitment to provide all pupils with the richest possible curriculum; and teaching that will foster high attainment, and promote self-esteem, confidence and a capacity for life-long learning.

CONTEXT

The context in which a school exists will significantly influence the head's vision for the school, and, in the long run, affect their ability to respond positively and bring about its successful implementation.

In terms of context it has to be admitted that some schools are significantly harder to work in than others because of their particular circumstances. These might include:

- A record of underachievement regarded as irretrievable by the school community

---

[2] Every Child Matters is a phrase no longer used by government.

- An overly challenging community, or one apparently indifferent to education and reluctant to engage in partnership with the school

- Difficulty in appointing and retaining able, well-qualified staff

- Disproportionate cohorts of families living below the poverty line

- Historically poor resourcing, exacerbated by the lack of community support

- Racial or political tensions within the community that impinge on school life

Formal evaluation of schools in such circumstances, despite the application of systems claimed to be capable of identifying the real value added to pupil attainment, may not always take full or proper account of the adversity and challenge faced by teachers in that context, and the extent and nature of the demands on leadership.

However, one thing is certain: whatever the circumstances and context of a school, it will not prosper without an assured and guiding vision.

A MORAL AND ETHICAL CODE

For a school to be worthwhile, it must be imbued with an unequivocal and positive moral sense. This would ensure that moral and ethical values are made explicit throughout the whole curriculum, and in spiritual, moral, social and cultural programmes and activities. Through their behaviour, adults would model high moral standards and demonstrate supportive working relationships with each other. There would also be illuminating reference to community, national and international matters, from issues of conservation and preservation to concerns regarding the promotion of human rights. The school's moral code and values should be exemplified through the children's whole educational experience.

HEADSHIP IN PRACTICE

The educational reforms of the past three decades have called for a radically different type of leadership: visionary and innovative, intellectually rigorous and enquiring, analytical and evaluative, competent in the management of the complex business of institutions, creative in the professional development of personnel, outward-looking and active in the making of professional networks.

MANAGEMENT AND ADMINISTRATION

The management of a primary school today is far more complicated than in the past. It calls for the esoteric skills that one might associate with the control of a medium-sized or larger business, including managing large budgets and bidding successfully for specific grants; organising staff provision – significantly enlarged in recent times – and related industrial and professional obligations; using costly resources effectively; and mastering complex legislation.

THE MANAGEMENT OF PUPILS' LEARNING, ATTAINMENT, ACHIEVEMENT AND PROGRESS

Schools are committed to ensuring that every pupil reaches and maintains the highest academic attainment possible for them, realising that potential in relation to all areas of the curriculum. Educators' pious hopes and good intentions are no longer sufficient or acceptable. Pupils' attainment and progress are scrupulously monitored and evaluated against realistic but ambitious targets, based on rigorous, nationally accredited criteria. The progress and attainment of specific groups are tracked with equal care. Where shortfall or underachievement occurs in relation to individuals or groups, then corrective action is applied and again evaluated.

These measures of quality assurance require sophisticated monitoring systems, the expert use and interpretation of data, the scrupulous maintenance of records, and informed understanding of the implications of data outcomes for teaching and learning and curriculum provision generally.

Responsibility for quality assurance will usually reside with a senior member of staff, probably supported by one or more colleagues. In addition, the head teacher will need to be comprehensively informed and ultimately accountable for not just the practical effectiveness of the monitoring systems, but, more importantly, for the way in which the school responds to what these are telling them about pupils' education.

PERFORMANCE MANAGEMENT

A school's success depends largely on the quality of teachers' performance in the classroom. Securing quality assurance in teaching performance (and the ways in which teachers carry out other allocated responsibilities) remains a major and often challenging responsibility of school leadership. In the chapters dedicated to individual head teachers, it will be seen how learning and instruction-centred leadership can provide powerful structures to support, develop and enhance the professional capacity of teachers.

Although the performance management of this critical area is widely shared, it is also at the heart of the head teacher's role; the final responsibility for assuring the quality of teacher performance lies with them. The head is ultimately accountable for dealing with, and remedying, inadequate performance.

THE MANAGEMENT OF CURRICULUM

There is a strong correlation between a head's vision for the school and the curriculum shaped and provided for the pupils. The quality of the curriculum is one of the major determinants of a school's worth. Together with the head teacher's responsibilities for teaching and learning, assessment and evaluation, and the promotion of staff personal development, it is central among the factors which ultimately define the effectiveness of their leadership. When national curriculum requirements are modified (as in September 2014) another major responsibility for head teachers is evident: to guide and support staff through the challenges of major change.

Schools may appear to have little room for manoeuvre in determining what children should be taught. Never before has there been such explicit, definitive and expert mapping of the content of the curriculum by the agencies of central government, backed up by unprecedented and prolific guidance for teachers on what should be taught, and, in some respects, how it should be taught.

Even so, in a curriculum which has expanded in recent years, head teachers have to make initial, even-handed decisions as to what is in and what is excluded, what is accorded high priority and what is seen as marginal. As with most areas of primary education today, there will be corporate concern in schools about how the curriculum is organised and provided for. Staff make important contributions to this, but head teachers will be looked to for clear thinking and decisive direction.

COMMUNITY INVOLVEMENT

For many head teachers, genuine engagement with their communities is likely to prove as challenging, demanding, and possibly exhausting, as any part of their multi-faceted role.

There is a long tradition of primary schools engaging with their communities in various ways, including:

- Encouraging parents and carers to take an active part in their children's day-to-day education. Parents need to be informed about children's learning and curricular activities and their purpose, and be supported and coached in ways that will enable them to engage practically with them at home.

- Showcasing for parents and the wider community the pupils' work, play, sports and creative activities.

- Making the school and its facilities accessible to the wider community for leisure and learning purposes.

- Contributing to community activities and events through the efforts of staff and pupils.

- Enriching the curriculum and life of the school by involving members of the community who have particular expertise and skills to offer.

- Educating pupils about their community: the factors that define its nature, life and development; their place in it and how they can contribute to it.

This perception of community relationships and involvement has grown over the years to a stage where some schools describe and formally declare themselves as 'community schools'. However, practice varies widely from school to school.

The government has now made it mandatory for schools to work to promote 'community cohesion'. But legislation apart, head teachers today simply cannot afford to hold their schools aloof from the concerns and aspirations of their community as, in an age of transparency and dialogue, these increasingly impinge on what they do as educators. However, the business of promoting community cohesion is as varied and diverse as the communities involved; for some schools it will be more complex and fraught and call for different sensibilities and approaches.

LEADERSHIP AND SUCCESSION PLANNING

Succession planning is a relatively recent concept being promoted by government agencies. It proposes that schools must actively nurture the leadership capacity of staff. Ofsted has highlighted the necessity for schools to accustom teachers to the notion that they will, over time, succeed to positions of leadership, and to put in place practical arrangements and strategies that would provide for this. Local authorities have worked with schools to facilitate the process in various ways:

- Deputy head teachers and other senior staff shadow head teachers in other schools for periods of time to enable them to become familiar with different styles and approaches to leadership.

- Head teachers are encouraged to assume acting or temporary headships of schools in particular circumstances, with their deputies taking on the vacated role of head 'at home'.

- In some cases, experienced heads are leading federations of schools, with senior staff filling the headship role in the schools themselves.

- Highly skilled teachers are being released from their schools for periods of time to support and work alongside colleagues in schools encountering difficulty.

This drive to provide for leadership development and succession planning adds not only to head teachers' portfolios of responsibilities but makes fresh claims on their capacity for vision, generosity of spirit and the will to look outward.

CHAPTER TWO

CLAIRE ROBINSON

St Thomas More Catholic Primary School, Kidlington, Oxfordshire
Boys and girls aged from 3 to 11
Pupils: 235

Claire is dedicated to the involvement of the school in the wider education community and the development of its international perspective.

Claire Robinson transformed a beleaguered school, one that had forfeited the trust of its community, into one officially credited as 'Outstanding'. In the process, she demonstrated the importance of ensuring all staff have a profound understanding of primary education, sustained by research into their own practice, and their involvement in consultative teams across a group or cluster of schools.

Commitments to a broad curriculum and the effective management of rigorous assessment and evaluation, have been key factors in the marked enhancement of pupils' achievement and attainment.

From the beginning, Claire and her staff have worked consistently to make and sustain a creative partnership with parents and the broader community. They believe that pupils' high attainment and their enthusiasm for learning is attributable to an important extent to the development of this school–parent relationship.

Enhanced funding realised through entrepreneurial initiatives has contributed notably to the richly resourced whole school environment and its impact on the children's education.

Because of domestic circumstances, Claire left school at sixteen and began working in an insurance firm. She continued to study, through day release and in her own time, gaining A levels and an Open University degree. She progressed to senior management level, dealing with a wide range of people, 'from the casual and undecided, to executives of corporate business companies. You'd go in, do your work and you'd leave and that was it. There was nothing deep about it. I wanted something more than that, something that truly mattered. So I did a PGCE, became a teacher. I never looked back.'

Her first teaching practice in a middle school on a challenging estate in Oxford was a chastening experience. Often left unsupported in total charge of volatile Year 6 classes, she unexpectedly found herself accused by a highly aggressive parent of making a comment that impugned his son's sexuality. ('I had merely enquired whether it was really necessary for him and his friend to go to the toilet together, and then return and disrupt the work of the rest of the class.')

The head teacher, attempting to mollify the intimidating parents, turned a minor issue into a show trial, taking evidence from every pupil in the class. This left Claire unsupported and vulnerable, cast in the role of 'dodgy defendant'. In the end, it was the children 'who came to my aid, insisting that my accuser was simply paying me back for reprimanding him earlier for swearing'.

Claire was learning significant lessons: the crucial importance of establishing good relationships with children and demonstrating they were valued; the consequences for authority figures of taking easier, perhaps more showy, options; and how this can cause a loss of trust and diminished morale on the part of staff.

She recognised the deeper understanding that negative experiences afforded, and the insights to be gained from observation and reflection on the behaviour of others in difficult or challenging situations.

Claire's second teaching practice in a primary school confirmed that:

> Classroom management comes from within you and nobody can actually teach you that bit. They can give you strategies, but it's part of who you are and how you conduct yourself with children. If you've got that you can learn the rest.

> Teaching is something of a performance. You have to be able to do that in front of children who are increasingly attuned to the visual with an average concentration span of ten minutes. Teachers have to adapt and vary things, to call on different strategies, to match teaching styles to varying learning styles.

The leadership styles she observed on her teaching practice fell short of what her School of Education had led students to expect as commonplace. What teachers needed was to be self-motivated, to have a clear idea of what they wanted to do and where they wanted to go. 'Teaching is not for the faint-hearted. It calls for a firm sense of purpose, dedication, self-awareness, and a readiness to seek out advice and to learn from others' practice.'

She mentions a newly qualified teacher in her first term for whom the implications and demands of teaching were only then becoming clear. She was in a job she hadn't given serious thought to in advance, and now realised her heart wasn't in it and she didn't want to do it.

We had given her all the support possible but we did not attempt to persuade her to stay. Teaching is a hard job and we are doing no favours to anyone if we pretend it's all right if you just get by. It isn't all right for the children to just get by; their life chances are being affected by what you do with them, every day.

Claire regretted the waste of time not only for the young teacher but for all those professionally involved with her. Colleges of education need to make their students better aware of the real nature of teaching. They need to be 'comprehensively aware of the circumstances of schools to whom they relate, and the demands upon those who teach there. They need to provide, with their cohorts of schools, as wide an experience as possible of diverse teaching contexts for their students, especially if they are likely to begin their careers in challenging urban schools.'

Her experience convinced her that the quality of leadership determines the fate of schools. In Claire's first appointment – which had a benign laissez-faire leadership – there was an undemanding ethos and an absence of challenge, where 'teachers should feel free to express themselves. This meant in effect that you were given your classroom, and got on with it.' For a newly qualified teacher this was comforting and unthreatening in some respects, but early experience soon led her to re-appraise and re-evaluate the situation.

She realised that institutional and individual professional development were contingent on an infrastructure geared to whole school development, decisive and generative leadership, informed guidance on curriculum and pedagogy, collegial working and coherent planning, the requisite resources and rigorous appraisal systems. That early experience was an epiphany for her.

In her fourth year, Claire was appointed Deputy Head of a one-form entry primary school in a challenging semi-urban environment. She took up her position under an acting head, the latest of several short-term, trouble-ridden head and deputy appointments. Once more she was to learn about leadership, now largely through observation of highly fallible, crisis-driven management and practice. She now found herself in a blame culture, with all her efforts placed in supporting beleaguered staff.

Just months after her arrival at the school, a clearly untenable situation led the governors to appoint Claire as Head Teacher.

HOW HER EXPERIENCE INFLUENCED HER WORK AS A HEAD TEACHER

Claire was formulating a clear vision of what she wanted for the school and for the local community. In a changing and often turbulent society, a school must be at the heart of the community, taking the place once occupied by the Church, and working through its own particular mission.

Making effective school–community partnerships is crucial to children's education, so feeling that she had a broken school to mend, she set out to impress upon disillusioned parents the importance of establishing a shared dialogue between them. She promised the parents that she and her staff would take no important decision about the life of the school without inviting parents in for information, discussion and a full exchange of views.

It is a policy she has never deviated from, and one that has often been stressful and challenging. She would seek out those parents who were vehemently voicing complaints about the school, often about exaggerated or misunderstood issues, and insist they come and explore the matter with her, until agreement and reconciliation were arrived at.

In this way, over the years, she and her staff have demonstrated to parents, and to the community at large, that for them every child matters; that their sole concern is for their care, enrichment, development and empowerment.

Claire insists that service to a community must extend beyond 'tribal' boundaries. She appointed a teaching assistant, a displaced Romanian who was previously a teacher in her own country, who did marvellous work in EAL with their children. Over the years she was nurtured by the school to full teacher status.

Her worth to us was inestimable. But when I heard of a neighbouring head teacher unable, despite all his efforts, to fill an urgently needed post, I arranged for her transfer to his school, one that in those days would be described as a competitor. I did so because I passionately believe that every school in its own particular community must work in true union together to support each other. People talk about a fractured society. Only by a genuine coming together can we heal and improve society for the sake of our children. There must be a spiritual dimension.

THE SCHOOL MISSION AND THE CHILDREN

The school's vision and mission are shaped by the children's needs, rights and entitlement. In practical terms, this translates into provision designed to:

- Endow children academically to the fullest extent so they can fulfil their potential, and lead physically, mentally and spiritually rewarding lives in an uncertain future and a society difficult to envisage.

- Help children become reflective, self-aware, resourceful people, at peace with themselves; able to communicate with, relate to and get on with others.

- Enable them to be tenacious, persevering and resilient, aware of what they must do to succeed and achieve, and to progress beyond their own previous best.

The last aim arises from Claire's concern about the tendency of children, boys especially, to become disaffected with learning and endeavour as they move up the school. One of the main reasons for this is their constant exposure to a testing regime which measures, matches and compares individual performance to others.

The school vision and mission can be realised only if vital elements are securely in place. These are:

- An enriching curriculum

- Unremittingly high quality teaching

- An inspiring and generously resourced learning environment

- A climate and systems conducive to learning

- Assessment integral to children's learning, and processes to monitor individual progress and development

- A school philosophy that constantly asks: Is this the best we can manage? Can we do better still?

TEACHING AND LEARNING

Teaching and learning are inextricably bound together – something, Claire maintains, it has taken educationists time to recognise. The first Ofsted frameworks made it possible for teaching to be highly graded in contexts where the learning was often no more than satisfactory. 'We know better now,' she says.

She researched the nature of teaching and learning in schools noted nationally for their good practice, and visited many of them to observe their work at first hand. From these visits, Claire selected and adapted methods, approaches and techniques that would suit the needs of her school, staff and children. She was constructing an elaborate teachers' toolkit which they could dip in and out of, that equipped them to use and adapt a range of strategies to meet the needs of all their learners. What she gained from her learning tour helped shape the nature of the school's training through the formulation of CPD and training programmes.

The total training package included a study of the theory of Thinking Skills and practical ways in which these could be used to enlarge children's learning. Training was provided in using strategies and tools that enabled children to reflect on and enhance their learning, which was supplemented by a range of workshops run by international experts, covering the latest research on neurological development and its implications for children's learning. This was a transforming experience for teachers. There was intensive investigation of assessment, and how formative assessment could be made central to their teaching and to children's learning. There was also exploration of cooperative learning as an instrument for securing the active participation of every child in class. This was followed by the formation of a partnership with another school to share and trial the strategies.

Lessons were observed and videoed and then subjected to scrutiny and analysis – supported by intervention and guidance from an Ofsted inspector. This process called for honesty and sensitivity. Although people remained guarded, the process encouraged deep reflection. At the outset, a teacher commented that concern for colleagues' feelings would incline her to grade lessons as 'good' whereas Ofsted would be more likely to rate them 'satisfactory'. Claire responded that their basis for judgement should be Ofsted criteria alone; they would serve colleagues best by being scrupulously professional.

MONITORING TEACHING AND LEARNING AND LEADING STAFF

There is a comprehensive programme for monitoring and evaluating teaching and learning across the school. The head teacher is regularly involved in the process, together with coordinators who monitor subject responsibilities. They do paired monitoring, matching and evaluating judgements.

Claire has 'learning walks' with coordinators and teacher leaders, getting a 'helicopter view' of aspects of teaching, learning, curriculum implementation, the learning environment, and other aspects of practice, together with an evaluation of their particular areas of responsibility.

The school has established a network of peer-to-peer coaching monitors. For example, Claire moved an outstanding young teacher from Year 1 to Year 6, to provide the regular teacher there with a break from its intensive demands. The young teacher spent a week in the Year 6 class with her experienced colleague, in a kind of tutor/apprentice situation. She also had the weekly experience of teaching her specialism in creativity to older children. Moreover, the paired arrangement offered added experience of leadership.

Claire herself has not held a class responsibility for two years. Before that she had always taught a class, with some free time arranged for monitoring, coaching and general teacher support. 'The major part of my administration, management and organisation was dealt with outside teaching hours.'

In her first year of headship she was obliged to teach Year 6 almost full time, because a depleted budget did not allow for the provision of another teacher, and no member of staff was prepared to assume the responsibility of the Year 6 class.

That responsibility – a potentially crippling burden for a newly appointed head teacher in a seriously struggling school – led to some positive outcomes: it provided teachers with a model of high quality teaching; it allowed Claire to demonstrate to staff that she would not ask them to do anything she was not prepared to do herself; and it conveyed a strong message to parents about her dedication, industry and professional competence. Head teachers have to set a powerful example. For that reason, she still teaches across the school, because she insists she 'must continue to be a model to colleagues'. This obliges her to maintain the highest possible standards of competence. To enable her to do so, she participates in all staff INSET and does everything possible to keep abreast of developments in curriculum, teaching and learning, and pedagogy.

You have to treat teachers with the care and solicitude you bestow on children. They need to be acknowledged and thanked for what they achieve. They need to be supported in practical ways to do their work. For example, teachers appointed to take up posts in the following September receive a paid-for INSET/ Induction package they can access in the preceding summer term. In similar fashion, all staff receive training and resources to make it easier for them to teach impending national initiatives, not just to show them what they have to teach, but to help them see and be confident about how to implement it in the classroom.

Claire has instilled in staff the notion of accountability, and has made it a central tenet of the work and life of the school. When she came to the school the teachers were adamant they would not teach Year 6 children because they viewed the workload as excessive and the responsibility for the outcome of SATs as intimidating. The attitude was almost as strong in relation to Year 2. She was concerned that teachers perceived there was more work involved for those classes, so she decided that each year they would report the SATs levels for every year group to the parents. There was a risk here, because parents inevitably began to draw comparisons with their child's original performance and to challenge when they felt progress was inadequate or was not being maintained.

She persuaded teachers that *all* staff were accountable, because everyone needed to know where the children they were about to teach had come from in terms of attainment, and where they had to go in terms of progress.

She moves teachers regularly so that they know they are not guaranteed to stay with the same year group every year. She discusses this with them individually and collectively, and takes account of where they would like to teach and what their preferences are. She makes the decision in their best professional interests, but also first and foremost, in the interests of the children.

Head teachers need to acknowledge that whilst they may be perfectionists, that does not mean that others are necessarily wrong. They have to accept that different styles may be equally valuable and be prepared to adapt to them, to listen and respect other views and to have empathy. 'Above all, you have to keep in mind where you want to go and where you have to go; to be passionate about it and not be driven off track.'

She quotes a particular incident as an example:

> *A few years after my arrival we were judged to be an 'Outstanding School' that is 'Outstanding' in every single respect. We were elated and celebrated as a team. The following February we had our termly internal assessments of pupil performance. I went to the staff – and perhaps, with hindsight, I might have handled this differently – and asked which they preferred: to go through the evidence with them individually or collectively. They decided we should do it together.*

> *With detailed statistics for each teacher, I pinpointed the children in each class who were achieving well and up to target and congratulated teachers on that. Then I identified children who were not making adequate progress. I said that obviously we could not allow this to continue, had a preliminary discussion on*

action and provision for each child, and asked teachers to go away for a day or so, reflect on the matter and come back with a completed programme for implementation.

That evening I had a request for a meeting from four staff, led by my senior teacher, to discuss my action. I insisted that this meeting should take place on an individual basis, since I judged – correctly – that their concern would vary along an emotional continuum and was best and most profitably addressed separately with individuals. This led to their response that since I had refused to meet them collectively they would have to 'consider what further action they should take'. (A good example of how easily apparently innocuous matters can escalate to confrontation and entrenched stances.) But I persisted, explained my reasoning and found all, save one, were satisfied to see me on a one-to-one basis. In discussion, two dismissed the matter as a storm in a teacup.

The grievance was strongly articulated by the senior teacher (who is still with me). 'You are never satisfied,' she said, 'no matter what we do or how hard we work. We have been judged an outstanding school, but that is still not good enough for you. Nothing is good enough for you. You keep on asking for more and more.' I went back to the teachers, apologised for not tackling the issue differently and said, 'The point is not whether things are good enough for me; it's whether they're good enough for the children.'

I acknowledged again what they had done to make us outstanding, but pointed out that that could never mean we had arrived, that there was no further to go. Our concern had to be for all the children and their attainment, and that had to be carried through in constant monitoring of their progress and positive response to what it tells us. I reminded them of what to do to ensure no child falls below what they are capable of.

It would have been easy, and tempting, to soothe and mollify staff; to say, 'You're right – I am being unreasonably demanding. We are outstanding; we have earned the right to rest on our laurels for a while.' But that would be a wholly unacceptable path to follow; one that would become a downward slope from which it would be difficult to regain the high ground. As Head Teacher, I would have failed absolutely in my duty to them as staff and, even more damagingly, in my obligation to the children. We must be constantly about self-improvement. That must be the purpose that drives us – and inspires us.

AN ENTITLEMENT CURRICULUM

Learning depends on experience. A diminished curriculum, comprising basic or core subjects, is likely to provide diminished experiences unless that limited handful of subjects is taught with unusual inventiveness. A broad, inspiring curriculum is more likely to help children attain and achieve, particularly in those basic or core areas. A rich curriculum does not mean constantly accumulating new or additional curricular elements; it means presenting a diversity of experiences at the highest level possible across a range of learning areas.

We are urged, for example, to enable children to become Level 5 writers, children whose commonplace oracy or talk is pitched at or around Level 3. Writing at Level 5 implies a capacity for oracy at Level 5 and the only certain way in which that will be developed is through Level 5 experience. In other words, through an enriching, stimulating, challenging curriculum and not just through the imposition of new techniques and commercially driven solutions.

We are actively involved in experiences like the Forest School. Here children are educated in woodlands, engaging in activities linked to the national curriculum. It is suggested that benefits to children attending Forest Schools include improved physical and motor skills, improved language and communication skills, improved knowledge of the environment, improved social skills and increased confidence and self-belief.

Once a week the school engages in a creativity afternoon. Children are in groups of fifteen to twenty on a cross-school basis; that is, from Year 1 to Year 6. The learning activities include: pottery, philosophy for children, natural history, modern languages, drama, music, outdoor study and so on. They are not national curriculum based, but obviously have strong connections. Over time children can sample everything on the menu. Creativity units are taught by staff, including some experts from outside the school, as their specialism. Staff can express themselves in an area where they have particular expertise and skill, gaining valuable experience of teaching across a wide age range, and working with children whom they would not normally encounter.

We are an International School accredited by the British Council. As a result we have been involved in activities linked to schools in other countries – Italy, Germany, Spain and Romania – and we have a developing link with a school in Kenya. Each term we select a continent and study it in detail. Teachers make links with that continent in all their subject planning. We study and become actively engaged with aspects of its culture and lifestyle, music, art, and dance. We have interns, students and teachers from other countries, who reside with us for the term, get involved with the project, and teach aspects of their culture and language. In the past year we have had Korean, Japanese and Spanish interns.

RESOURCES

Claire is adamant that the 'right and best resources' are vital to effective learning.

We returned last September to find, without warning, seventeen children seeking admission to the school, five of whom had no English and four with extreme special needs. Such an occurrence changes a school community in significant ways. Having spent part of their summer vacation planning their resources for specific circumstances teachers were now faced with a very different situation. There may have been a time when a response would have been, 'Oh well, we'll manage; we'll fit them in somehow,' but that won't do anymore. Ours is a school where every child matters and has to be fully provided for.

We had in store the materials and resources necessary to cater for the newcomers, particularly for language development, simply because our commitment to high quality resources is reflected in practical provision for all areas of the curriculum. It was necessary to support staff teaching the EAL arrivals with personnel equipped to contribute to their language development. So I went to that particular ethnic community and engaged a qualified person to work with the children in the classrooms. Their progress in basic language acquisition soon made them broadly independent members of the class, able to involve themselves in the learning process. What we needed on that occasion was found outside. We had to be resourceful in acquiring it, and yes, such events impose strain on teachers and their classroom communities.

We provide whatever teachers need to enhance children's learning, to support their complex and demanding work. The wide-scale physical expansion made to the school is a tremendous resource for children, staff and the wider community. I think this has added incalculably to the range and quality of education available to our children.

Claire has no doubt that the most vital resource available is the staff. They are the key to everything.

> *You can have highly competent and dedicated heads with great visions and ambitious plans worked out in detail, but without staff who can bring it about, they come to nothing. This is much truer now that teaching has become more complex and challenging, and only practitioners of the highest quality will serve.*

She sees her task as nurturing and developing staff, devising a programme of CPD for every individual that will advance their personal expertise and careers, taking into account their individuality and to some degree, the circumstances of their private lives. A head teacher requires wisdom, a finely-tuned intelligence, sensitivity, acute awareness, maturity, compassion, resolution, consistency, and, at times, steel – a determination to deliver to the limit of their potential.

ASSESSMENT

Assessment is now seen as being at the heart of good teaching and successful learning. Teachers need to analyse children's work and accurately identify, from what they do and what they say, where they are on a learning continuum and what must be done to move them on. In addition, the teacher must encourage the pupils to be reflective and appreciate their progress in learning through constructive feedback, and provide them with strategies for identifying the skills they must cultivate to take that learning further.

The elaborate nature of the school's assessment procedure indicates the extent to which it is integral to the learning process and to children's attainment, achievement and progress. It comprises the following measures:

- Training for assessment is made an important part of INSET and teachers' CPD.

- Children's progress is scrupulously tracked through standardised testing and analysis of target outcomes, and through regular, rigorous assessment of their ongoing work.

- Each term the head teacher reviews, with individual teachers, the progress of every child, identifying those who are underachieving and the likely causes, setting programmes for progress and development.

- Each term the parents are informed of the outcomes of the SATs in relation to their own child.

By being informed about their child's progress, parents are able to consider ways in which they can contribute to their child's learning. It also demonstrates the school's determination to be accountable. At the beginning of each academic year, teachers are updated about each child's learning in the class they are to teach. They know 'precisely where they have come from and where they are expected to go on the learning journey. I remind them that they are all, in effect, Year 2 and Year 6 teachers, because we all share responsibility for final outcomes.'

Claire always gives the Year 6 children their SATs results before anyone else, including their parents. She believes it is the children's right, and a way of making sure that they put these results in perspective: their own personal data which is intended to help measure their progress and ensure it continues, rather than a yardstick that will determine their future or set them apart from their friends and classmates.

> Some children are afraid to open the envelope. I have children who are initially devastated at what they regard as failure on their part; children who cry, 'Why didn't I get a Level 5?' That's not coming from the school – that's coming from the parents. It is self-inflicted. We have to help them cope in such situations because they are going to encounter them again and again, because they sit tests throughout their school life. We have to help them value what they are achieving and appreciate what they are capable of. The reward comes in seeing children go away smiling and reassured, and in the relief of parents who are grateful for our recognition of their children's worth.

OUTREACH AND AN ENTREPRENEURIAL ROLE FOR SCHOOLS

Circumstances now oblige schools to be outward-looking and entrepreneurial. However, Claire claims that many head teachers reject that notion and insist that the sole business of schools is the education of the children in their care, fearing that 'dealing in the marketplace', or even large involvement with other schools, may dilute commitment to, and diminish concentration on, their essential work.

> The government makes public our 'balance sheets' in the shape of inspection reports and league tables. So, like it or not, we are pushed into the marketplace, with our brochures and our websites. More to the point, we have to attract enhanced finance, increasingly on a serious scale. Few of the things I have talked about – the transforming curriculum, the quality of resources, the

enriched environment, the additional external professional input, our growing internationalism – can be realised to the degree that we want without funding significantly beyond our basic allowances. So yes, I am entrepreneurial. But first we get our ideas and aspirations and then we think about how we are going to fund them.

She works as a school improvement consultant to eight schools. This is not merely an example of an entrepreneurial venture, but of reaching out to a wider educational community beyond the school itself. Her consultancy fees are used in their entirety to enhance her school's financial resources; in educational terms, her expertise not only supports the work of other schools, but enlarges in various ways her own professional experience and awareness.

ACCOUNTABILITY AS A HEAD TEACHER

Claire sees these as her main lines of accountability:

GOVERNORS

She accepts, without question, her obligation to be accountable to them, and says that at their best they can be highly supportive. She works constantly to keep them fully informed and as practically involved as possible. However, this relationship is not always easy; it's time-consuming and not always productive. You cannot expect or demand too much of governors – they are volunteers and often in full-time work. Most critical is the relationship between the chair and head teacher, and Claire adds that in that respect, she is 'blessed'.

THE LOCAL AUTHORITY

Legally she must respond to the various requirements of the local authority, which seems to her to be increasingly driven by the demands of central government, and therefore less able to be a creative influence on schools.

CHILDREN AND PARENTS

Above all, she regards herself accountable to children and their parents. These always come first, no matter what. 'If something is right for our children and their school, then we'll do it. So whatever the national initiative and however great the degree of accountability that accompanies it, we will implement it in the way and to the extent that best serves our children.'

HOW SUCCESSFUL AM I AS A HEAD TEACHER?

Claire says that head teachers must regularly confront this question unflinchingly. For all the inherent complexity of the question, there are plain criteria for providing answers:

- Am I leading a school that succeeds in doing for all our children the very best they deserve?

- Are we educating them fully and appropriately to flourish in an unpredictable future?

- Is my leadership the best that all my staff are entitled to?

She stresses, 'Be wary of any head teacher who talks purely from a personal perspective about what can only be, in the final analysis, team success.' Avoiding the fact of her own election as National Head Teacher of the Year, she offers the following as the most tangible evidence of whole team success:

- A school that has been transformed from a failing place, increasingly abandoned by parents, to one that is now widely sought after

- An 'Outstanding' Ofsted report

- Consistently high levels of accredited value added to our children's performance

- Consistently successful performance by our children in national tests

- A school that enriches its community

Claire speaks passionately about her role as head teacher and offers a vivid insight into what drives and inspires outstanding head teachers.

She absolutely loves the job, being with children, believing that by the time they leave the school she and her staff will have changed their lives for the better and enriched them, perhaps forever. She loves the endless variety, the excitement of working with staff, of relating to the community, of teaching itself.

She says she has never worked so hard in her life, from early hours to late at night, though she admits that part of that is self-inflicted by virtue of her heavy consultancy role.

She promises her family it will be easier in future, but admits it never will be, 'because there is always something new to be done, something extra we can achieve'.

She talks about her 'dark night of the soul':

> I have sat alone, shaken, in this room and wept, after encounters with parents who have chosen to be abusive and threatening over matters totally outside our responsibility and beyond our control. I have struggled and felt I have failed with seriously damaged children, and, sometimes, have had to call on all my resources to come back for more.

> There are times, when in the face of hostile opposition, your convictions can waver and you can be tempted to take the more comfortable way out. But that cannot be the way of headship. You must remain true to your vision and beliefs, even if that may be personally bruising at times.

She concludes:

> Headship is a lonely occupation in many ways, but at the end of the day there is no job to compare with it. It matters to me more than I can say, and I am, and always will be, passionately devoted to it.

CHAPTER THREE

JOHN RONANE

Ickford Combined School, Buckinghamshire
C of E school for boys and girls aged 4 to 11
Pupils: 115

In recent decades, many local authorities believed smaller schools were not economically viable, and constituted a drain on resources which seriously disadvantaged larger schools. Influential educationists were not always convinced that schools of the size of Ickford could deliver a broad, relevant and appropriate curriculum, or offer the resources and professionally empowering contexts likely to attract able and ambitious young teachers. Some even thought that small schools were susceptible to intellectual and educational decline.

John's professional experience, almost exclusively in London, led him to assume that if headship were to come his way, it would be in a large urban school in the capital. But life is seldom predictable and he finds himself a head teacher of a smaller school located in a picturesque setting on the border of Buckinghamshire and Oxfordshire.

Ickford Combined School powerfully refutes the above claims and perceptions and provides some insight into what can be achieved by a smaller school. John has established himself as a dynamic, inventive, indefatigable head teacher, who has gathered about him a skilled and enthusiastic staff, who match him for commitment. He ensures that the school offers the children a rich, highly relevant and up-to-date curriculum, a stimulating and enticing environment, and diverse opportunities for learning.

In John's time there the teachers have changed and the environment has been significantly improved. It is a happy place, and visitors remark on the calm atmosphere and the sense of caring and community.

Tracking data shows that attainment has improved, but he and his staff are committed to maintaining improvement and making greater progress between stages.

Ours is a wonderful job and vocation. That feeling is reinforced by the memory of standing in a trench, knee-deep in mud, shortly after dawn on a bitter January day, trying to warm my hands so they would not stick to the shovel. Without education my life would be very different, and I value it immensely and all it has done for me, and what it does and can do for our children.

John was born in Bow, London, and attended a local primary school, before moving on to a Boys Grammar School, where he remained in a middle stream throughout, academically and intellectually unchallenged.

He left at sixteen with eight O levels, but it was never suggested to him, either at school or at home, that he might take his education further. This left him with an enduring and, at times, debilitating sense of insecurity.

He began work as a labourer on a building site, doing back-breaking tasks such as heavy lifting, carrying and trench digging.

At the age of twenty he decided he needed to master a trade that would offer more steady employment. Having rejected bricklaying, he was persuaded to become a black taxicab driver and began the Knowledge – learning his way about London. He thought it 'the best part-time job in the world'. However, after six years he became disenchanted, unhappy and unfulfilled with the work.

'In my heart,' he says, 'for reasons that were not always clear to me, I knew I had always wanted to be a teacher.' He was admitted to a teacher training course at Hammersmith College. 'It was the beginning of an extraordinary, transforming journey that continues to this day.'

His commitment to teaching meant huge sacrifices in his personal life and it remains a source of concern to those closest to him. 'I cannot stop,' he admits. 'I am driven by a fear of failure, by a sense that I may be revealed to be an imposter in a world and a profession where I am not entitled to be.'

This insecurity has imbued him with a deeply rooted need to be valued, indeed loved. As a student teacher he discovered that the harder he worked, the more successful his teaching became, the more the children enjoyed being taught by him, and, in turn, the more highly regarded he was by their parents.

He believes such self-doubt derives from an overactive imagination. He constantly reflects on things, analyses them, sometimes excessively. In other spheres of activity, such a trait may prove a hindrance, but in the classroom a fertile imagination is a valuable gift.

The lessons I taught, and continue to teach, often emanate from that restless imagination and, at their best, manifest themselves in creativity. I am always thinking of approaches and ideas to bring the curriculum and learning to life in ways that engage and captivate children.

Such ideas often involved risk-taking – not in any way a danger to the children – but went beyond the commonplace favoured by many colleagues. He would march children all over London, up and down the escalators of the Tube, and encourage them to walk with their heads up and their eyes open. When educationally worthwhile films were released he would negotiate discounts, and take his whole class together at weekends. They dressed as Tudors and went to castles, they canoed up canals, they equipped themselves in the appropriate historic style and fought the Battle of Stamford Bridge across the playground. They ate roast quail and figs at their Roman Christmas banquet, and, on a never-to-be-forgotten occasion, secured an audience with the Pope.

None of this was ever totally unplanned, or happened off the cuff. He believes that teaching of enduring quality is rarely shaped that way. Such ventures and enterprises could not have happened without the enthusiastic and occasionally bemused support of parents, and the approval and backing of the head teachers for whom he worked – and to whom he remains grateful to this day. He feels he has been blessed in those who led him.

These ideas encouraged the pupil voice in the classroom; they inspired activity, movement and practical learning; they allowed for spontaneous changes to plans and the celebration of success. He himself celebrated children's success outside of school, reciting their poetry and reading their stories to friends in the pub. There were occasions when his sense of pride in their achievement moved him to tears.

John sees himself as relatively conservative in his educational outlook, and something of a traditionalist. He supports the emphasis on accountability, and regards the work of Ofsted as necessary and valuable in the raising of achievement.

Throughout his training and teaching career two aphorisms have inspired him: 'A rising tide lifts all ships,' and 'Children don't care what you know, until they know you care.'

Regarding the first maxim, he was fortunate in that he started out at a decisive time for education: the introduction of the National Curriculum and the other reforms. These transformed people's understanding of what could be achieved in schools, and the progress and advances possible that would enrich all involved: teachers, the children they taught, and their parents who hoped and dreamed of what they might realise and achieve. For him, it has been a challenging and thrilling journey, which has empowered him to enhance the experience of all those with whom he has worked, both teachers and children.

In terms of the second, he is convinced that children can invariably sense the degree to which a teacher cares for them, not merely for their well-being, but for their success and achievement. When he set boundaries for them and high expectations, they did not object. Rarely did a child fail to complete homework, or to read at home every evening. All those he taught understood that certain things were not negotiable, and accepted that because they trusted him to be doing what was best for them. They felt safe and happy – and they learned.

LEADERSHIP AND MANAGEMENT OF SCHOOL AND STAFF

The mission statement John has chosen for his school is concise: 'Inspired to learn, motivated to achieve.' It encapsulates his teaching career. However, he would be reluctant to share the uncut version: '... terrified of failure'. That, he stresses, is a personal mantra, inseparable from his personality and the experiences shaping his life.

Emphatically, he does not want his staff to fear failure; he wants them to be confident about taking risks. He also wants them to understand what poor performance means to the children, and therefore he wants them to be unfailingly focused on the quality of learning in the school, putting that at the heart of everything. They must ask themselves at the outset of all they do: What is likely to be the impact of this on the children's learning, on their attainment and achievement?

He observes lessons on a regular basis. He frequently walks into classrooms, spends time observing carefully, and talks to both teachers and children about the purpose and possible outcomes of what is taking place. Observations are graded, and records maintained for purposes of evaluation and development. The staff cannot be caught unprepared as they receive a school schedule at the beginning of the academic year on which the lesson observation weeks are set.

When he first came to the school, the teachers were largely unaccustomed to being observed. Younger staff were receptive to the idea and welcomed feedback, which they found constructive and encouraging. The two most senior staff were resistant and treated the innovation of observation and evaluation with disdain. It is telling, he says, that neither was successful in the course of external review and they are no longer teaching.

Over three years he had built a great team of teachers: positive, enthusiastic, and inexhaustibly hard working, with a competitive edge about personal performance. When he was reforming the staff structure he found that newly qualified teachers (NQTs) were far more knowledgeable, enthused by his vision, and determined to create an outstanding school than those with experience, who often saw the school as a 'cosy village retreat' where they could wind down their careers.

John says he is always honest and transparent with those who work under his leadership; applicants are left in no doubt about the high expectations held of all who work at the school.

ASSESSMENT AND EVALUATION

At first there was no consistent planning or assessment; the amount of each was determined by the whim of individual teachers. To ensure consistency, he introduced computer software for planning and for formative assessment, which, for a while, managed to satisfy governors and Ofsted that things were being put in order. Despite these tools making planning and assessment less onerous for the teachers, monitoring showed that their use remained erratic.

Having new teachers enabled him to make a fresh start. Rather than trying to persuade reluctant teachers to use computer tools, he began his second year at the school with a simple system based on teachers' marking for continuous formative assessment, and end-of-term tests in literacy and numeracy for cumulative assessment.

Performance management is rigorous and robust, and linked to learning. Therefore, it is essential to have an accurate assessment of children's progress, particularly when the outcomes may affect teachers' remuneration. To eliminate the problem of insecure levels of assessment and suggestions of grade inflation by staff, each term he gives the whole staff a day out of the classroom in order to moderate all the test material. To facilitate this, John organises a day for the whole school to take part in a visual literacy project, an outing or a similar activity which he arranges with the help of those staff who are not class teachers. Consequently, the teachers are happy that the children are being assessed correctly, and all accept responsibility for the progress of the children they teach. They understand that rates of progress vary, but acknowledge the need for informed and accurate judgements. They realise that their historical data may not be reliable, but are confident now that their data is 'honest'.

THE CURRICULUM

John has a duty to follow what the Department of Education stipulates. However, he is puzzled by colleagues who, 'slavishly read and act on every dictate that comes in the post or across the Internet'. He works hard to keep abreast of curriculum development, but he is convinced that the school is developing a curriculum that 'will need very little tinkering, with regard to changes by government'.

The school curriculum is built on the foundation stones of literacy and oracy; John says schools must give children good language and literacy skills. He encourages them to read as much as possible, to speak with confidence and good sense in a wide range of circumstances. He seeks to cultivate in them enquiring minds. He was able to change his life because his mother bought books from jumble sales and accompanied him to the local library each week. She also corrected his speech and expected him to be well mannered. John insists that staff speak properly to children at all times, and that staff always use grammatically correct language and offer a model of good, appropriate usage. He says, 'The mantra, "Every lesson is an English lesson," probably holds true in my school.'

Standards of teaching and learning in numeracy are high, and teachers work hard to ensure consistency in strategies and practice. He has invested in external expertise to work with the staff, particularly with problem solving, using and applying mathematical knowledge and algebra throughout the age groups. This investment has proved very worthwhile.

The teaching of science has been completely overhauled, with children carrying out 'real' investigations. In addition, their Science Week last year culminated in a Mad Scientist Day that not only had them all dressed in costume, but also raised several hundred pounds for a children's hospice.

John's goal is that every child leaves the school competent in another language, able to read music and play at least one instrument. Ideally, he would also like each child to be as healthy as possible, to have played a number of different sports, and to be confident using a wide range of technology. To that end, they have enriched their curriculum through good quality language, music, PE and ICT teaching. He employs a languages specialist who teaches French across every year group, including Reception. She is also the class teacher for Year 6, and her work is testimony to his belief that 'charismatic, hard-working, organised and intelligent people can inspire children to enjoy learning and achievement'.

He loves music and deeply regrets that as a child he was not encouraged – or even coerced – into learning to play an instrument. He is determined that the children in his care will have such opportunities, and that this will not be reliant on being able to afford private or peripatetic lessons. He employs, as a teaching assistant, a parent who is a professional violinist; using the thirty violins that the local authority provides, she gives a weekly whole-class lesson for every child in Key Stage 2. In addition, every child in the school learns to read music and play the recorder.

I hope that in my rather conservative approach I am helping to develop real musical skills, rather than subjecting children to endless lessons of two-finger beat clapping and fights over who will get a turn on the glockenspiel!

John successfully manages a decreasing budget and has raised funds for improving the ICT provision in the school, creating a dedicated ICT room, a wireless network, some Blackberry Playbooks, thirty laptops, visualizers in every classroom and LED projectors. The scheme of work enables teachers and children to work together on podcasting, film creation, music creation, 3D drawing and video game creation. Aided by one of the parents, they also plan to develop a computer program for enabling children to write their own software.

John is not convinced that 'the future of teachers is in jeopardy and we are soon to be replaced by the tablet computer and Google'. He believes in embracing technology and using it to benefit all children. The problem is not so much in teaching children to use new technology – he allows Kindles in school and welcomes mobile phones for use in some lessons – but in guiding them in its responsible and appropriate use. Schools will only be able to do this if they engage with parents and work together to ensure that children become responsible 'technological members' of society. It is not what the computer brings to the child, so much as what the child brings to the computer.

He is concerned that cyber bullying is a growing problem in society and a potentially lethal blight for communities. He knows that the Internet and the mobile phone have forced modifications to bullying policies and procedures in all schools during the past decade and a half, and is determined that bullying will not be tolerated in any classroom or school where he works.

The children use a three-step approach to dealing with someone who may be treating them unkindly.

Step 1: This begins with a hand held up and the clear words, 'Stop it!'

Step 2: Tell the person you don't like it.

Step 3: Tell an adult.

Only when they feel it necessary do the children involve an adult. Once this happens, they are promised support and action. This approach, embedded across the school, empowers children to stand up to bullying and to develop their own confidence in dealing with those who choose to antagonise them.

The school has a dress code. He does not permit hair gel, hair dye or extreme haircuts. (This initially upset some parents, but is now accepted.) Children who have what may be considered cult/status haircuts or items of jewellery, may feel empowered to dominate other children. He celebrates individuality and admires those who are different, but does not want this to be a means for unduly influencing others. He has seen many children considered cool or tough, simply because they were permitted to dress in inappropriate costume. 'Stripped of the garb, rather like Samson stripped of his hair, their power is diminished.'

PLANNING

John says that in spite of being someone who can manage pressure and react quickly to changing circumstances, he long ago learned the value of good preparation. He expects his teachers to plan their lessons and to be well prepared to teach, but he doesn't examine their plans.

He trusts his teachers to plan in a way that makes them confident they are properly prepared, and which supports the school ethos of transparency and accountability. When John looks at planning, it is usually because he has seen something in a classroom that he is unhappy about, or has been really impressed by, or because there are indications that individual children are having problems.

The staff have created their own system of storing their short-, medium- and long-term plans on their computer network, and all use it. The planning format is based around the three questions: What do I want the children to learn? How will I teach them? How will I know they have learned it? He believes that more needs to be done to ensure teachers are really clear about what they actually want the children to have learned by the end of a lesson.

MEETINGS

'One of the delights of becoming a head teacher was that I could implement a policy of holding only necessary meetings and rarely having long ones!' John does put regular meeting times in the diary, but if there is nothing of note that requires a meeting, he would rather not waste his teachers' time.

He tries to ensure that everyone has a voice at meetings, and a culture of shared learning and team commitment. This does not mean having to go through every policy and document with all the staff, so that they gain 'token ownership' – that can be a waste of time. He can tell staff, and the governors, that he is taking full responsibility for the creation and implementation of a policy.

John does not attend the most important meeting in the school. During Thursday lunchtimes the teachers eat together and debrief their week. The deputy head leads the meeting and everyone understands that whilst concerns can be raised and questions asked, it is not a moaning session, but an opportunity for telling each other of the successes there have been in individual classrooms that week.

OUTDOOR LEARNING AND EXTRA-CURRICULAR PROVISION

The school is situated in a village surrounded by fields, near a river and woodland. It offers 'a wonderful outdoor environment in which the children can learn a great deal just through playing and using their imaginations'. John says the challenge for staff is to make sitting in a classroom for much of the day more worthwhile for the children than being free outside.

Whenever John is uncertain or doubtful about educational matters, he is driven to improve his knowledge and understanding of the issues. In his early years in teaching John was a 'learning-through-play' sceptic. However, he was so impressed by the work of early years expert Elizabeth Jarman, as a deputy head, when the opportunity arose, he chose to teach children in the earliest stage of their education. Teaching this age group opened his eyes to children's formative years, and he now believes strongly in the need for schools to create effective learning environments both indoors and out.

To this end, John has transformed the school's outdoor environment. With his thirty Reception children, he created an outdoor space using pieces of timber, railway sleepers and halved ale casks filled with rocks and water. The children delighted in making huge spiders' webs from bamboo poles and masking-tape, wearing newspaper hats all day and building ships, stages and aeroplanes. 'They made camps and dug holes looking for gold and bones, and when they were not in Neverland, they ran a market stall!'

He learned from completing the London cabdrivers' Knowledge that understanding is retained more effectively through physically engaging in the learning. Riding around on a moped for two years left him with an indelible map of London in his head, which still enables him to find his way around, even after two decades.

He asks teachers to treat the outdoor classroom as an extension of the indoor. Teachers must be prepared to be outside with the children and engage in what they are doing. 'Child-initiated learning both indoors and outdoors is most successful when it is facilitated by informed adults, whether play is directed, or the children are engaged in free "choosing time".'

His tracking data indicates that in the past three years, the boys in Key Stage 2 have outperformed the girls in literacy and numeracy, contrary to more general experience and expectations. He suspects – though he has no concrete proof of this – that the extensive opportunity the children have to take part in outdoor physical activity may have had a positive impact on the boys' academic performance.

Each morning, after registration, the whole school meets in the hall for a brief act of worship, preceded by 'Wake 'n' Shake' exercise. The Year 6 children design dance routines and teach the rest of the school, with the staff participating as well. John joins in, but only on very rare occasions: 'I don't feel the need to court popularity by trying to be the most "down-with-the-kids" head teacher.'

The school offers a range of extra-curricular activities: the Head Teacher's Activity and Breakfast Club every morning before school begins; lunchtime ballet; after-school tennis; evening Taekwondo; cheerleading, hockey and football clubs. The majority of the clubs, five of which John himself organises and runs, are free to the children. Other clubs, led by external coaches, are kept at a minimum cost. The school also employs a specialist PE coach to provide cover for teachers during their PPA time, ensuring that all children have at least two hours of scheduled PE per week.

RELATIONSHIPS WITH PARENTS

John's relationship with the parents at the school has not always been easy but has improved steadily over a three-year period. As a teacher in four schools and a deputy head in two, he was accustomed to being popular and held in high regard. He soon discovered that becoming a head teacher, and taking over a village school in need of change with a long-established staff, was a challenging and turbulent experience. He found that his previous reputation as a successful class teacher and a deputy who got things done counted for nothing. It has taken several years for him to finally feel accepted and valued in his role as school leader.

Parents receive a record of their children's attainment and development at the end of each term. The reports sent out after Easter explain how well the child is learning and give targets to be aimed for by the end of the year. These are backed up by regular parents' evenings.

John has an open-door policy for all parents, and makes it clear that he is happy to discuss any matter with them at mutually convenient times. At the beginning and end of the school day he makes himself available on the playground, and often answers questions or queries at this time. He will meet working parents very early in the morning or in the evening. He shows all prospective parents round the school and tells them what the expectations are in respect of uniform, homework, punctuality and regular attendance. Having clear guidelines on punctuality and attendance has made a huge difference to many children's progress and attainment.

He has gained the support and the respect of the majority of parents because they know he works hard to improve the school for their children. When he wanted a new classroom suitable for the Reception children, he dug out hedges and fences by hand; he also spent part of his summer holidays paving and fencing a new outdoor learning area.

He opens the sports hall each morning at 7.45 AM and invites all parents to drop their children at school early to use the equipment and play games, supervised by him. Although this ties him into being at school early, it enables staff to be free for preparation and for helping each other in advance of the day's work.

NETWORKING AND EXTERNAL RELATIONSHIPS

John admits that networking may not be a strong point for him, but accepts he must adapt to sharing practice and being open to learning from others.

John has taken on the role of Chair of a partnership trust, involving a large local secondary school. He sees this as a step forward in his own professional development, plus it will allow the schools to procure services at competitive rates. The Trust intends to work on common themes and shared needs so that they can design effective CPD. Although committed to the group, he has made it clear that he would feel obliged to withdraw if it were in the best interests of his school, his staff and his children.

FUNDING AND THE HEAD TEACHER AS ENTREPRENEUR

Faced with a diminishing budget each year, John needs to be creative in how he manages it. He believes that the notion that only schools with a large number of SEN children need money is wrong, as is penalising small rural schools such as his through allocation by postcode. The assumption that only children from low socio-economic backgrounds have special needs is also wrong. He is well aware of the correlation between poverty and underachievement, but many children in areas of economic deprivation are being denied opportunities, due to low expectations, a culture of excuses and even a failure of professionalism.

> *Without doubt, challenging underperformance among staff had a huge impact on my school. It created an opportunity to improve the standards of teaching in the classrooms, and reduced the costs of staffing in the budget.*

> *As ruthless as this may seem, this has had a huge benefit for the children. Not only has teaching improved, and made a measurable difference to what the children achieve and their progress, I have also been able to spend money on improving the environment and the resources available to make teaching more effective.*

John plans to improve the environment so that it requires very little financial commitment for the next ten years at least. Then he hopes to spend the majority of the budget rewarding teachers for the quality of their work.

A small school has limited room for promotion, so maintaining a staff of outstanding teachers means paying a competitive wage.

> *I would love to see the profile of the teaching profession raised, particularly at primary level, and to see attractive salaries for good graduates. I think standards at teacher training colleges could be improved, and I am in favour of robust performance appraisal if it makes it possible to reward the best, and to weed out those who do not make a proper impact.*

John has tried raising funds through sponsorship and by seeking possible funding streams, but this is time-consuming and not always fruitful.

CHAPTER FOUR

LOIS CRANE

St Mary's Church of England Combined School, Aylesbury, Buckinghamshire

C of E voluntary controlled school teaching children aged 4 to 11
Pupils: 395

Lois's account is notable because she offers a profound exposition of what constitutes effective headship: shrewd, well-founded advice on the leadership, management and professional development of teachers; thought-provoking views, based on long practical experience; and deep reflection on the critical issues that perennially challenge educationists.

Prominent among the factors that have helped to make Lois Crane an outstanding school leader are:

☐ consistent concentration on the continuing professional development of all staff and the use of carefully organised processes for its achievement;

☐ a highly informed understanding of what makes for effective learning, derived from constant observation, analysis and classroom based research and the impact of high quality teaching in relation to it;

☐ the development of a richly resourced, imaginative and innovative whole school learning environment;

☐ a strong emphasis on team work and the development of leaders;

☐ an effective partnership with parents, nurtured by constant application and the formulation of a clear understanding of mutual responsibility;

☐ a dedicated practical involvement with the wider educational community.

Lois Crane's primary education was at a school that offered opportunities for creativity and a range of educational visits.

Her grammar school had high expectations: an insistence on standards of behaviour, appropriate manners and conduct, and academic achievement. These beliefs, values and aims are appropriate for her own school, St Mary's C of E Combined School. Central to the school's philosophy is a commitment to acknowledging excellence and challenging poor performance. 'Children have only one chance at primary education. Neither staff nor children must allow any of that precious time to be wasted. They must share a clear vision of what can be achieved and a determination to bring it about.'

Lois deplores the tendency in modern education for dumbing down, the acceptance of minimum standards. She sees a widespread reduction in the expectations schools have regarding the potential and capability of children. This tendency she partially attributes to the growing number of one-parent families. She insists she is not condemning individuals, but making a judgement based on observing the heavy demands of single parenthood. Although many single parents cope, doing an excellent job in bringing up their children, it is harder managing a family alone, maintaining discipline and standards. One single mother of three boys confessed that ultimately it was easier giving in to their incessant and often highly unreasonable demands. Such patterns of parenting have negative consequences for child development, leading, in extreme cases, to 'lawless' areas of society.

Lois never imagined having a university education; there was no tradition of that in her family nor among the majority of her friends. So from the Lower Sixth she went to Teacher Training College. At the end of a three-year course, she went back to teach at her own primary school, where her former head teacher was still in charge.

Apart from having to present a weekly 'forecast book', teachers were left to their own devices so far as planning was concerned. She had no INSET at that time (1971). Contact with parents was extremely limited: 'The parents left their children at the school gate. We saw them once or twice a year and at the Open Evening.'

Four years later, Lois moved from what was an Education Priority Area to a more affluent area: the school had a swimming pool, the parents drove large cars, had much higher expectations and interacted more with the school. The head teacher exercised a little more leadership; they met as a staff and 'somebody would talk about a course they had been on'. What they had learned would cascade down to the others.

Her first promotion, a Scale One post, gave her responsibility for the school library, and ignited her interest in children's literature and literacy in general. She also coordinated and managed girls' games.

When Lois became pregnant she had to leave, 'to the chagrin of the head teacher'. She spent the next ten years out of school: 'In those days you didn't come back when you had a baby.' Being at home benefited her own children; once they were beyond middle primary school years and no longer so demanding, Lois decided to return to teaching.

When she did, the National Curriculum was in place. She remembers fraught teachers struggling with the huge subject folders, 'obliged to ensure that highly detailed modules drawn from across the broad curriculum were taught, and within particular time frames'. But as Lois had been teaching part-time as a Section 11 teacher, she 'sort of absorbed the National Curriculum' and welcomed the radical and challenging demands its delivery imposed on teachers. It provided a rich and coherent framework for teaching and learning; an attempt to define essential concepts, skills and knowledge. It was a necessary instrument for assessment and evaluation, and a guide to progression and continuity in children's attainment and achievement.

It was mandatory for Section 11 funding to be used for language acquisition and general educational assimilation for children for whom English was a second language. With the advent of the National Curriculum more INSET was provided, and teachers were required to avail themselves of it. Lois had an afternoon a week devoted to this. She and other colleagues with similar Section 11 responsibilities met to discuss their work and share ideas and devise learning materials for the children, although there was little specific guidance on this.

Her return to teaching was marked by the large-scale reduction of male teachers in primary schools. Whilst she feels the lack of 'gender balance' diminishes the range of educational provision available to primary children, especially older boys, she welcomes the skills that women bring to the profession.

Lois had been working with and leading staff in the course of her Section 11 work, and subsequently for the coordination of literacy. A complicated structure of layered leadership was developing, with subject, year and phase leaders. She and her colleagues gradually, sometimes painfully, mastered the business of leading people, although they were often very different in terms of personality, experience, involvement and commitment. They developed skills and strategies for getting the best from all staff, including those who were reluctant or recalcitrant.

They learned the importance of positive leadership; of working alongside people; of identifying their capability and skills, however limited, and building on them. They understood the importance of high expectations and refused to accept anything less than their best. They also found that some people rejected the challenge to aspire to expectations.

To build team responsibility, she had everyone produce an explicit statement of what their specific business was: its aims, objectives and substance, what every individual's role in that was, what capabilities and strengths people were bringing to the work and how they could enable themselves as a team collectively and individually.

> *There was nowhere left for people to hide. But, at middle level leadership and management, the extent to which we could exercise direction over colleagues was constrained to a degree that is now no longer so for me as a head teacher.*

At the same time, working as a Section 11 advisory teacher, she was becoming more informed about a diversity of cultures and children: their home circumstances, the different faith systems to which many subscribed and the implications of this for their school experience. She endeavoured to get to know the communities, to become part of them.

> *When children had days off to celebrate the great feasts, such as Eid and Diwali and Ramadan, I accepted invitations to visit families and share their commemorations and meals. By the time I had finished my rounds I would be surfeited with food. The children loved the fact that a teacher was coming into their families and sharing their celebrations. They talked about it for months afterwards: 'Mrs Crane came to visit us for the Feast!'*

As a subject coordinator, Lois attended the occasional meetings of senior staff. (They were not called senior management teams in those days; that came in later through Ofsted Inspections.) A new form of hands-on, supportive leadership was emerging. When she vehemently disagreed with a head's decision, he asked her, 'What would you do then?' and genuinely took account of her response, rather than being confrontational.

Lois became Deputy Head Teacher of what would now be categorised as a 'coasting school', situated in a relatively affluent neighbourhood. The head teacher had been in position for over twenty years. After a cursory interview, she secured the post over an internal candidate favoured by the head teacher. (At that time she did not appreciate the significance of a governing body overruling the head teacher.) The staff took the outcome badly, deliberately excluding Lois whenever possible. Lois found that the unsuccessful colleague, while not overtly obstructive, would openly criticise her when possible and was 'making bullets for others to fire'. What brought matters to a head was a hostile criticism made by the particular colleague before the whole staff, about a school journey to France. Lois had organised this trip for her top year class, the school's first educational expedition abroad.

Lois seized on this incident to establish her position, to clarify her role and her perception of the obligations attached to it. She opened a discussion on the ways in which she intended to work for the benefit of the school, the children and all the staff who taught there. She explained the educational aims and purpose of the visit in detail: her class was making a broad study of France, its links with Britain, and the two great twentieth-century wars that had involved the countries in partnership; they were also engaged in thematic work around the Bayeux Tapestry. The visit vividly reinforced the work already done by the children and provided a powerful stimulus to further research and creativity. This successful French educational journey demonstrated her organisational capacity and her ability to win over parents. She was ready to involve other staff in partnership in such enterprises.

By the end of her first year, she had established herself, in professional terms, with the staff, clarifying to colleagues the educational purposes of her work and actions. Lois was willing to seek and take account of their views and opinions and she provided, unobtrusively and subtly, effective professional support to colleagues who sought it, in a school where the prevailing ethos did not encourage collegiality and interdependence. Above all, she established herself through 'revitalising rituals', making familiar routine things such as morning assemblies interesting and engaging.

Now, as head teacher, she ensures that new demands and official initiatives are seen by staff not as an additional workload but as a challenge and an opportunity to shape teaching and learning in as interesting and productive a way as possible. As an example of this she cites two initiatives promoting community cohesion.

One involved an exchange of pupils with a special school for severely disabled children. The second involved a partnership with a large inner-city school with a high proportion of Muslim children. Year 5 children from St Mary's went to the partner school for a day and shared lessons with children from different cultures and significantly different backgrounds. They worked with partners (Year 4) on ICT assignments and played games on artificial grass – a novelty for the majority of the visitors. At St Mary's, the visiting children shared a wide range of learning activities, including an assembly – an experiment that was greeted with apprehension by some staff and especially those from the inner-city school.

Neither initiative was an easy option; some teachers thought the second especially risky. However, both occasions demonstrated her belief that such initiatives, arising from imaginative and fresh approaches, added new interest and meaning for children.

Over that first year as a deputy head teacher, she sensed staff gradually moving towards her, largely because she was always ready to be explicit and transparent, and provide support and encouragement to colleagues.

At that point, the head teacher secured a secondment and Lois became the acting head teacher.

It was the best thing that could have happened and a wonderful opportunity to revitalise the life of the school. The secondment was to be for a mere two terms. I simply wanted to get on and do what was very necessary for the school as a whole.

She had already attended some of the governing body's sub-committees and knew about their roles for particular development. They, in turn, were aware of her views and aspirations, and when the secondment came, gave their blessing to do what she wanted to do. Most importantly, the staff were ready to contribute to transforming change:

- They set up a school council.
- They put an assessment and tracking system in place where none had existed before.
- Lois organised 'job chats' for all staff, including teaching assistants, to discuss their work, professional development and aspirations for the future, and to explore how they saw themselves fitting into her 'big picture'.
- She appointed two new members of staff who she knew would respond positively to sensitive guidance and coaching, including one highly skilled in teaching sports, an area conspicuously lacking in the school.
- She embraced parents, offering them a partnership in their children's learning and sharing ideas about translating this into reality.
- She engaged the school in the Investors in People initiative.

Then the head teacher returned. Despite acknowledging what had been done and promising to maintain the progress made, things soon reverted to where they had been. His dislike of Investors in People meant that the initiative eventually perished; he also struggled to come to terms with the school/parent partnership.

Lois and the staff, energised by their achievements and excited by the realisation of what more could be done, were determined to preserve what they had worked so hard to bring about. 'It is very difficult to be innovative and transformational if you are not at the top, if you do not have executive power.' Gradually the staff's new-found enthusiasm waned, through a lack of commitment and encouragement. Lois, back in her marginalised deputy position, was forced to withdraw now that there was so little she could do in terms of staff leadership and development.

Now that Lois knew she was 'capable of making a real and important difference to a school, to all who worked there, and the children and the community it served', she could not happily accept this regression to what had been. She had come to recognise and appreciate more fully some of the elements and skills essential to effective leadership and the efficient management of an institution – though she could not claim to have fully mastered any of them. That only comes over time, from reflection and response to practical experience, from a readiness to learn from mistakes and setbacks as much as from success, from a commitment to collaborative professional endeavour and, probably above all, from a learning disposition in a school that is a thinking organisation.

In that period of acting headship, other leadership qualities became evident to her:

- Above all is managing the school effectively and efficiently, from day to day; making it a pleasant, ordered, stimulating and enjoyable place for staff and children. 'Without that, the best of intentions and the grandest plans will run into the sand.'

- The head teacher must show staff their love and enthusiasm for teaching. They must talk about the principles of effective teaching and learning, and be prepared to demonstrate them in practice. They must help staff be successful in their practice, enable them to recognise and celebrate what they are achieving and support them practically in developing strategies for improving performance.

- Head teachers should formulate a vision for the school, and share that and its values with colleagues. Having a priority of high standards and attainment commits staff and pupils to doing all they can to realise and maintain them, and persistently fight against unsatisfactory performance and underachievement.

- Staff should take responsibility beyond their classroom domain; their capacity for leadership will be supported and developed in relation to particular initiatives and teams.

- Head teachers should systematically delegate management tasks and monitor their implementation to ensure the effective running of the school. As part of CPD they should:

  - Clarify the purpose and value to the school, staff and children of the initiatives, see them through to a good conclusion, and apply the lessons they learn to their future practice.

  - Reach out and build effective relationships with parents, keep them informed about their children's education and progress and help them play a genuine part in it, in partnership with the school.

  - Seek and accept advice, expertise and evaluation from accredited external bodies.

HEADSHIP

The next logical stage in Lois's career was headship. Even though she felt that she was now adequately equipped for the position, in her own time she achieved an MA in Education, since she assumed that a degree was necessary to make her eligible to apply.

Within a year, Lois was appointed Head of St Mary's C of E Primary School. The school, previously 'a tiny first school in the middle of Aylesbury and on the verge of closure', was moved by the county authority, in partnership with the diocese, to cater for children on the new Fairford Leys Estate, becoming a two-form entry primary school.

This transition had been extremely well managed and resourced – the retiring deputy head teacher was unstinting in working to ensure an efficient changeover. In the formidable task of establishing a new school, Lois received generous support from the local authority, which paid for the deputy to be free of class responsibility for two terms.

Some staff left during the transition, but other teachers applied, attracted by the prospect of working in a new school. Lois found herself in a position where she could take a huge step forward in putting together a strong team, committed to the success of the school, rich in potential, eager to learn and to advance their own professional development.

She perceived the core purpose of the school to be developing the children to become effective, successful learners and achievers. This would motivate staff and children, inform parents and draw all staff together as a learning community. If teachers are to serve children professionally then they must hold the highest expectations for them and do everything possible – academically, cognitively, socially, morally and spiritually – to enable them to fulfil their potential in all they do. Anything less is to fail them.

Children should not come to school because it is a convention, a social expectation, or because their parents insist they must, but because they will find there something of true and abiding value, of undreamt-of possibility.

They set out to make children reflective learners:

> From the very beginning, our focus was on the quality of our teaching and the children's learning, on the promotion of their metacognition. I believe that metacognition – the capacity to examine one's own learning, to identify what makes it effective, to master the strategies that underpin it – is absolutely essential to the effective learner.

This is not easy; it is a highly sophisticated process whereby children are taught to evaluate what they do, to make sound judgements about the quality of their learning and what they can do to make it more effective. In other words, we help them become 'agents of their own learning'.

We spent a year embedding the process, tutoring and coaching the children, helping them to understand and become engaged in what they were doing, providing them with enabling strategies.

In all classes, children learned to talk about their work and their learning in an analytical and reflective way. They discussed and reflected with their teachers on lesson objectives and intentions, working to arrive at an understanding of their point and purpose. At the conclusion of lessons, they reflected individually and collectively on how successful they had been in what they had done, how far they had realised the lesson objectives, the factors that had helped and hindered their progress, the strategies they had called on in their learning and what they might do in subsequent lessons to improve performance and attainment.

The teachers and learning assistants were wholly involved. Key factors were dialogue between teachers and learners and the provision of carefully structured, accessible and 'learner friendly' feedback, both oral and written. Each classroom had a lesson board to remind them of routines and strategies which they would frequently refer to.

Then the school focused on the emotional dimension of learning. The children reflected on the impediments, other than the purely cognitive ones, to their learning and attainment. Staff taught them to identify and recognise these impediments: a failure to concentrate and persevere; a lack of confidence and awareness of what they could achieve; a readiness to be satisfied with less than their best; a reluctance to think things through, to evaluate and be rigorous. Then they would discuss strategies for dealing with them. It was a complex and demanding process.

We were making big demands of the children and their maturity, but ones, I was convinced, that they were capable of meeting, at each individual's particular stage of development.

At first the children struggled with it, because they were not accustomed to reviewing and reflecting. Nor did they always have the vocabulary to articulate their reaction and responses. Gradually, they learned to identify what worked and what didn't. Staff used questionnaires at the beginning and at the end of the year to ascertain the progress made by the children. An analysis of the questionnaire demonstrated significant advances made by children in terms of their capacity to be reflective and more autonomous learners.

This increased focus on teaching and learning had important outcomes beyond the enhancement of children's attainment, personal confidence and self-esteem as learners. It drew the staff together into a powerful common enterprise, and promoted collaborative practice and exchange of ideas about teaching and learning. Everyone was involved, teachers and learning assistants, no matter how experienced, whatever their status. Everyone contributed something of value and significance from their own classroom evaluation and research. They were all learning and growing professionally together.

For her own part, Lois was developing those leadership skills she had first identified at the end of her brief period as acting head: the need to keep oneself as informed as possible about curriculum development and current educational matters; the absolute necessity to be an effective manager of school business from day to day; above all, the need to formulate and share a vision for the school. She was gradually learning and mastering the skills of leadership of a big and expanding school on a daily basis: leading and managing a large and diverse staff, using the kind of collegial teaching and learning process described above, and navigating the rapid and immense changes in education which obliged staff to look outwards and to be more accountable.

She summarises this developing repertoire of competencies:

- The capacity to access, analyse and interpret relevant and important data and use it for the benefit of the school as a learning institution.

- The ability to master budgetary systems and use financial resources most productively to serve the needs of the school.

- A readiness to accept that managerial, organisational and personnel related decisions must be made only on comprehensively informed awareness.

- Head teachers must develop leadership and management capabilities and qualities in staff, and empower them to use these appropriately and effectively, through teams, structures and systems established to provide quality assurance and high performance.

- An understanding of how to establish, maintain and learn from reliable and rigorous systems of evaluation of the work of the school.

- An eagerness to learn from, and be influenced by, the outcome of regular school self-review and authoritative external evaluation.

A readiness to make productive professional networks, designed to increase their professional knowledge, widen their perspective, and thus add value to the school.

An ability to establish and maintain a dialogue with parents and the wider community, based on a consensus about the school's vision which clearly exhibits strong values and beliefs and a common responsibility for the education and welfare of the children.

TEACHING AND ENCOURAGING TEACHERS TO LEAD AND MANAGE

The modern, successful school depends on shared, delegated leadership and management. Lois constantly reminds her staff that leadership does not reside in her office, and that as head she cannot, and most emphatically does not wish to, attempt to do it all herself.

Her policy for sharing the leadership and management of the school, and for training teachers to progressively assume the various roles and functions involved, begins with a clearly established 'no-blame' culture in relation to the leadership responsibilities delegated to staff.

As a result, people feel appreciated, valued and respected; they feel confident about expressing themselves and doing things, knowing that if things go wrong, the school will deal with it as a community. They feel able to be creative and innovative, to take risks, because where outcomes are not as intended and hoped for, then matters can be changed or adapted, but put right.

All staff are given chances to lead and manage, starting with lesser responsibilities, through which they are supported, resourced and encouraged, but with a clear mandate to be in charge and to take action. Over time they are trained and coached to take on greater responsibilities, knowing that their ability is recognised and that they are valued and trusted.

Without that dedicated team of staff we couldn't do the things we do or achieve what we have achieved. Your success as leader is largely dependent on them, individually and collectively. That is why I appreciate and value them so much. They know I take notice of what they say; they know I take their ideas and use them.

The language they use is important. Instead of asking people to 'take on' or 'be in charge of' tasks and assignments, she quite deliberately ask them 'to lead', 'to be the leader', with all that implies in terms of status, responsibility, accountability and, above all, trust – trust in them as leaders and trust in their proven capabilities. This applies to every member of staff.

If children are falling below expected levels, for example, those who are underachieving in literacy, they use the ALS (Additional Literacy Support) intervention programme. She gives the leadership of these to the teaching assistants. They are trained to do it, and learn how to track progress, analyse outcomes, implement the programme appropriately and report developments to her. They work in small teams in the classroom, accountable to the designated TA leader, and are responsible for making it work. They know she trusts their competence and dedication. And the more chance they get to exercise leadership, however small the beginning or apparently minor the assignment, the better they become at it, the more informed they become as practitioners, and the more skilled and confident they become professionally.

Whatever roles people play in the school, they learn to articulate the purpose, importance and essence of each role and its place in providing effective teaching and learning. An example of this is the collective response to behaviour management, where all staff seek, through their specific role, to nurture in pupils: a sense of personal responsibility, pride in oneself and one's work; determination to do what is right and good; tolerance, respect and concern for others; and commitment to making the best of the wider school community.

Lois places great stress on the concept and practice of people working in teams.

> Many teams operate in the school because we do so much. Sometimes their existence is relatively brief – the time it takes to run an initiative or assignment. For these, teams come together for a specific purpose and disperse at its conclusion. Other teams have a longer lifespan or are permanent; their membership may change as circumstances demand. There will be, for example, a senior management team, teams with particular administrative functions, teams that are responsible for the care and maintenance of the school, teaching assistant teams, curriculum and monitoring teams and so on.

People often belong to more than one team. The personnel and the teams are interchangeable. That was one of the things that greatly impressed Ofsted in the course of the school inspection: the range of teams established for specific purposes, but often overlapping with other teams in terms of their objectives; also, the capacity of people within those teams. Team members were well aware of the critical nature of their inter-dependence. Lois says, 'We all know that the existence of a weak link endangers every-thing. Where it exists, it is not just my and the senior team members' responsibility to recognise and rectify it, but that of other leaders who may be more immediately or more appropriately related to it.'

As leaders they are all involved in an elaborate system of performance monitoring and observations: the senior management team, phase leaders, curriculum coordinators, teachers engaged in peer observation, class teachers responsible for the leadership and management of TAs and so on.

She states: 'Commitment to the team is a sustaining force for us.' Team members are interdependent and mutually accountable. Talking about her care of staff in personal and professional terms, her Awards for Teachers system comprises written messages formally read out in assembly to thank people for contributions they have made to the welfare of the children and the value of the school.

> *I try to be specific. The awards, my 'Thank Yous', are directed at individuals or teams for particular services. Children recognise what is happening: that teachers are being appreciated, valued, and honoured. Slight though the gestures may be, I know they matter to teachers.*

One member of staff told Lois that she carried her first award letter around in her wallet for two years.

> *The more I value them, the more I acknowledge their contributions in terms of leadership and management, the more I am able to ask them to do that extra thing, to go the additional mile. And the more experience they have of leadership, of seeing initiatives through to a successful conclusion, the more confident they are about innovating and setting up their own.*

Some of the staff exercise aspects of leadership and management in connection with other schools. This has come about through Lois's induction as a National Leader of Education, with an obligation to support struggling schools on a one-day-a-week basis.

When she first got involved she was surprised at what was not in place in many schools; for example, she had to help staff inaugurate systems for monitoring and evaluation, for lesson observation and feedback, and for effective pupil assessment and tracking.

Subsequently, her staff became involved with other schools 'in needy circumstances'. Teachers visiting St Mary's from those schools observe lessons, discuss pedagogy and teaching and learning with St Mary's staff, and take back learning materials for use in their own schools. Curriculum leaders, especially in the core subjects, spend time in the schools, working with colleagues to provide guidance and expertise in a practical, hands-on way.

Lois believes that such experience is invaluable in providing for 'succession planning' – training and preparation for teachers who will wish to take on larger responsibilities, including headship, a little later in their careers.

At the time of my first visit to the school, Lois had already invited comments from staff about leadership:

> Could you write down six things about leadership that you consider are the reasons why our school is successful and effective. This can be in terms of my leadership qualities and attributes or the leadership of the school in general. We need to know what staff think and I promise not to let it go to my or the leadership team's head. We are not asking what doesn't make us effective; we are just looking for the best qualities.

The response from staff, both teams and individuals, covered a wide range of issues. The following is a sample of representative viewpoints:

- SMT is supportive, both of each other and their teams; they also quickly cascade information.

- We are not afraid to say what we think – we know we will be heard!

- You don't let us stand still. There's:

  - CPD which you actively encourage for all.

  - All those challenges – achieving the Artsmark or Healthy Schools award, running special events – all of which keep us pressing onwards and upwards; we don't rest on our laurels.

- The 'We're all in this together' approach.

- Leadership is approachable and open to new ideas and always available to offer help and suggestions.

- Good delegation and great team spirit (everyone is approachable, friendly and very helpful).

- All members of staff are valued and treated the same.

- All work gets done to a very high standard and yet the atmosphere is still relaxed.

- Respect and encouragement is given to all members of staff.

- Up-to-date with current thinking/initiatives.

- Leadership is aware of pressures of other roles in school and prepared to lighten the load as necessary.

- Head motivates staff by example, praise and attitude.

Although some of the responses might seem trivial, they are highly significant and informative. They are the things that are genuinely important to teachers, the things that sustain and motivate them, the things that make them tick. They seem to suggest that systems on their own, no matter how impressive, won't do. Leadership and management seem to need the human touch.

RESOURCES

Lois talked at some length about the use of ICT and its transforming impact on children's learning. She stressed the power of visual impact for children, the nature of their expectations in relation to the presentation of information and ideas, influenced by the media revolution, and the implications for the ways in which learning is delivered to them. She believes that schools will have to take greater account of the fact that children are increasingly visual learners. She even goes so far as to suggest that for some children, reading a story book doesn't really work anymore. They may need to be introduced to the world of learning and books through other media.

For children attuned to the visual image, more and more of their reading is of things that flash in front of their eyes. The Aztecs in a picture on a page of a book in front of them is fine, but the Aztecs moving about on screen is even better and more powerful ... have an Aztec in the classroom!

EXTERNAL RELATIONS

The school values relationships with parents and the community, and has created partnerships that support the children's learning and development. Lois believes that the Christian ethic that informs their work can contribute significantly to the dissemination of a values system that offers a unifying and life-enhancing philosophy for the school and the families it serves.

Last year parents were invited in on two occasions to 'tell the school how they might do things better'. They intend to continue this practice at intervals. They are also inviting parents of children in the Early Years to come and observe teaching and engage in discussion and explanation about its form, practice and purpose. Later they want to introduce the initiative into other year groups.

> What I have never wanted is parents outside the gate complaining about what they regard as typical shortcomings. I want them to know that if something is wrong we wish to hear about it and sort it out.

PERSONAL QUALITIES THAT IMPINGE ON LEADERSHIP

Effective leadership cannot be complete without reference to the personal qualities and attitudes of the leader/head teacher. The head is the one who builds the team and it is inevitable that their personal qualities, dispositions, attitudes, life view and philosophy impinge on that and significantly affect the members of the team in one way or another.

Their public persona, the leader's overt behaviour, also provides a model for colleagues, many of whom bear leadership responsibilities themselves. She reflects dispassionately on some of her own personal qualities that she believes significantly contribute to her style of leadership:

> I am always consistent, so people know they will always get a positive response from me; I'm not going to be nice one day and bite their head off the next.

> I am enthusiastic and have boundless energy. I am assertive and good at making decisions, but I don't make them quickly; I weigh up evidence before I act, and once the decision is taken, I stick with it. Although my leadership is based on strong unchanging principles, I believe I can also be flexible and adaptable in terms of style to match events, demands, occasions.

I am excited by my work. I see every new demand and initiative not as a burden but an opportunity for discovery, growth, development, enrichment. I am always looking for new ideas and fresh approaches to problems.

I am sensitive to others and acutely aware of my teachers' workload. I am concerned to support them through that. But I am not a touchy-feely person. I don't want to be part of people's personal lives. I don't want to be part of that kind of tittle-tattle. But if staff have personal problems where my support and intervention would be helpful, then I will never fail them.

I am a punctilious person in my management and I train my staff to be the same in terms of time management, delivery dates and so on. I expect them to deliver what they promise and have committed to, ensuring we know it is realistic and doable, just as I do personally in my work.

I am a great and unremitting enthusiast for the school, which also means for the local community I lead: children, staff, and, where relevant, parents too.

CHAPTER FIVE

MAXINE EVANS

Rush Common Primary School, Abingdon, Oxfordshire

Non-denominational school for boys and girls from 4 to 11

Pupils: 415

Maxine Evans brought to headship a set of beliefs and convictions that appeared at the outset, at that time, to be inordinately radical in relation to important aspects of the role. Her extensive, high level experience in the world of business and a rigorous and cerebral approach led her to analyse, challenge and, where necessary, significantly adapt some traditional beliefs and practices. She advocated a theory of leadership markedly different from generally held views of headship.

She expresses clearly argued reservations about what she regards as an over-emphasis on the teaching role of head teachers, for all her manifest giftedness in this respect, and her capacity and willingness to bring it into play in developing the professional competence of staff.

She believes the emphasis she has placed upon the responsibilities of the head teacher for the oversight and management of the local life of the school, and the development of distributed leadership to underpin this, have been greatly instrumental in the transformation of an often good, but underachieving, school to an outstanding one.

Among the major innovations she has fostered has been the development of the school in outreach terms as a successful and profitable agent of INSET and CPD of teaching staff.

But, essentially, all her work is driven by a powerful commitment to the provision of children's successful learning, attainment and achievement and a belief in the capacity of teachers to bring it about through inspiring practice in the classroom.

Maxine, who grew up in a disrupted and challenging home environment, remembers her schooldays and teachers as her salvation, a transforming influence in her life. Her primary school head teacher had a passion for music and determined that every child would learn to play music and find a place in his recorder orchestra.

Maxine graduated to the violin and found a mentor in a peripatetic teacher, Gretchen Curtis, who ferried her to play in orchestras far and wide.

> *I was never at home on Saturdays. This teacher had seen something in me, and took me under her wing. Coming from a working-class home where there were few books and no holidays, that primary school, and my experience of music and orchestras with Gretchen, opened another world to me – a middle class world, where parents nurtured their children and supported them.*

Within a year of taking up the violin she was playing in competitions, yet nobody from her family ever saw her play until her mother attended her graduation and heard her perform in the orchestral concert. At sixteen, Maxine won a scholarship to Dartington Hall to study music and English, despite her stepfather's determination that she should leave school and become a breadwinner.

Later, prevented by injury from becoming a professional musician, she went to Bath College of Higher Education and became a teacher. During her time at Bath she 'played music everywhere', not just for the love of it, but to earn money: in the pit at the Theatre Royal, in operas and musicals, and in a quartet that performed at weddings. A primary head teacher invited her to teach music in his school every Wednesday morning, 'so I used to bunk off to go and teach primary-age children'.

Having completed a four-year B Ed Hons course, Maxine went straight from college to take up the post of Head of Music at Kings of Wessex Upper (13–18) School which, she reflects, probably seemed quite outrageous. However, she felt that the range and richness of her experience at Bath – she organised, administered, conducted and led orchestras; ran a Saturday morning art school; taught choirs; did occasional music-related work for Somerset County Council; busked on the streets; and played in Bath Abbey – suggested that she was confident enough to manage the role successfully.

When she arrived, all music in the school was taught in a hut. By the time she left three years later there was an imposing purpose-built music department, transformed at the instigation of an HMI who had observed her work. In that time she had built up a seventy-piece concert band and a full-part choir. It was a great time for the school, for music and for her.

Then after three years, newly married and 'having worked myself to the bone', she decided she needed a different kind of professional experience. She became Primary Consultant with a computer software company, Research Machines (now RM Education), with the task of selling a new and sophisticated piece of technological equipment to schools. The link was that she had been part of a Somerset pilot project in ICT in music, had set up a recording studio in the school, and introduced computing equipment in all the classrooms.

RM used fast-tracking, monitoring, mentoring, coaching and training for their employees. She moved swiftly round the organisation to different areas, working with new people and meeting new challenges. She was soon managing increasing numbers of staff and being given the coaching and the resources to enable her to grow. She found the enormity of the RM job petrifying at times, leading a staff of nearly eighty people, in a project designed to make RM outright market leaders in their field.

She learned to perceive things holistically, incorporating relevant external factors and aligning them with what they were doing in a way that reinforced and further empowered the company. 'It seems to me now that I was learning to do what people describe as "thinking outside the box".'

What she does now at Rush Common School – spotting and nurturing talent, succession planning, and capacity building – had been bread and butter stuff at RM. She spends half her time thinking about people's professional development, what they need and how to ensure they get that. 'I'm not interested in courses necessarily,' she says, 'but in the needs of individuals, in finding talent, and then putting the staff in place to make sure they maximise that talent.'

When yet another series of initiatives from central government arrives, rather than feeling in despair or overwhelmed, Maxine analyses them in terms of 'where, how and whether they fit in to what we are trying to achieve in the school', and responds to them and exploits them accordingly.

> *Working alongside gifted colleagues, I learned that it's okay to be different; to adopt approaches that are not always traditional, conventional or by the book. I recognised there is a right time, an opportune time, to do things; that leadership is about clarifying what it is you need to get done, identifying the best people to get it done, putting in resources that will help them get all the systems in place for them to achieve the targets, empowering them to get on and do it, and coming back to make sure they are still on track.*

At that time, she was seen by those who did not know her well as rather distant and stoic in attitude, conveying a first impression of being tough and ruthless. But underneath that uncompromising exterior, she is 'a bit of a softy' – and always accessible to her team.

In her final role at RM, in charge of over 200 people, the first thing she did before she sat at her desk was to 'walk the talk': she went out with team members to see customers, mentored them, and showed them she could handle the business she was expecting them to manage, because she believed 'you get the best out of people if you lead by example'.

The organisation, however, believed that the higher in the hierarchy you were, the more detached you had to become from certain levels of activity. She, on the other hand, was convinced that, as a service industry, one had to become closer to the customers and be involved with the teams one led.

She devoted a disproportionate amount of mentoring care to a casual and underachieving employee, because she perceived potential that was worth investing in. His subsequent achievement validated that. 'But,' she emphasises, 'had he not been worth it, I would have got rid of him.'

She occasionally spent too long over the caring process and wasted time. Knowing how much to invest in someone was another important lesson she learned at RM: 'How long are you prepared to tolerate what isn't working, or good enough, and to count the cost?'

> *That applies as much in school as in business, in terms of output and in terms of the children and their needs and entitlement. It is a question many schools are still not prepared to ask and answer.*

Twelve years after joining the company – by now the first female executive director and in the process of being seconded to Harvard – she resigned, in order to care for her second child. After twelve extraordinarily demanding years, she felt it was time to go, to do something different.

One significant event influenced her. She was commissioned to present an award for high achievement in ICT to a primary school on behalf of RM. On arriving at the school, she was invited by the head teacher, without notice, to conduct the entire assembly for over 500 children. She unhesitatingly went back to her music and they did a singing 'round' related to technology and constructed a machine from sounds. 'The children were enthralled and captivated; it felt fantastic.' That experience stayed with her through the next year; she had realised how passionate she was about education.

At the invitation of the then head teacher, she went to Rush Common Primary School, at a much reduced salary, as Business Manager of their tentative entrepreneurial work in offering training consultancy services. They were tentative because they were attempting to launch themselves into the unknown. As educationists, they knew they had something valuable to offer, especially in the developing field of training for higher-level Teacher Assistant status.

At the end of a year, with the training business expanding and earning substantial income, the head teacher offered Maxine the position of Senior Teacher and subsequently Assistant Head on the business management side, the only official post of responsibility in the school. There was no provision for a deputy head. As much as Maxine admired the head teacher for his shrewdness, charisma, humane and caring relations with staff, and charming authority with parents, she did not care for his particular style of leadership: he invested all leadership responsibility in himself and rejected the notion of a formal management structure.

> *The school could only go as fast as he wanted to. Everyone, the school itself, was wholly dependent on him for too many important things. A formal business meeting would be constantly interrupted – he would break off repeatedly to answer his mobile phone; people would come barging in with requests and problems and our agenda would perish as he took the time to respond to them. He was bewildered at my frustrated insistence that we could not meet for business unless he would guarantee no interruptions.*

Her appointment was a recognition that in times of radical educational changes, primary schools, especially ones as large as this, urgently needed structures and an organisation fit for purpose. Leadership invested in a single person, no matter how admirable or heroic, would not do.

After a career largely spent in the world of business and commerce and with only limited teaching experience, her appointment was not welcomed by some long-established members of staff, not least because it suggested an emerging hierarchical structure. However, much of the dissent never became explicit or visible to her because the head teacher insisted on the staff's acquiescence and patience.

In her career with RM, she visited hundreds of schools and observed diverse and often inspirational practice, varied structures, organisational innovation and enterprising activities to raise funds. She had witnessed different forms of headship and leadership, much of it notable, and some outstanding. Staff, on the other hand, were reluctant to acknowledge or take advantage of such experience; many had remained in the same school, in a particular room with an unchanging pupil age group. Worse still, they had never visited or spent time observing another school.

Now, as part of performance management and development at the school, and to avoid this kind of parochialism, every member of staff, from school helper to head teacher, must make at least one awareness-raising visit to another primary school and observe an aspect of practice relevant to their personal area of responsibility. Additionally, twice each year every member of staff is required to identify, assimilate and master a core competence in relation to their work.

The head teacher then announced he was taking early retirement. He did not relish the impending changes in the world of education: workforce remodelling, staff and structure review, the extended services agenda, a new Ofsted framework. However, he had thought carefully about planning succession, and made it quite clear that he saw Maxine as the right person to implement the necessary changes for taking the school forward.

He took steps to prepare her for the task, persuading the governing body to accept her for a couple of terms as acting head teacher, which gave her time to grow and test her suitability. He then created a situation where she had to prove to staff her quality in terms of teaching and learning. At short notice, he asked her to teach a class for a week, covering for an absent colleague. It was not so much her high quality management and organisational flair that mattered in her role as assistant head teacher; what staff really wanted her to demonstrate was her ability as a teacher. Clearly her performance as a teacher earned her colleagues' respect; once the period of acting headship was completed she was appointed as Head.

A DIFFERENT STYLE OF LEADERSHIP

Maxine's 'meteoric' career development, both in business and in education, happened because:

> All the way along, inspirational people recognised my potential and enabled me to realise it by providing what I needed and giving generous support. I passionately believe that it is the right of everyone to have nothing less than that. It is my job as Head Teacher to see that every child who goes through our school benefits from the very best we can give them, and that when they leave us we can be absolutely sure that they will never look back and think we could have done more for them. My vision for this school is that it is wholly in the business of improving life chances.

The business I am in is ensuring that I find the best and surest way for this school to achieve that vision on behalf of every child. I had that; I was given that by wonderful people – and it is every child's right to have it too.

Maxine found the NPQH 'good for networking, being exposed to different people, other potential leaders'. However, at that time NPQH training focused largely on teaching and learning rather than on the real business of headship: managing a diversity of crises and challenges proficiently and ensuring that the school functions effectively and realises its vision.

Very little of her day is involved with teaching and learning:

I am surrounded by years and years of experience of successful teaching and learning. The people who were engaged in NPQH had spent their professional lives immersed in teaching and learning; they were comprehensively informed and highly expert. It was very seductive for them to continue being absorbed by it and submerged in it, in an unchallenging comfort zone. What they needed was to identify the quality of their financial management and its creative application; their understanding of the complex operation of running a school; and their knowledge of people and how to manage, nurture, coach and develop them.

A major part of headship is facilitating expertise and creating the circumstances, conditions and support so that highly skilled professional teachers can exercise their craft to the very best of their ability. Maxine spots the best people to do a job, empowers them to do it and then monitors them. She asks critical questions: Are the outcomes what we had hoped for? Are they as good as they could be? How can we be sure of that? Why have you chosen to do things in that particular way?

These are not questions to catch people out, or to put them under pressure, but to ensure that we remain reflective and self-critical, and arrive at answers that illuminate things for us about our practice, our teaching and learning, and help us keep on improving.

This notion that the head teacher's responsibilities lie elsewhere than in the area of teaching and learning runs counter to some of the current views of leadership. Some suggest that such a stance may diminish their credibility with staff. Therefore, a head teacher must also be able to show not just that they can teach well and command all the skills and technology of contemporary pedagogy, but that they have a passion for it and can engage effectively with children and with their learning.

One of the first things she did after her appointment as head was to demonstrate her practical expertise in teaching by leading an extended team project in the Early Years and Key Stage 1. She had been concerned that pupil outcomes as measured by SATs were very good at Key Stage 2, yet absolutely dismal at the end of Key Stage 1. She thought she knew why this was happening, but needed to identify the causes and establish courses of action that would lead to a major improvement, particularly in writing. Together they created a project focusing on the implications and effects of transition at different stages in EYFS and Key Stage 1. They also created a computer system for monitoring and tracking pupils' progress, identifying assessment points throughout the year. She played the leading part in devising the project, was practically involved at all times in its implementation, monitoring and evaluation, and was a working teacher in the classroom.

What mattered was not that she had demonstrated to her staff that she could teach 'with the best of them', but that as head teacher and leader she had identified and acted upon a serious issue that needed urgent action. Her solution proved successful – standards were raised and the children's attainment significantly improved.

As the head teacher she had some hard, uncomfortable things to say about the quality of teaching and learning that had led part of the school into an unacceptable situation.

> *The staff hated it because their view was that we had been doing fine up until now and why did they have to go through all this unpleasant stuff. It was uncomfortable because now it was obvious that in some classes children were seriously underachieving. Some teachers found themselves confronting awkward truths. But a head has to do more than simply 'unzip' things and make explicit what is going on. A head has to take action, and lead the staff in taking action.*

For Maxine, headship and leadership are about dealing with the hard, demanding issues (such as unchecked underachievement) that can blow a school off course if they are not dealt with. It's about meeting the constant challenges, overcoming the impediments and crises, and clearing the way for staff to get on with the thing they are expert in and suited to: teaching and learning.

What emerged – the need for monitoring and tracking systems, for gathering data, and for interpreting what that was telling them about children's attainment and progress – led her to conclude that:

High quality teaching in the upper school was obscuring less competent perfor-
mance elsewhere; received data was not being acted upon or being analysed
for the critical information it could have provided in relation to children's at-
tainment and progress and teacher performance.

The greatest problem was that there was no structure, no system and no capacity within the organisation to take essential action on what her investigations were revealing. When the school was faced with external demands or when something was going wrong, there was no one ready to take things on. The organisation exhibited a kind of paralysis, yet within the school were some outstanding, highly capable people, some of whom were quietly and instinctively managing to minimise what could have been serious consequences of an inadequate organisation.

Maxine needed to sort out the professional and attitudinal features that were at the heart of the underachievement issue. The first thing was to unite the staff in understanding the school's mission.

I said to them, we have no choice, other than doing the very best job we can for
all of the children in this school. And they would say to me, 'It's most important
they have fun.' I used to reply, 'Yes, it's important, but it's not the most import-
ant. The most important is that they make progress.'

Once we'd got a plan, my message was quite simple: 'You do have a choice. You
can opt in and stay, or you can opt out and go, but you can't opt out and stay.'

Although the initiative to raise attainment in EYFS and Key Stage 1 established her credibility as a leader, manager and teacher, something more than a successful project was required if the school was to achieve the levels of excellence she envisaged. It needed an infrastructure that would provide distributed leadership; corporate coherence in terms of action, effective monitoring and evaluation processes; efficient performance management; and continuity and progression in teaching and learning throughout the school.

She put a management structure in place, comprising Operations, Teaching and Learning, and Pupil Welfare and Support. Each had a designated leader heading up each section and was formally supported by a staffing structure. Operations was responsible for the management of the front office and all administration, for the library and anything to do with extended services. In Teaching and Learning, leaders were accountable for ensuring high levels of performance. Pupil Welfare and Support included the SENCO role, but was also responsible for liaising and working with all the multi-agency services to coordinate shared action on important aspects of child provision; this extended beyond the purview of the school and eventually incorporated the Every Child Matters agenda. She says it would be tempting to attribute that particular development to her foresight about what was coming from official quarters, but it was actually down to her belief that it was the right thing to do for the children.

Her radical restructuring of the school management system – or, rather, the creation of a structure where one hadn't existed – was facilitated by government legislation and mandatory requirements for workforce remodelling and staff and structure reviews. The staff who made that transformation possible were already in the school. Over the years they had been allowed to slot into limited positions because that suited the existing organisation. What was needed was someone to release and motivate them.

Restructuring meant that some staff decided the change and the challenge wasn't for them so they went. This freed up room for fresh appointments, for people who wanted to be part of an exciting, innovative development.

> I retained the longest serving staff, including five who were to assume the main leadership posts, whilst some younger staff, who had been cosseted and pampered, went. I am committed to cherishing staff, but my approach is not the cuddling arm about the shoulder or the assurance to a sobbing teacher that of course she can have two days off to recover from a relationship trauma. It is a cherishing and a professional concern, expressed through consistent action and support, that will enable them to achieve their professional potential, grow in terms of true self-awareness and personal esteem and learn to teach their children more effectively.

To do this she had to recognise some teachers' potential and to arrange training and coaching, setting targets that would bring it to fruition. In some cases, she had to manage people out of the system, because it would be better for the school, and ultimately, better for them.

> That doesn't mean just getting rid of people without a qualm. A leader has responsibility for doing the best in all ways possible for all staff. So managing out meant a variety of things and strategies, a kind of contract or pact with staff that would enable us to agree on the course of action that was best for them: finding schools or other employment more suited to their dispositions, inclinations and talents.

It isn't easy and doesn't come naturally. A leader must have conviction and determination; must do what has to be done, based on mature reflection and judgement, for the good of the institution and for the betterment of the children.

> *It is not uncommon to find staffrooms where a cohort of influential staff, often long established, refuses to give any credence to the aspirations of a newly appointed head, or subtly but determinedly hinders attempts at change. In such cases, heads must separate the 'bullet makers' from the 'bullet firers'. The latter reveal themselves and are more easily dealt with; the former need to be identified and dealt with uncompromisingly. Heads who struggle and flounder do so because they lack the courage to see things as they are, the vision to realise what they might be, and the resolution to take the action that will make it so.*

That doesn't happen by reflecting exclusively on teaching and learning. Nor does it happen without added funding to provide for promotions, the additional personnel and support, and the adjustments created by restructuring.

Government had funded some aspects of workforce reform, but significantly more funding was required to establish and maintain the wide-ranging structural changes Maxine wanted. This finance was forthcoming from the school training arm and the business she had put in place in her first role as Assistant Head.

RECRUITMENT AND DEVELOPMENT

Not only must schools develop capacity within, they must also actively recruit from outside, not just to fill inevitable departures and gaps, but to attract talent that will revitalise existing practice. This has to be made to happen. If schools are struggling to recruit, they must find compelling reasons why people would want to work for them and then publicise them so that people know. At Rush Common, it is because the school is recognised as an establishment that grows and develops people, that invests in learning at all levels, that has a mission to improve life chances, not just for the children, but for everyone who belongs to the organisation.

> *If staff want to grow and develop and be somebody, they come here. We don't need to advertise; people send me their CVs.*

They proactively inform schools of the range of training they offer, such as guidance on the Mentoring and Development of Newly Qualified Teachers. (They had recently hosted fifty NQTs, who were tutored by one staff member on teaching and coaching active learning in Mathematics.)

Other examples are Maxine's own work in supporting schools in Special Measures, and supervising coaching for teaching assistants.,

RELATIONSHIPS WITH PARENTS AND THE WIDER COMMUNITY

Maxine perceives the relationship with parents as a vital and inescapable, often challenging, aspect of headship.

> *This is an estate school, with a large amount of council housing and a high proportion of one-parent and needy families. This combination often gives rise to complicated scenarios.*

Head teachers frequently find themselves in challenging situations which call for resolution and a determination to uphold the principles and defined codes of behaviour; for example, having to physically separate loudly swearing parents who are fighting in the playground in front of alarmed and distressed children.

It is the duty of schools to establish a clear understanding with parents of the responsibility they share with the school to do only what is best for the children. That includes explaining to parents how they are expected to behave in the school, and how adults must model for children the behaviour expected of them.

When Maxine came to 'unzip' what this school was about, she was shocked by the sheer range of parental responses: the wide spectrum of parental involvement, care and concern about their children.

> *It is not for schools to make moral judgements about parental standards or attitudes because, after all, which of us could claim to be a perfect parent?*

> *They are our clients and we have nothing less than a sacred obligation to do the very best we can for their children. That is a truism we can all accept, but there are dimensions beyond that schools and head teachers cannot ignore.*

Notable among these are parents who believe they know better than staff how their children should be taught, and how the school should be run; parents who are not interested in their children's education, who actually neglect their welfare; middle class parents who lavish toys and expensive technology on their children, but find it harder to invest time in them, to talk about what they are doing in school, to read with them, to give them, in fact, real care and love.

EXTERNAL RELATIONSHIPS

The school has other significant external relationships. In common with many schools, the head teacher often takes on a 'front-of-house' position. This is notably so of Rush Common School's relationships with business and commerce. There is a strong link with the local authority in this respect because of the significant amount of training and staff development outsourced to the school.

The school also has links with commercial companies in the wider community, something uncommon in primary schools. They set up a project where the Year 6 pupils created their own business called Youthful Greens, with the objective of securing the 'Eco school, healthy school' status. The purpose of the business was to grow and sell a range of flowering plants, notable for curative and environmentally enriching properties. Apart from the creative and conservational value of such a project, she and the teachers involved were keen that the children should learn something of the practicalities and complexities of setting up and running a business.

She had various professional contacts contribute to this. The Chief Executive Officer of a large corporation talked with them about their proposed business, and got them to clarify their ideas, intentions and practical plans.

Maxine trained them to 'pitch' to a number of different organisations for sponsorship for their project. Then she had another CEO visit and discuss with them how to construct a business plan. Every month the children went for a rigorous progress report of their business project, meeting with him in the imposing boardroom at the company headquarters. They used company technology to present their reports, found themselves exposed to hard and challenging questions and were expected to explain why aspects of the plan had fallen short of expectations or why they had failed to meet specific targets.

At the end of the business's first year, Youthful Greens triumphantly declared a profit, only to be told by the CEO, who was tough and uncompromising with them, that it was simply not good enough because they had not taken steps to reinvest profits in the business.

It was a far from comfortable ride for them, but an enriching experience that took them significantly beyond 'zones of proximal development' and was genuinely productive in learning terms. This enterprise not only established links that opened the school to a wider world, but significantly expanded pupils' learning and broadened their education.

Maxine has established similar working relationships with five organisations who offer partnerships and joint ventures with the children. In turn, she advises the organisations on how they can work more productively and creatively with schools, and, in the process, extend their business and help to nurture the competences, skills and dispositions that will make for more fulfilled, able and creative workforces in the future.

> *This outreach work can be very demanding and at times frustrating. Not all head teachers are prepared to get involved in arduous endeavour of this kind. This is symptomatic of an inertia that characterises some headships. It seems to me that many heads find themselves in secure and comfortable square boxes that they can adequately fill, but that incrementally become more diminishing and confining in terms of creativity.*

> *When I find myself in situations where, for me, there seem to be no solutions to particular problems, or, worse still, no new beckoning avenues or fresh and promising routes to explore, then I realise I am too involved in the game, too much in danger of becoming locked in my box. I need to think afresh, to reflect on different options, to be revitalised, to look outside my box.*

> *I tell this to NPQH candidates on their final residential course. It is all too easy for head teachers – and their staff – to become institutionalised, to lose the drive for invention and creativity. I, and of all my staff, go regularly to see what other schools, recognised for outstanding practice, are doing. That, I believe, is at the heart of professional renewal.*

DEVELOPING LEADERSHIP SKILLS

Maxine has no doubt that had she not implemented distributed leadership, the school would have been in danger of stagnating and good teachers would have unwittingly continued to contribute significantly below their potential. Implementation was a major step because she did it with the staff who were already there. To manage that she had to do a number of vital things:

- Identify those people with the potential for leadership, the high quality talents and skills implicit in that, and the will and capacity to take on responsibility.

- Make clear what was required, convince them they could do it, and, in the process, flag up that she had identified something out of the ordinary in them.

- Ensure that they saw and understood the need for change, were prepared to commit themselves to the enterprise, and had confidence in their ability to lead and manage beyond their classroom environments.

- Provide the necessary practical and moral support for colleagues who hitherto had been overdependent on centralised decision-making and direction-giving.

- Engage personally with the project in a way that would model effective leadership for them.

People only learn leadership by actually leading, by seeing duties, tasks and enterprises through to successful conclusions. Budding leaders start small, in contexts which are less demanding. Maxine develops potential leaders by identifying what they are good at and by giving them a chance to lead in areas that will benefit from their input.

Curriculum leaders, for example, are made responsible for monitoring resources, for keeping acquainted with developments in their particular area of expertise, for securing the best possible provision and for working closely with colleagues to achieve coherence of material across subjects.

Maxine makes it clear to them why she is selecting them. Usually they do things which are necessary to the prosperity of the school and these are often things that they can do better than she can.

> Then I resource them, and trust them to get on with it. I keep an eye on things from afar and evaluate outcomes with them at the end. We identify what they have achieved and added to their leadership repertoire. I praise them for what they have accomplished and we reflect together on what the next logical development for them may be and the training and coaching that will require.

From a corporate point of view, this gradual process is tailored to suit individuals, based on their stage of professional maturity and their particular skills.

THE CHILDREN'S LEARNING

The school is confident that all their children, without exception, are making good progress. The evidence is clear in their work, their attainment and the value-added measures that place the school in the top ten per cent nationally.

The children leave the school with senses and spirits attuned to awe and wonder; they are confident, responsible and caring, with a strong desire to learn. They believe that learning is cool. They are all independent learners and highly competent in the use of ICT.

Maxine believes that ICT can transform teaching and learning:

> ICT is a tool – for the school, for staff, for the children, for the community. Its purpose and its power is about enabling. We have spent a lot of time ascertaining where technology can do certain things more effectively.

> There is a mass of good subject content available on the Internet, but the real power of ICT is that it opens endless horizons.

> Arising from our belief in that philosophy, we are one of a small group of primary schools in the country who are BECTA accredited for the use of ICT. This year we have enabled all our children to access certain tools and resources at home. Ninety-seven per cent of our children have access to broadband at home, so we've opened up resources for them to use out of school. We have something called Education City, a collection of cross-curriculum activities, a whole host of resources and materials they can access at home to reinforce the work they are doing in school.

Maxine sees music as another significant feature of the school:

> Music was a decisive influence in my development, so it would be natural for me to hold a special place for it in the school. Music can be expensive, especially as children become more accomplished and need the often sophisticated resources to maintain progress. That is beyond the reach of many parents, so we have to do what we can.

> Though we are still some way short of my vision for what we can achieve, important foundations are being laid. At Key Stage 2 we have an active choir of over a hundred children, with regular choir practice as part of the curriculum.

From Year 3, all children can learn to play keyboard and we are providing sub-stantial instrumental teaching.

In addition, Maxine believes that children in the contemporary world need to engage in the language and culture of others. The ability to speak another language is a trans-forming one, so the development of Modern Foreign Languages matters greatly. There are three language specialists on the staff and there is language teaching from Year 3 onwards. From the Foundation stage there is 'language tasting' – the games, activities, greetings, naming, songs and nursery rhymes that are a familiar part of young learners' experience and everyday routines.

Currently the language tasting involves Japanese, supported by a teacher from the London School of Japanese who works with the children for two days a week over eight weeks. 'We have a number of Japanese children in the school and this was a marvellous way of drawing them in. I also feel that our children will mature in a world where languages such as Japanese and Spanish are likely to be predominant.'

RESOURCES AND THEIR MANAGEMENT

In common with the other head teachers in this book, Maxine identifies teachers as the key resource. She is emphatic that unless the right investment is made in staffing, and talents are identified, nurtured and developed, 'you could waste a whole host of money investing in other things and other resources'. Maxine insists they pick people very care-fully, seeing them as a fresh and stimulating resource, an asset to be developed and nurtured carefully.

The school generates considerable income. It takes a large body of 'additional teachers' for professional training; they run graduate teacher programmes (GTP, now School Direct), and school-centred initial teacher training.

Sometimes I take risks and overspend and get my fingers burned. But we can square that and make it up. What would be absolutely criminal for me would be to come out with a surplus. I see schools with surpluses and I wonder what they can be thinking.

Though they receive financial remuneration for a portion of this training, people have questioned their commitment to training programmes on such a scale. But Maxine says that this is neither a drain on resources nor a dilution of the quality of teaching and learn-ing they provide for their children.

ACCOUNTABILITY

Maxine is accountable to her governing body and regards herself as managing them in some aspects. Their relationship, she says, is very different from the one they had with her predecessor, who managed them well, to their mutual satisfaction. Theirs is now what she describes as 'a work in progress'. She has persuaded people with particular skills – a lawyer and an accountant among them – to join the body.

When they offered her the position they wanted her to be transparent in terms of what she was doing in the school and to engage them in the process. That was very acceptable to her, because she is essentially consultative in her approach. Equally, she expects them to be skilled in providing the challenge and support she needs. She makes the point that if they are not skilled in that respect it makes it harder for her to do what is best for the school and the children. She is accountable to them, but says it would be incorrect to say they manage her. 'However, as they grow into the job, they will be more competent to do so.'

The most helpful management she has had has been from her School Improvement Partner. Selected after rigorous examination of the candidates available and having satisfied demanding professional criteria, the SIP provides Maxine with the quality of management, guidance, advice and challenge she wants, and that the governors cannot yet provide. Through all her career, Maxine has looked for people who will stretch and develop her. This partnership is realising their hopes, because the SIP's work models the essential features of leadership and management so far as teaching and learning are concerned, and reflects much of what Maxine strives to do as an effective head teacher and leader. The SIP has helped them to realise they are better and more capable than they had ever believed themselves to be.

CHAPTER SIX

GWEN LEE

Christopher Hatton Primary School, Camden, London
Non-denominational school for boys and girls from 4 to 11
Pupils: 220

Christopher Hatton Primary School is, as Ofsted judged, a classic example of outstanding practice and provision in every aspect of primary education: through leadership and management; teaching and learning; value-added pupil progression; curriculum, assessment and evaluation; staff development; quality of environment and resources provision; succession planning; and parental and community partnership and involvement.

Given that formidable litany of achievement, acquaintance with the school leaves one with a powerful impression of a particular quality and dimension that is difficult to pin down. There is a great sense of sanctuary there, in educational, humanitarian and spiritual terms, created for children and families who have too often known adversity and hardship.

There is no doubt that Gwen seeks to develop a school that offers children transformative opportunities for a richer and better life, in ways that are not easily measured in terms of their worth and quality.

Gwen went to a small primary school in a Victorian building hardly changed since her grandfather's time, and then to the grammar school in the same town. However, her two older brothers – 'every bit as intelligent as me' – failed to qualify for the grammar school and instead went to the secondary modern school. This piece of domestic history left a deep impression on Gwen and has influenced her educational philosophy and belief. 'Those who failed the 11+ on that day were lost.' It cost her brothers the chance of a university education. They were not expected to go to university or have any aspirations about higher education. The unfairness of it remains with her still.

The situation is terrible. Grammar schools and all selective schools are great for the people who succeed and go to them. Grammar school was very good for me – it gave me the chance to go to university. But it is unacceptable that so many others are denied that chance of education. Education should be inclusive, not elitist. I don't want anyone to feel limited or excluded. Children, young people, should not have boundaries set about them, yet too many have by society and by family.

Gwen's village was in an area of high social deprivation. She was the first in her family to go to university. Hers was the 'working-class girl' story; she grew up 'in material poverty, but knowledge wealth'. Her father especially was very keen on learning. He was self-educated, 'went to lots of courses, studied industrial history, was fascinated by everything, and was a real lover of the outdoors'. For Gwen, he was a scholar driven by a passion for discovery; a role model for her.

Her parents did not have the opportunities Gwen had. Their house had few books. 'We had the *Encyclopaedia Britannica*, from which I did many of my projects. My father hated television, so little time was spent on that.'

Inspired by the art teacher at school, Gwen read art history at Leicester University. This teacher would bring her students all the way from Durham to London to visit galleries, museums and art exhibitions. Gwen says, 'I still love to visit galleries and museums. Art is very important to me. It's something I bring into school and nurture and support. There is evidence of that throughout the school and in the richness and diversity of the children's experience and work.'

Her school, in the heart of the city, offers great educational opportunities for its largely deprived children. Gwen and her staff take advantage of the location:

London is a great city; you can never grow tired of it. We walk out of our school and we see something different happening every time. Five minutes' walk from here – with all they have to offer in terms of beauty and wonder and every area of experience and learning – are the town and the river and the architecture. I am not a religious person, but I am fascinated by the great churches and cathedrals. The opportunities to bring inspiration, enrichment, and true learning into the lives of deprived inner-city children are endless.

It is her capacity to respond to and engage with all of that, and wanting to use her creativity and imagination, that led her eventually to teaching and to primary education.

You simply can't be bored as a teacher, because you have thirty different per-sonalities before you and a diverse and changing curriculum to teach. I love discovering new topics. I can't wait to teach them, to impart them to children, to engage them in the wonder of it all. I love planning lessons that will do that most effectively and successfully. And I think just as hard about the plans and lessons that don't work so well sometimes, and reflect on what can be done about it.

For Gwen, teaching and learning remain at the heart of headship, not just as an ideal, but as something to be substantiated. 'They need to see me doing what I am talking about. I am head learner; head teacher and learner.' She wholly rejects the idea that head teachers are, in effect, leaders of business more than the curriculum: 'If that is what being a head teacher was about I wouldn't do it. For me, it is about teaching and learning, above everything.'

This viewpoint is not unreservedly accepted by the other heads; some point to the sheer size of their schools as a huge impediment to any useful teaching on their part.

Gwen came into teaching at thirty, having travelled widely, living and working in various parts of the world, including Australia, India, America and Vietnam. She happily admits that 'the long summer holiday allows one to travel so widely and to enhance the life of the spirit and the imagination'.

Gwen has strong political views: 'Inevitably, growing up as I did at the time of Nelson Mandela, the miners' strike and issues of that nature, I seemed to spend my youth march-ing. I was very active.' However, her staff grew up in a different time:

I find it slightly shocking that I have teachers who have never been on a protest march in their lives. In my time, we had a very clear-cut enemy. There were many things to criticise and much to be critical of; there was much social injus-tice, a lot of inequality and resistance to feminism. Some female teachers said to me, 'We wouldn't describe ourselves as feminists.' I felt like strangling them. That means the media have taken ownership of that word and turned it round and corrupted it. To be a feminist simply means you are entitled to and have equal rights. It is a piece of recent history; in many countries it is part of their present.

Gwen has always had a strong sense of social justice, and thinks that teachers have to possess that awareness:

It is our role to ensure that children can go out into the world and know what their rights are and how to set about ensuring they get them; they have to be enabled to stand up for their beliefs, to have a sense of justice and to have an understanding of the political system.

Political discussion – political education in a sense – is part of the school curriculum, an element of the topics the children study. When the London Mayoral Election was set in motion, Gwen, with her staff, decided the occasion should be used as a means of contributing to the political education of their older pupils. Year 6 children went to the Houses of Parliament and gained a sense of its purpose, its political significance, how it worked and its implications for them, their community and the country at large. This then became a starting point for the work that followed.

The Year 6 children developed their own political parties, devised their own particular politics, made and filmed their political broadcasts and publicity, designated their potential Ministers for Education, Health, the Environment and so on, campaigned to the whole school and presented their arguments.

We found some attempts at bribery and corruption going on and we had to deal with that. It was, in fact, a valuable occurrence to encounter, experience and address. Finally, the whole school voted. As a project it provided a genuinely worthwhile opportunity for speaking and listening skills and for developing a range of writing forms.

Through assemblies and the broader curriculum they teach children about the great political events that have taken place in our own time. They do so especially because many of their children are refugees who have been through horrific experiences in Somalia, the Congo, Afghanistan and other parts of the world. 'They come with stories, with personal experiences to make you weep. They must begin to know about history and to understand the implications for themselves and for others.'

EARLY TEACHING EXPERIENCE

Gwen completed her PGCE at the Institute of Education in London. For her, teaching was the way into a wider and more diverse society.

She often tells the children of her own early education, where everybody was white, everybody spoke English, and very few people moved schools (highly significant for children in a school of extraordinary pupil mobility). She explains that it was a cause of excitement when once in a lifetime somebody new joined the class. The children's response is usually one of astonishment and sympathy: 'Gwen, how boring for you!'

She is still fascinated by the different cultures she encountered when she started teaching:

> *Suddenly I was being immersed in alien cultures, a totally different world that you've got to be curious about and take into account. Different people's experiences and cultural backgrounds – that was one of the things that really hooked me into teaching.*

She was also hooked by the thrill of 'passing on of learning to a great, responsive, enthusiastic and captive audience'. Teachers need to be performers, both in passing on learning, and in being part of and sharing the learning process as well. 'Learning can never be about the filling of empty vessels.'

Gwen began her teaching career in a junior primary school in the city of Westminster. Within a year she assumed coordinating responsibility for science, a core subject curriculum area that fascinates her, and which she still loves teaching.

She was then appointed to the school's senior management team. Her familiarity with managing people in her previous work in the business world and her readiness to seek out new opportunities, contributed to her rapid promotion and helped her cope with a leadership role involving the management of other staff.

Her young, dynamic head teacher was very good at identifying people with talent and ability, encouraging them and giving them responsibility. She learned a lot from him, but he was not the kind of head she wanted to be. He was autocratic and good at getting rid of people – necessary in certain circumstances – but less good at nurturing people. She also benefitted from the example of an excellent deputy head who was very good at time management and structures.

Gwen says her staff would describe her as highly organised and systematic – characteristics she sees as central to successful headship. Being structured and systematic gives more freedom. 'There's so much going on and you're juggling with so many things that if you don't have a system you're just going to crash.' She believes that since she began teaching circumstances have changed greatly in this respect in a relatively short time. 'The levels of accountability are so much higher now.'

After five years at her first school, Gwen moved to the deputy headship of her present school, which had been open for just over two years. She was attracted by the opportunity to help create a new school. However, in the summer vacation preceding her first term the current head teacher left to take up a post elsewhere and Gwen and the school were left leaderless. She also learned of difficulties and of the two previous deputies who had remained for less than a year.

The local authority seconded the experienced deputy head of a large primary school to the position of acting head and subsequently to the substantive role, 'so we walked through the door together, not knowing anything about each other'. However, the partnership flourished because they had different characteristics and complementary strengths.

This head teacher was a 1970s-trained, 'old-school' teacher; very good at the nurturing side, very good with staff, and dedicated to children learning through a project approach and the richness of the creative arts. She lived by the creed that if the head teacher and the leadership team look after the staff, they, in turn, will look after the children. Gwen came from a very different type of school and a very different form of leadership so she did not understand that style of leadership at first. However, she learned a great deal from her new head teacher about the importance of nurturing and fostering staff and taking care of them professionally and, where appropriate, personally. But despite her people skills, that head teacher fell short in terms of organisation and management, whereas Gwen was systematic and organised. Gwen managed the curriculum and the assessment and pupil tracking systems, the evaluation, recording and documentation. She ensured that policy was formulated and implemented, and that accountability was expressed in a formal and methodical way.

> This was commonplace for my generation, accepted as something that needed to be done and done properly, in a way that wasn't readily acknowledged by teachers who had flourished in the systems and approaches of the seventies.

Her career to that point coincided with the advent of the National Curriculum, inspection, SATs and league tables – developments that served a serious and important purpose: the need for rigour, concern about children's learning, and the progress they were making in terms of attainment and achievement. This evolutionary shift changed the landscape of primary education. No longer could children slip through the learning net, with gaps in their understanding and knowledge. As a consequence, teachers are now much more thorough in terms of assessment, monitoring and evaluation, and have a profound understanding of the crucial link between teaching and learning.

Gwen assumed responsibility in the school for these transforming and sometimes wholly new developments, using a set of guiding principles coming from the philosophy of her guru, the great explorer Ernest Shackleton.

SHACKLETON'S TEN STEPS TO SUCCESS

1. Never lose sight of your goal

2. Be a good example to others

3. Be optimistic and self-confident

4. Take care of yourself

5. Be a team player

6. Show courtesy and respect to others

7. Deal with your anger and avoid conflict

8. Celebrate your successes and have fun

9. Be brave

10. Never give up

> *Shackleton was a fantastic leader of people. If you follow his management techniques then things will be all right. I think his ten principles are as apt for children as for adults. He speaks to them as directly as he does to adults.*

Gwen points to the vital sense of partnership that characterised her relationship with the head teacher, before she eventually assumed the role:

> *We recognised and valued each other's strengths. She identified my strengths and fostered them; she respected my ideas and responded to them. I felt nurtured by her, and I learned a great deal from her. For example, I had come from a school where parents were kept outside, to a school and a head who believed they had a critical role to play, who wanted to give them access and genuinely involve them in their children's education. Now parents are free to spend the first fifteen minutes of the day in the classrooms with the children; they come in all the time and are very much part of the school. But it only happened as a result of a great deal of outreach work on both our parts, working together to change the image of the school.*

At the outset Gwen was excited to take on the role of deputy head, with two and a half classes in an empty building. Teaching Year 2 was her first experience of teaching infants. Her main task, though, was to devise the curriculum for the new junior department and to select and purchase all the resources and equipment, including the furniture ('which is why it's all nicely colour-matched and distinctive in each classroom').

Although the staff was much smaller then, she and the head teacher decided they would place a permanent, full-time teaching assistant in each class; this was distinct from the system of allocating such support for a few hours here and there, which was common at that time. They wanted to create genuine teaching partnerships in each classroom by establishing continuity and coherence of practice. Soon after, they added bilingual, SEN and 'intervention' support.

PREPARATION FOR HEADSHIP

The head teacher encouraged her towards headship, going so far as to request of the local authority that they should be recognised as joint head teachers – a notion perceived then as too ahead of its time. She received further support from a successful school inspection which highly praised her management of the role of Deputy, including her responsibility for staff development. Her preparation for headship was 'here, on the job, in partnership with the head, in a rapidly expanding and developing school, together with attendance at courses and the opportunity to visit and observe models of leadership and practice in other schools. The local authority was particularly helpful, identifying and nurturing people when they were ready for headship.'

She found the fast-track NPQH training helpful, but probably less informative than the more extended version would have been, as it focused more on her showing what she could already do and had done. She firmly rejects the suggestion that the training 'turned out clones':

> Head teachers aren't the kind of people who are cloned. People who are ready to be cloned wouldn't survive as head teachers. The reality of the job, the essential need to get on with people, to really understand what teaching and learning are and to bring them about, would be beyond the reach of unthinking, programmed clones.

THE EXPERIENCE OF HEADSHIP

When Gwen became head of the school she was in an environment she had helped create and working towards goals she strongly believed in. She was respected by the parents and the community and supported by the governing body that had appointed her. She had a three-year strategic plan, considerably influenced by her reading and study, and by the INSET and courses she had taken. In her first year they focused on accelerated learning. 'A fancy name,' she says, 'for what is essentially good teaching and learning, underpinned by the emerging body of research about engaging children, making their learning memorable and enduring, in sound emotional and physical environments.'

Her CPD is done in yearly blocks. The whole of the first year was concerned with everything important about teaching and learning. Over that time, Gwen would introduce and lead on various elements of the theme, such as connecting up learning. The teachers would then try out what they had covered in their classroom practice, and the next week share and analyse their experience. Their teaching and thinking were underpinned by a strong theoretical basis; they were, in effect, a learning laboratory engaged in action research.

Gwen regards her teachers as key researchers:

> They have to be thinking about their pedagogy and its interface with the children's learning, thinking about what they are doing and why they are doing it. We are a learning team that learns together. We are a learning school.

Over that year, because they were all exploring the same things, they gained a sense of cohesion. For example, they were all finding various ways to use music in expediting the children's learning. From their observation of how children learned, they found little evidence for the notion of children being exclusively or even predominantly 'one style' learners. As a result, they were able to refine their practice.

She expects teachers to be perennial learners, continually trying things out and reflecting on what they are doing and its outcomes for children's learning. She states, uncompromisingly, that 'if people aren't competent, they have no right to be in front of a group, particularly of inner-city children, who already face enough barriers to their learning. To teach in a school like this, you have to be an excellent teacher. Inevitably, there will be people who are in the wrong business, perhaps in the wrong school.'

ASSESSMENT

In the second year of their three-year plan they addressed assessment because they could see clearly how it linked to the principles of learning and to accelerated learning.

However, Gwen regards SATs as highly pressurising and disproportionately expensive in terms of money and time that could be used more productively in other areas of education. When used solely for assessing children, both primary and secondary schools must feel confident about the assessment data they receive and the information it provides about children's attainment and progress. These days, teachers are knowledgeable about assessment and assured in its implementation. They see the kind of assessment represented by the SATs as only part of the picture. They do Assessing Pupil Performance (APP) assessments for progress, which is more diagnostic in terms of children's attainment; they look at and evaluate a range of children's work, which enables them to determine if outcomes are a one-off or indicate more general development. Much of this they learned or had confirmed by the year devoted to their theoretical and practical evaluation of assessment. They could see how assessment is part of the learning cycle.

> It's about peer assessment, self-assessment, defining clear success criteria for the children, understanding the purpose of what you are teaching, teaching the children to be assessors and evaluators of their work, their attainment and their progress, and the strategies and learning modes that bring these about.

Good teachers instinctively did most of this, but were not always conscious of what they were doing. They wasted hours with extensive marking, 'writing masses of comments that the children seldom read and not allowing time for marking feedback'.

In the final year of their three-year plan they reviewed the curriculum they taught in detail and how it might be most effectively delivered.

Gwen says, 'We decided to adopt a thematic approach. I am well aware that you need to be a brilliant teacher to teach the curriculum in a thematic way and not allow it to go pear-shaped.' Teachers now have substantial knowledge of the subjects they teach and how to incorporate that knowledge into themes that cross over subject boundaries, identifying related ideas and skills to promote learning.

She and her staff found that the children's learning was disjointed:

> We would teach them history, but they couldn't always make meaningful connections between history and other curriculum areas. So when they came to write recounts, they seemed to have nothing to write about. But take, for example, Antarctica as the focus for your thematic study, draw in Shackleton, read his diaries with them, and you begin to create genuine contexts for their recount writing.

There are a number of criticisms of the thematic approach: themes may become bloated and incoherent, curriculum balance is not always secured, connections between themes are often difficult to identify or may be tenuous, continuity and progression in children's learning can be lost amid the elaborate structures of a range of themes, the process may become repetitive, with learning minimised or stalled altogether.

As these were concerns, this determined the sequence of their three-year plan.

> *If you have good teachers, working with a good and purposeful assessment policy, then they know exactly the skills they are going to teach. For each theme we identified the skills we wanted to teach across the year for each year group. When teachers planned their topics they knew the skills they had to include and where to fit them. Then when we went back to the National Curriculum, which we hadn't looked at for a year, we found it really rather good, a valuable curriculum resource.*

Having an 'Outstanding' Ofsted Inspection liberated them and encouraged them to be adventurous. 'It was my head on the block and I was perfectly willing to stand up and defend and justify what we were doing, where we were going.'

In the current year the school is examining the curriculum more deeply, examining the skills of enquiry, problem solving, personal learning and thinking – the skills that pupils need to take into secondary education – and how these are to be defined in terms of the curriculum.

Although they had been building those skills into their planning, Gwen was not convinced that people were wholly secure about certain aspects. In what ways would such skills differ between year groups? What would be the significant differences between thinking skills in Year 1 and Year 4? What would the implications be for practice, teaching, learning and resources? What would the indicators be of children's progress?

For this reason, CPD or INSET focuses on this issue. Teachers are placed in problem-solving situations. Having identified, classified and graded the skills they use to solve their problems, teachers design a mini-project related to their class theme, teach that to the children and video the process. The various videos are analysed and evaluated by staff in INSET sessions to identify the skills used by the children, and to ascertain their effectiveness, appropriateness and performance levels.

The INSET process continues throughout the year, with regular evaluation of the teaching project and the skills involved. Then the staff move on to the development of emotional intelligence, as this is important in the lives of children who are massively deprived in material terms; this development helps to nurture their self-awareness, self-esteem and sense of personal worth and value, and builds on all the skills that help them survive the adversity that is common for many of them.

She speaks feelingly of this:

> In the twenty-first century we should not have children living in such poverty, in so crowded a way. It shocks me that I have families where the mother, two brothers and a sister are sharing one room and in the other room there's the father and two older brothers. Such situations should be totally unacceptable. How can children in such circumstances do homework?

The school is a safe haven for children living in poverty and denied access to open spaces. It is a community school where parents are drawn in and become involved. 'Parents have a much bigger impact on their children's progress than schools can have.'

A VISION FOR THE SCHOOL

She wants the school to be a centre of excellence for children in terms of teaching, learning resources and general experience, 'because that's what the children deserve and need'. Her vision of the school being at the heart of this community means that for many families it has become the place where parents can meet each other, get advice, celebrate their own and other communities and ethnic groups, overcome the fact they do not speak English, exercise their cultural skills and cooking, be comfortable, and have their hopes and wishes for a good education for their children realised. Gwen insists it must be a place where they can feel safe, motivated to learn, leave there 'feeling ten feet tall', confident they can achieve, that they will be the first of their family to go to university if they wish.

MOTIVATING STAFF AND ENCOURAGING THEM TO LEAD

The staff work closely with the University of London's Institute of Education, helping to develop their students. The school welcomes NQTs, holding weekly development and support meetings, nurturing and training them, and making provision for them to visit other schools. Gwen cited her literacy and numeracy coordinators as examples of how teachers are developed and then encouraged, motivated and supported to be leaders:

They came as newly qualified teachers and are now lead subject teachers for the local authority. The Numeracy Coordinator made a book and video on Talk Maths, which is being used by teachers throughout the borough. The Literacy Coordinator, who devised a similar teaching aid for the Letters and Sounds Programme, team teaches with colleagues through the school and has been responsible for all the training in guided reading for the teaching assistants, and support staff.

She describes them as 'absolutely brilliant teachers, who are more than happy to say to colleagues, "Come and watch me do it." '

She sees staff growing professionally, confident that others come to observe them work in class as colleagues, not as critics; they learn from each other in a two-way process.

SPECIALISATION

Specialisation was problematic for Gwen, worried whether she was deskilling teachers by denying them the chance to teach certain subjects. But just as she herself was not a competent teacher of music, so most teachers will find themselves unable to teach certain subjects to the degree that the children need and are entitled to receive. This, she argues, is inevitable if teachers are expected to be able to deliver as many as ten increasingly complex subjects.

The school employs skilled people for specific areas of the curriculum, such as art, ICT and music. These specialists teach across the school but in some cases teachers work alongside them or observe them at work. This happened with the ICT specialist, where there was a perceived need for staff to make cross-curricular connections with ICT and to be confident with the children using laptops in the classrooms.

These specialists are usually qualified teachers, though there are exceptions: the art specialist is not qualified. Gwen is adamant that there is no question of teaching assistants teaching a class during PPA time, a practice that is increasingly common. 'Teaching is a profession and must be about a higher professionalism. I won't have teaching assistants taking over from qualified teachers. I know that schools are being encouraged to do this, but it is downgrading education.'

MANAGING RESOURCES

For keeping on track, the bursar advises her on what she can and cannot do. They prioritise what is needed for curriculum purposes, for their teaching and learning. For her, and for the children, the teachers represent the most vital and valuable resource. Therefore the budget is managed to ensure that training and development is of the highest quality.

The Literacy Coordinator, an outstanding teacher, is being released full time from class responsibility to work with colleagues across the school. Members of staff travel abroad (sponsored by the British Council) to observe creative teaching. Each year, two members of staff spend a fortnight teaching in a French school for immersion purposes and French teachers come to observe English teaching in the school. The school's deputy head has been to Cuba as part of the International Leadership Programme.

In terms of finance, Gwen accepts that head teachers have to be entrepreneurial. The school has to raise money to provide an enriching experience, including the provision of educational visits and school journeys, but she does not think fundraising is the best use of her time.

Every summer, the school hires a cinema and takes the whole school to see a film. This harks back to Gwen's art teacher, who brought her and other members of her class to London to visit galleries and see exhibitions that, in other circumstances, they would have had no chance to experience.

However, as many as thirty children in a class is a challenge when it comes to enrichment activities. Gwen explains:

> Look at the diversity of needs in a school like this: a very inclusive school. There are children with severe needs, children with Down's syndrome, children with severe speech and language disorders, children with all kinds of special demands on them. If we could afford to reduce the size of groups we could take the children off and do all kinds of interesting and worthwhile things. There is such a rich environment nearby. Think of the museums that we could use if we had more resources in terms of personnel and money.

> Nevertheless, the school has developed links with Warner Bros., the film company. They provide an annual sum, so that all the children can be taken to the theatre to see a professional theatre production. Last year the children went to see a pantomime. There is no possibility these children would normally go to the pantomime at Christmas, so we take them.

ACCOUNTABILITY

All schools are accountable to a range of constituents, but the concept of accountability is far from straightforward.

When asked to whom she is accountable, Gwen responds immediately: 'The children most of all, but there are layers of accountability. The governors, of course, but they come and go. Our governors are fine, but personally I don't really see the point of governors. I spend my time just telling them what we are doing. They don't have the knowledge; they don't have the time. They can be a waste of energy.'

The School Improvement colleagues from the local authority are another layer of responsibility. Gwen has had four in her time as head teacher, two of whom gave good advice and support. 'You don't want someone to come and say, "This is your problem," but, "This is your problem; try this." ' She fears that the role of the School Improvement Partner, where it still exists, has become judgemental and less supportive. In addition to which, the preparation and paperwork required is exhaustive and time-consuming.

Accountability is easily dealt with when a school is doing well. But what happens, how is accountability rendered, she asks, in circumstances where a school is apparently seriously underachieving for reasons wholly beyond the control of staff?

She cites as an example the extraordinary level of pupil mobility in the school, and the impact of this on performance and test outcomes. During the course of the year, twenty-six children joined Year 6 (a twenty-five pupil unit) and twenty-four left. That is a 200% turnover of children! Other inner-city schools are also in a similar situation. It is difficult to fully comprehend the challenge this poses for a teacher, especially in maintaining children's progress and achieving required levels of attainment in state examinations.

> That is why, when we talk about accountability and the immense emphasis placed on SATs, I almost despair of our situation. If an inspector asks me to explain drops in standards and levels, I say I can't unless they are prepared to take account of the fact that many of the children will have been with us for mere weeks, at most a couple of months, before they are tested.

Apart from the challenge confronting teachers of integrating yet another child, identifying where they are in their learning, where the gaps are, and how they must be programmed to progress, the situation has an enormous effect on the children.

For a group like Year 6 it is about a constant shifting of the sands, a shifting of friendship groups, a change in the pecking order. One child can affect the dynamics of a class. They come in new, with heaven knows what history and experience, having to learn the way we work and the behaviour system.

Practically every child in that Year 6 has a tragic story to tell – the deaths of parents, truly horrible things that have happened in their lives. How do they even cope with the business of coming to school? Sometimes I wonder about how I can 'sell' yet another traumatised newly arrived child to a teacher. I say to my governors, if I could choose which children had to leave us and which stayed, then I could deliver 100% level 5s!

There is a positive aspect to the mobility issue: the occasional parents who come to complete higher study and doctorates at the International College and bring their children to the school.

They are professional people, lovely families with children who have been educated and provide great positive role models in the school. But whatever the situation, the staff and I still have the highest expectation for every child in the school. I firmly believe they can achieve and I'd be after them if I thought they were striving for less.

One of the girls I taught here for three years while I was Deputy has just won a place at Oxford. I shall be inviting her into the school to mark her achievement and to talk to the children about aspiration and achievement.

BEING A HEAD TEACHER

Gwen reflected on the role of a head teacher:

It's an amazing job, a mad job, a job where every day you find yourself in seemingly unbelievable situations.

She recalled doing a Victorian topic with the children. She had found the original head teacher's log books in the archives and discovered that, essentially, the problems remained the same: inspectors coming in with their demands and parents coming in because their children had gone home and moaned about something. In reality, the job has changed out of all recognition. She and her fellow head teachers are cast in a role that calls for the highest professionalism. It used to be very much about the cult of personality, but that, she says, won't do the job any more. 'It's too subtle and complex for that.'

> It requires head teachers to be innovative, at the cutting edge of things, leading a team to search for, discover, evaluate and try out the new. It is about wholeheartedly having a go at things. It is about good management and structure, and scrupulous organisation.

Gwen would not wish to be head of a large school. 'I do not wish to become more of a manager and less of a head teacher. I would miss too much the regular close contact and working with children.'

CHAPTER SEVEN

JOHN FOLEY

Green Meadow Primary School, Selly Oak, Birmingham

State school for boys and girls aged 4 to 11

Pupils: 425

This account of John Foley's perception of and approach to headship is perhaps best summarised by what I found most striking about him and his work: his unfailing and passionate commitment to children's education, driven by a belief in human potential and a child's absolute right to the very best that schools and society can offer. This comes through strongly in the never-failing enthusiasm which has sustained him in own teaching and relationships with children, and in the joy and sense of fulfilment that school leadership has offered him.

John's experience and professional development reflect and represent, in important respects, the seminal changes and notable advances in primary education over the past four decades. His ability to adapt and embrace initiatives has meant that he and his schools have managed change effectively, based upon a notable capacity on his part to reflect on and learn from all experience.

John's leadership has been shaped by a belief in the vital need for a collegial working ethos in a school, and his understanding of the means, infrastructure, and processes to support it. Added to this is his determination to accept nothing less than the highest levels of professional performance from himself and his colleagues. For John, this has meant a single-minded and absolute dedication to the business of his own school, and his aim to make it an outstanding centre for education.

John Foley grew up in inner-city Liverpool. His father, a docker constantly struggling to find work, was the breadwinner for his wife and large family; his mother also worked part-time. John describes her as:

> *... the driving force, the one who was there most of the time, the encourager, the supportive presence when things went wrong. She wanted us to do well, for*

our own sakes, with a fierce passion. She set us moral standards, gave us codes of behaviour in a world where all around us there were rogues – 'scallies' as we call them in Liverpool. But she saw to it that we were not part of that culture; that we had clear, good standards to live by. That is what kept us going.

He speaks warmly of his schooling:

We had a great Catholic experience and education. It was a time when the parish was flourishing and the school was the central point of a marvellous community.

In that deprived environment, the nuns who ran the school provided the children with a wealth of experience: they were taught to read; they were enriched by contact with stories, music, drama and role play; they went on educational trips. The nuns imbued them with a sense of endeavour and tenacity, and a determination to see things through to a conclusion – which his staff would say he retains to this day. There was firmness there too, and strictness about values and moral standards.

Alongside all of that was material want:

Money was incredibly tight; treats and presents were largely unknown. There were no books in the home, not because they were not valued or desired, but because they could not be afforded.

The school was the vital force in his generation's education. Long before it became commonplace, children were encouraged to take books home, not merely to support their reading development but as a source of enjoyment.

I could read and became the role model for my siblings, sharing the stories with them and 'teaching' them to read, supported by our mother, who read with us all.

John was successful in the 11+ examination and secured a place at the 'second best' grammar school in the city, run by the Christian Brothers teaching order. His success meant that his parents had to struggle to pay for the school uniform. The grammar school was a place of severe, 'sometimes brutal' discipline.

There was a terrible sense of fear. It left me with the unshakeable conviction that anxiety, stress and fear, and the absence of security, warmth and real support inherent in such a regime, are wholly destructive of children's, indeed anyone's, confidence and capacity to learn. That has been one of the factors that has impelled me all my professional life to try to provide for the children for whom we are responsible; to provide them with circumstances and support that will make learning irresistible and rewarding for them and not something intimidating.

He is anxious to be balanced about his secondary education:

There were, in that tough school, teachers who shone out, who inspired the pupils. The Economics teacher 'ignited us'; he was extraordinary. When he left halfway through our Upper Sixth year we were devastated by his going, by the loss to us; we felt betrayed.

I accept that teachers do move on, and we have to let them go with grace and a blessing, and find and train others to succeed them.

John was successful academically at school. Despite the school suggesting that he ought to leave at sixteen and find a job – low-level banking or insurance – to help support his straitened family, his mother insisted he went into the Sixth Form. It was difficult studying amidst a growing family in an overcrowded council house – 'There was one room with a coal fire. After the others had gone to bed, I would stay there until one or two o'clock in the morning doing my homework and studying.' His hard work secured him four A levels and he won a place at Manchester University to read Law.

However, personal family circumstances meant he had to forego university. Instead he found employment working for Gola, a firm which sponsored Liverpool Football Club. This was a kind of dream period for John.

I met Shankly and Paisley, the great Liverpool managers and players, and had regular tickets for the games. It was like being famous without being famous. It was seductive, enticing, but it didn't satisfy me. I realised I wanted something beyond that, something more worthwhile.

Then the nuns from his old primary school asked him if he would take charge of the school football team on Saturdays. At the end of the season, having looked after the team at weekends and trained them in the evenings, the school offered him a job as a student teacher – 'a kind of teaching assistant really' – with the implication that if the period of probation was successful and satisfying he would go for teacher training.

One member of staff who had taught him eight years previously, and who had been something of an idol for him, had grown jaded and cynical. John vowed that he would never let himself stagnate like that.

The loss of a teacher a few months after joining the school led the nuns to offer him a full-time teaching post, with responsibility for the top juniors. Despite the prospect being overwhelming, it never occurred to him to refuse the offer. Doubtless he made many mistakes, but the head teacher (the Reverend Mother) made it clear she had confidence in him and in what he was doing.

BECOMING A TEACHER

He found it daunting, but he 'grabbed the chance with both hands', searching for different ways of doing things, taking risks and trying ventures in the way he later encouraged his staff to do. He wanted them to realise they learn from mistakes, from what seem to be negative experiences, and to realise they do not have to be perfect or infallible because they are in a high-achieving school.

From the beginning he wanted the children to find the experience of learning enjoyable and interesting. He wanted them to look forward to coming into class, to find a world there that made them reluctant to leave.

He worked at home at night, making teaching and learning materials. He used literature and story to stimulate their interest and inspire their imagination. At the same time he was striving to make their mathematics relevant, intriguing and meaningful.

When he was a primary pupil himself, it was common practice to have the brighter children sitting at the front of the room, while the less able were distributed back through the class in declining order of merit. The least competent, the ones most in need of help and close exchange with the teacher, were at the very back and least well situated to have their needs attended to. Even as a child, he sensed there was something unacceptable about that. From his earliest days in charge of a class, there would be no such regime.

He did not attempt group work as he felt that was beyond him. However, he made a valiant attempt at tackling basic science – highly innovatory in a primary school at that time – and there he encouraged paired work.

He saw the need for careful observation of children's performance, for good management and for purposeful and appropriate discipline. He was learning about pedagogy. He was given more freedom than a teacher would have nowadays to manage his classroom.

Alongside the praise, he was encouraged to reflect on what he was doing and how effective it might be.

From the outset, he did everything possible to equip himself for the work: reading, learning from experience and giving up vacation time to attend residential courses that he sought out himself and paid for from a meagre salary.

John's encounters at the College of Education with a number of influential educationists convinced him that teaching was a vocation.

This was what I was put on earth for, and all my experience since, all the relationships I have formed, the children I have worked with, the outcomes we have brought about, confirm for me that I have been privileged to be a teacher.

John reflects that from the beginning of his career, he has been:

impelled by my determination to do what was best for every individual child and to have them achieve beyond what often seemed to be a too-readily-accepted 'that'll do' level. I thought that many, if not all, of the children were capable of more, often much more than was expected.

This philosophy has influenced John's practice through the years and shapes an important element of the culture of his school today.

DEVELOPING EFFECTIVE PRIMARY PRACTICE

From the beginning of his career, he sought to put together a 'toolkit of professional skills', constructed not only of INSET but from observing and selecting the best practice of colleagues working in different schools and changing contexts. In his second appointment, in an open-plan school, the nature of the building allowed teachers to observe each other, to work together and to share practice. He also learned from observation what not to do, and to analyse and be critical of varying types of practice and pedagogy. In situations that were often far from ideal, John was studying, striving and experimenting with the problems and challenges of achieving efficient classroom management and organisation and providing effective teaching and learning with large classes. He was constantly refining his strategies and skills; for example, trying to ensure that an open-plan classroom, limited in space, with other classes impinging on the area occupied by him and his pupils, could be made into an ordered and well-provisioned place for different styles of teaching and learning.

He was also struggling with the immense task of providing adequate curriculum coverage, especially in those subjects where his own knowledge and expertise were limited. He was weighing teaching input against pupil enquiry, discovery and practical activity. He was learning how to provide for differentiated learning and how to structure assignments that would ensure learning and progression for diverse levels of attainment and understanding – especially approaches and resources that would ensure an effective response to children's special educational needs. He was exploring styles of organisation and time management that might help him to solve the class teacher's perennial problem: how to have intensive and productive one-to-one exchanges with pupils in classes of thirty or more individuals.

The most formative of such experiences and professional enquiry came from his work in a large, three-form entry primary school:

> I had taken a sideways move as Literacy Coordinator to enlarge my professional experience and to learn about working with a very different ethnic group; the school intake was almost entirely Muslim children, the majority from socially disadvantaged backgrounds. I prepared myself by paying for an in-service course on multicultural education, including the teaching of children for whom English was an additional language.

Here he worked under a head teacher committed to equal opportunity, to serving the needs of a disadvantaged multi-ethnic community, and dedicated to parent involvement.

John benefitted from working in partnership with a group of other senior staff who were concerned to realise the head teacher's aspirations.

> It was the period of the Callaghan Ruskin Speech (1976). It became clear that the world of education was about to be turned upside down.

A group of teachers with major posts of responsibility came together to discuss, plan and implement. They put together a curriculum designed to guarantee progression and continuity in children's learning. John accepts that what they produced might not have been as complete and sophisticated as subsequent government models, but it provided substance, purpose and direction where little had existed before.

They implemented a system of behaviour and discipline based on values that were understood by the children and to which the whole school subscribed. They made sure that positive models of behaviour were always available to the children. They turned the aspiration of parental partnership into reality by providing training in English and reading for parents. This enabled them to acquire and develop mastery in basic English language, to learn to read, and to understand ways in which they could share and help in their children's language development.

As Literacy Coordinator, John resourced this initiative with the appropriate language materials which were emerging on to the market for the first time, including a wide range of dual language texts for pupils and parents. They set up INSET for staff on the teaching of English as a Second Language (as it was referred to then) and provided particular training support for non-teaching staff, so their work with small groups of children was purposeful and directed.

This period confirmed the following for John: the need for an organised curriculum and a system of monitoring pupil attainment and progress; how much could be achieved by a network of similarly minded and dedicated young teachers working together to a common purpose; the value of genuine partnership with parents in relation to their children's education.

It was enlightening for him to educate children from an ethnic group very different from those he had taught previously. He saw that the children from that Muslim community were formed by values and experiences as powerful and positive as those in his Catholic community. They were just as focused and ambitious in their wish to learn and achieve. At the same time, he and his colleagues struggled to accommodate some of the dominant values and attitudes of the community in which they were working, and were obliged to accept that agreement and reconciliation would not be quickly achieved with issues such as corporal punishment, given the children's religious training out of school.

Deputy headship in a one-form entry Catholic school provided instructive experience for when he became a head teacher himself. As he only had a vague and insubstantial job description, the head teacher made it clear that proposals for educational initiatives from him would be unwelcome if it meant teachers had to undertake additional work.

John soon realised that this was a school where staff had stayed too long, had become complacent about their practice, were unaware of or were determined to ignore the large changes in education taking place about them, and where, because of the size of the institution, it was unlikely there would be enough staff with a different attitude to come together and form a critical mass to effect change.

CPD AND STAFF DEVELOPMENT

In 1986 a major government initiative, GRIST (Grant Related In-Service Training), was introduced to prepare and train staff for the education revolution. As Deputy Head, John was responsible for its implementation. He had a mandate and the funding necessary for putting the project into operation. At last, he was able to pull the strings: 'For the first time I now had the opportunity to organise the whole school for a major initiative.'

This was another addition to his 'toolkit of skills'. He found that the INSET provision for individual teachers, which required them thereafter to cascade what they had learned to their colleagues back at school, was ineffective, given that individual staff, resistant to change, were unwilling or incapable of revitalising or inspiring colleagues. Therefore, he changed the INSET to an in-house model, driven by identified needs in the school, where staff were obliged to share and find solutions to common concerns. The National Curriculum began to be an engine driving development, an eventuality that staff could not ignore.

Some worthwhile advances were made, but the process led him to later reshape his vision and practice as a head teacher. Real progress could not be achieved in a school where people, however zealous, were working in isolation. Leaders, however able and committed, need a few like-minded and dedicated colleagues to form a collaborative network. A significant change of staff may be necessary to ameliorate a culture of complacency and fatalism in a staffroom. If an institution is to change, then younger, fresher, more open-minded, more flexible staff – or at least a significant cohort of them – are essential.

In his role of SENCO, John had gained professional confidence and extended his repertoire of knowledge and skills – now he decided it was time to apply for headship. To some extent this was precipitated by his dismay at a divided and negative staffroom. 'I found it difficult to accept an unChristian, uncharitable and unsupportive ethos in what purported to be a Catholic school. It was a dreadful contradiction in terms.' Unsuccessful in his application for a Catholic headship, John was struck by the lack of consolation from his own head teacher. 'I resolved then that if I ever did become a head, the development, support and advancement of staff would become a priority; my school would be a "training" school.'

RESHAPING SCHOOLS

He accepted the headship of a state school in a notoriously difficult area. The entire intake came from what are now referred to as 'white underclass' parents, many of whom seemed not merely uninterested in education but positively hostile to the agencies that provided it. 'I had gone into headship,' he ruefully recalls, 'thinking that, with my experience, I knew it all, only to learn there were new challenges to face, not least the realisation that headship, especially in certain circumstances, can be an isolated and lonely occupation.'

John was strongly committed to the concept of a 3–16 education continuum, something difficult to bring about on a campus where other schools were reluctant to consider any form of amalgamation or partnership that might diminish autonomy or independence.

There were three schools on the site: the infant school, taking children aged five to seven, his two-form entry junior school and a secondary school. There was a prevalent sense that the school's business was 'to keep the lid on a social problem'. It seemed the governors were taking whatever teachers they could find, irrespective of quality. There were no structures to provide for quality control or assurance; in that pre-SATs era, governors had no real measure of quality. Some staff seemed to feel they were doing the children a favour just by being present to teach them. There was a handful of promising, newly appointed teachers, but they were in danger of being overwhelmed by the belligerent and threatening mood of the community; John had to spend time protecting staff from malcontent and aggressive parents, some of whom had to be forbidden access to the premises.

Having clarified his philosophy, intentions and aspirations, and spelling out that performance and standards on the part of teachers and learners would have to improve, he found that at the end of the first year two-thirds of the staff left, including a couple of promising teachers. It was a time for keeping one's nerve, especially in the face of uncertain governors, fearful at the haemorrhage of staff who seemed perfectly competent to them.

John knew that he had to appoint a group of good, enthusiastic teachers who would galvanise the school and the rest of the staff. In time, they came. He began the regeneration with a handful of high-flying teachers, who were prepared to work with others, be receptive and enter into partnership.

Underpinning this was the essential development he put in place as quickly as possible – delay was not an option. He told the parents that these changes would be non-negotiable and were in the best interests of their children. These changes were to be in terms of behaviour, conduct and discipline – a positive, assertive behaviour policy would be established. He encouraged a revised and carefully planned curriculum, which was hammered out and refined in regular staff meetings, seminars and INSET. He organised the staff into a couple of strong, collaborative teacher teams, with the more able and experienced staff responsible for the CPD of NQTs and other newcomers to the teaching force. As a consequence of these initiatives and developments, initially imposed top-down by him, pupils and teachers began to flourish. The number of children on roll began to rise. And over the next five years, the school changed for the better. Behaviour was transformed, pupil performance significantly improved and parents were largely won over. As the reputation of the school developed, it became easier to recruit accomplished staff.

However, one impediment that remained was the misrepresentation of Key Stage 1 outcomes, which provided a distorted and misleading picture of children's attainment. With the growing official insistence on evidence of value-added, this created an unmanageable demand on his staff at KS2. The practice of artificially inflating results – something beyond his control or influence that he believes is still widespread – made him decide to look for another headship.

GREEN MEADOW PRIMARY SCHOOL

In 1995 John came to Green Meadow Primary School, recently formed from the amalgamation of infant and junior schools on the same site.

The joining of the schools had already been efficiently carried out, with all that implied in terms of the rationalisation of accommodation, the merging of leadership and management systems, the reconstruction of financial schemes, the unification of staff and the formulation of fresh lines of communication with parents.

> But much remained to be done: the creation of an 'emotional and psychological' union of schools and staffs; the construction and implementation of a new curriculum; the rejuvenation of a tired and poorly furnished building and featureless environment; the need to dispose of a myth current among staff that the new school was not capable of aspiring to the excellence that had, in a distant past, characterised the separate institutions.

Even though this was a new school, there was a sense of weariness, almost defeatism about the staff. An indication of how things had been allowed to drift was that in the Early Years, all children wore school uniform; by Year 6 the number had dropped to under forty percent. Older teachers spoke wistfully of the school having been good in the past. John's challenge to them was: 'What do we do together to make it good again? And not just good, but better than that!'

John found several positive things to help him realise his vision for the school: some staff with potential for development, responsive and enthusiastic children ready to be inspired, and highly supportive parents, anxious for the school to move forward.

Almost as valuable was the fact that my predecessor, gifted with the significantly higher funding and the freedom over expenditure that Local Management of Schools (LMS) had brought, had chosen to save rather than spend.

He says, feelingly:

You might say that LMS kept me in headship. It is easy now to forget what a liberating innovation it was. It transformed schools. I found myself with £40,000 at my disposal – a considerable sum at that time. It allowed me to be creative as a head teacher in the way I had been creative as a teacher. I could be innovative and inventive; radical with the curriculum, the building and environment, and, in some ways, over staff appointment and deployment.

He set himself three vital goals: the first was to engage high quality staff and, where necessary, to move on teachers who did not buy into his vision for the school; the second was to create a rich, cohesive, inspiring curriculum matching the needs and potential of the children; and the third was to transform a dire learning environment.

He initiated simultaneous developments on a number of fronts for making his vision for the school clear to staff, setting out his high expectations in relation to the quality of teaching and classroom management. He spoke from an informed awareness of the nature of practice in the school, since from his arrival he had begun regular personal classroom observations. There were ongoing discussions in staff seminars on high performance teaching, constant in-class support and INSET to enhance teachers' technical development, and a refusal on his part to countenance underachievement. Inevitably, some teachers, unable or unwilling to subscribe to John's demands, left.

He recruited able, highly-skilled staff to add to those being developed in-house, thus building around him a powerful group who shared his vision and had the capacity to inspire others and transform the school. He stressed the importance of 'the collective message', eliminating the staff's notion that it all came from the head teacher.

THE CURRICULUM

The National Curriculum was the basis for the children's learning. They sought to make generous provision for the humanities and the creative and expressive arts, and they worked hard at the identification and development of general and subject-specific skills. The staff devised strategies and timetable arrangements to help solve the challenge of managing and tailoring an overcrowded curriculum, ensuring the most significant and valuable elements were preserved and properly taught. This led, over time, to the identi-fication of meaningful links between subjects, the humanities especially, and the creation of curriculum units or blocks of learning.

There was a general recognition that teachers, especially at the upper end of the primary stage, were going to struggle to deliver an increasingly broad, complex and demand-ing curriculum to a level that met the learning demands and entitlement of children, especially the more able. The teaching of some particular subjects called for specialist expertise. Staff were concerned about this at the outset; they feared – and it was an anxiety the head teacher shared to some extent – that the process would leave them deskilled in the teaching of important subjects. But, in the end, the children's interests determined the outcome.

The specialisation process began with ICT being taught across the school, with class teach-ers in attendance and working alongside the expert teacher. Although this specialist was an outsider brought in for the purpose, regular teaching to children across the school soon made him a fully assimilated member of staff. Over time, many teachers attained a degree of mastery in the subject that made them largely autonomous, but the specialist was available for expert intervention and support.

Eventually, the specialist teaching system was extended to include music and physical education. John would not embrace a wholly, or even largely, specialist approach to subject teaching, since he feels this 'secondary oriented' model would be incompatible with the cognitive development and learning dispositions of the majority of primary-aged children. However, the school now also uses specialists in the teaching of Modern Languages, and colleagues have to be ready to adapt their organisation and timetable to accommodate such developments.

The DfE national study of ten schools in 2007, 'Making Great Progress', recognised Green Meadow Primary School as making notable and outstanding progress in terms of chil-dren's attainment and achievement. The study identified the driving force of the school's remarkable success as a collective vision, an ethos and a culture, and the attributes that John and his staff worked unceasingly to put at the heart of all their work at Green Meadow.

The report stated:

- The schools had a moral imperative that all children will succeed. They assumed that every child had it in them to succeed. They did not accept background, race or gender as an excuse for underachievement. There was a positive 'can do' attitude. They made a strong presumption of success. They never said 'the kids we get here' or grumbled about the intake. The children thrived in this atmosphere and aimed high. They saw themselves as learners and expected to succeed because the staff did.

▦ There was a shared vision of their collective purpose and ethos. The schools had a pressing sense of mission, which united the staff and set the tone. The heads and senior staff lived and projected the vision. Since pupil success lay at the heart of the vision, staff felt obliged and inspired to make it happen.

▦ There was a precise knowledge of how each child is doing and what each child needs. A high value was placed on intelligence about the child's performance, aptitudes, strengths and learning needs. The single most effective thing the schools were doing was to track the progress of the pupils vigorously and individually.

The report acknowledged that the staff had made notable progress over the years in laying down an infrastructure for worthwhile learning across the phases. Major components of that infrastructure continue to include:

▦ Detailed long-term plans for curriculum progression in all subjects.

▦ Medium-term plans, a rich mixture that includes commercial and QCA schemes of work and home-developed materials. These resources are constantly enriched by teachers attending courses, or identifying useful resources for purchase. The process is generally supervised by curriculum coordinators and involves senior teachers, with a monitoring brief over quality assurance.

▦ Continuity between year groups which is secured by senior leaders, who induct new teachers into the team and its expectations. Detailed summative assessments at the end of each year are used to inform planning for the following year.

▦ Emphasis on key subject concepts, and a hierarchy of subject skills that children need to acquire to ensure satisfactory progress as they move through the school. Skills are learned for a clear purpose and are methodically built up, practised and refined so that more challenging and complex work can be attempted.

▦ Shared responsibility for improvement, both as a school and in relation to pupils. Each year group contributes to the effort. Personal targets set for all pupils are specific and challenging and they are followed up. This approach contributes to the development of teamwork and shared accountability for standards.

THE SCHOOL AS A LEARNING ENVIRONMENT

John says he cannot overemphasise the importance of the environment for the nature, quality and ethos of a school, and its potential for rich learning provision. Much of its value lies in that it is visible and constantly conveying powerful messages – not just in terms of learning, but about the value placed by the institution on pupils, staff, and on all those who work with or relate to the school in some way. Crucially, it allows parents an insight into some of the ways in which their children are learning. Parents at Green Meadow, previously accustomed to a drab and featureless environment, now saw a transformation inside and outside the school that was symptomatic of major advances in the education of their children. Some features of that transformation included:

- A Trim Trak adventure playground provided to enable 'fit minds' to be enhanced by even greater physical exercise: each child challenges him/herself by beating his/her previous best time for the course.

- A vegetable patch enabling pupils in school to grow plants or vegetables, which are then sold as part of the school enterprise days.

- In conjunction with Bourneville Village Trust, building a multi-use games area for the benefit of pupils during the day, and the broader community at night.

- An outside classroom/quiet area allowing one year group at a time to work outside the classroom. There are picnic tables at one end of the covered area with amphitheatre seating at the other.

- A multicultural rainforest area that enables pupils to be calm yet stimulated by resources from around the world. This is a hands-on exhibition whereby children are encouraged to learn by touch as well as by sight and sound.

Perhaps our greatest environmental asset is the school entrance. Our child-sized 'pencils' encourage you in, while concave and convex mirrors and lights add to the visual and sensory wonder of it all!

ENGAGEMENT WITH PARENTS

John's priority was to establish a partnership with parents regarding their children's education, and a practical commitment to make it happen – 'winning parents around and getting them on board'. He feels that this commitment and concern may arise from his mother's determination to further her children's education in the face of adversity, and the difference that made to him and his siblings. From his experiences in disadvantaged and often hostile communities, he knows that such partnerships are not easily forged.

At Green Meadow, the majority of parents were eager for dialogue and partnership. The school had previously been distant and guarded from parents – not an uncommon stance at the time. John and his staff set about changing this. He told parents: 'I want a seven-year progressive working relationship with you. I am not selling you a car. We need to build an enduring relationship.' He told them that, as in any partnership, there would be disagreements, differences of opinion and times of discord, but assured them the school would be unfailingly positive and civil, and committed to the resolution of issues.

Parents are invited to attend assemblies to gain an insight into aspects of their children's moral and spiritual education and the creative learning activities that contribute to it. They receive a termly topic letter, highlighting the work that is taking place and the level their child is working at. This enables parents to support children's learning at home. They also receive a monthly newsletter covering the ongoing life of the school and the children's learning experiences; this also includes examples of the children's work.

The school/home partnership, the building of positive creative relationships with parents, is a constant work in progress that depends upon maintaining the highest possible standards of education and provision for the children, and making these constantly explicit to the parents.

MANAGING PEOPLE AND ENCOURAGING THEM TO LEAD

The staff are determined that all children will succeed to the limit of their ability and potential, and that is largely dependent on the effectiveness and quality of day-to-day classroom practice. The priority for John and his senior staff is on developing, refining and improving teaching to ensure consistently high levels of learning and attainment.

A major proportion of their time is spent in classrooms: observing, monitoring and evaluating what is taking place; teaching and working alongside staff; mentoring and coaching; supporting their pupil assessment; and sharing in their planning and their own evaluation of what has been achieved. This requires far-reaching management decisions and the efficient deployment of resources. Three senior staff, freed of class responsibility, fulfil this leadership function across allocated year groups, with practical support from the head teacher.

Leadership is not confined to the senior management team. They exploit the two-form structure of the school by pairing experienced and less experienced staff, with the senior teacher having a stated responsibility for mentoring and leadership. Teachers also lead on subjects and other aspects of curriculum. Now even newly qualified staff are responsible for heading up the partnership of teacher/teaching assistant.

The TAs themselves are encouraged to take responsibility for aspects of their work. They have been trained to recognise the special learning needs of children in the early stages of their schooling – difficulties with language, number formation, motor skills or socialisation – and to help with these areas at non-teaching times, when they might otherwise be relaxing in the staffroom. They know that the accumulation of the occasional five minutes can have a significant impact on a child's learning.

The school has an ethic of corporate responsibility and accountability. Staff learn early on about leadership and are inducted into and trained in its practice. The school has a template for leadership development, based on four stages of development. It does not claim to be sophisticated, but it works.

Stage 1: They are new to leadership and management, so you tell them what to do and show them how to do it.

Stage 2: You ask them what they think they should do in particular circumstances and suggest possible options.

Stage 3: They identify problems and issues and come to you with possible solutions for discussion and evaluation.

Stage 4: They report back on what has been done.

This progression in leadership is used at all stages: 'You are in charge. You are accountable, but you are not alone.'

The head teacher's belief, philosophy, values and practice underpin the ethic, but there is also the corporate, shared dimension of leadership.

The effective leader nurtures leaders. Without that kind of organisation and management, a school today, so complex and demanding, could not possibly function effectively. Leaders must feel free to take the initiative, to make decisions and to act on the basis of their experience, observation and analysis. They can do that, secure in the knowledge that they are acting within a clear, rational, carefully constructed school framework and that they will not be blamed when honest mistakes are made, or things do not work out in accordance with the most scrupulous planning. I remind staff that none of us can be infallible or perfect, but within the supportive structure of a team, we can all contribute to the leadership and management of the school.

The greatest fillip of all is achieving success in what you do, and having that recognised and acknowledged. With achievement comes confidence and a readiness to take the next step.

KEEPING A CHECK ON LEADERSHIP

John stresses that the school is where he is to be found. There are professional meetings he must attend and INSET he avails himself of, but he says he is not a head teacher who gets involved in the running of other schools, or in helping with local authority business.

My compelling, all-consuming purpose is the leadership and management of Green Meadow School. I am accountable for the leadership and the best interests of a large and complex community. I do that by being here all the time, by devoting all my energy to it.

I want to know exactly what is happening. I don't want to make every decision, but I have to be kept in the loop. Staff have detailed job descriptions; they know what they have to do, and we hold them accountable. That sounds hard-edged, but it is how we are: accountability is linked to high standards, high expectations and a professional development ladder, on which teachers will be consistently supported.

It's about what happens in the classroom: the realisation of realistic but challenging goals, set for teachers and children. Here, teachers must be able to recognise levels of attainment. That comes through auditing and sharing, and through common enquiry about how we improve teaching and learning.

RESOURCES FOR LEARNING

The school spends generously on resources because they are crucial to the learning provided for the children. There is major expenditure on the whole learning environment.

They pay for specialist teaching in physical education, modern languages and music. They pay for high quality coaching in games, and make quite lavish provision for music and theatre workshops. They do so because they believe these things enrich the education and life experience of their children. The school provides comprehensive teaching and learning technology, and all the training necessary for the CPD of staff.

Although expenditure is high, there is no need for them to be entrepreneurial. John says, 'We have the funding we need at present to provide and maintain high quality staffing, environment, resources, activities and experiences.'

RELATIONS WITH THE WIDER WORLD

John recognises the school's accountability to the local authority (and through them to central government) and is ready to be part of a creative and constructive partnership with them to avail the school of the expertise and support they can provide. The deputy head teacher has the responsibility for maintaining close liaisons with the School Improvement Partner.

A main concern for the school in terms of external relationships is to keep themselves informed and up-to-date in terms of educational developments and research and to be aware of interesting practice and innovation in other schools.

It is a truism, he says, that relations with parents are crucial to the successful education of their children. In his first years at Green Meadow he and the staff ran numerous workshops for parents relating to curriculum areas and to the learning experiences of the children. At the outset there was an enthusiastic response from parents; he believes that much was achieved in terms of building parents' confidence and awareness. In time, however, attendance waned until a situation was reached where, on occasions, the staff leading and attending the sessions outnumbered the parents. They eventually found that the creation of informative, regularly-updated booklets for parents, highlighting the purpose of children's learning activities and suggesting ways in which they could be supported at home, proved more effective.

Governors, he suggests, can often be a burden – especially when they do not know the quality of staff in the school, and yet are ready to challenge his professional judgement of them! He welcomes those who are 'willing volunteers', those with professional experience, who can be useful in personnel, premises and finance committees. In his experience, many parent governors are preoccupied with the interests of their own children. They have to be reminded of the corporate, collegiate nature of the governing body and its decision-making processes. By and large, 'critical friends' are not really needed when schools are successful and can proactively engage its governors.

HIS VISION FOR THE SCHOOL

John's experience leads him to believe that all children, even those with the most pronounced special needs, are capable of genuine success that can be a transforming thing for them as human beings. He describes himself as haunted by the memory of children who sat at the back, were perceived as somehow 'ineducable' and were, perhaps with kindly intent, left unchallenged.

All his professional life has been devoted to creating schools, staffed by the dedicated and able, where children find all kinds of ways to succeed and achieve.

Reading about the success achieved by the primary school in Liverpool which he had attended as a child, he felt impelled to visit and congratulate the head teacher and staff on the magnificent work they are doing in 'circumstances that are as adverse as ever they were. Walking about those remembered corridors and visiting the classrooms where I had sat as a child, I felt a great sense of fellowship with colleagues who, like so many in the profession, are as strongly motivated by values and aspirations for children similar to mine.'

He wants the children to be happy, secure and confident; to leave the school creative, resourceful, able to solve problems and find solutions to things; to be curious and searching. If, in addition to all that, they achieve Levels 4 and 5, then that is a bonus to be desired. He wants them to value diversity and inclusivity, to take responsibility for their actions, to have a moral sense, to be sociable. He wants them to be 'learners forever'.

John worries that a contemporary generation of teachers, highly competent though they may be, may lack that sense of passionate vocation. He speculates that despite the 0–25 Education, Health and Care (EHC) Plan, they may have been over-programmed through their training, through emphasis on the need to meet externally defined targets and objectives, to such an extent that the children they teach are in danger of becoming subordinate to data and are no longer the centre of concern.

CHAPTER EIGHT

SUZANNE ALEXANDER-SOWA

St Thérèse of Lisieux Roman Catholic Primary School, Ingleby Barwick, Durham

Catholic nursery and primary school for boys and girls from 3 to 11
Pupils: 230

Suzanne is a notable example of a hands-on head teacher. She believes her role to be a predominantly instructional one, and her performance in this respect must provide a consistent and inspiring model for staff that will systematically enhance their pedagogy.

Her management of the school is organised so that most staff can assume responsibility for single, minor elements, while major aspects are delegated to teachers with part-time or minimal teaching duties. This enables Suzanne to spend a major part of her time in classrooms, mentoring and supporting the teaching and learning of the pupils.

The school has a very good standing and reputation with the local authority because of its high success in external tests and assessments and its 'Outstanding' Ofsted evaluations. It is particularly notable for its emphasis on the creative arts and especially music, where Suzanne's work and the children's enthusiasm and achievement demonstrate the value of specialist expertise.

Suzanne was born into a strongly Catholic working-class family. Her father, the son of a Hindu Dutch Anglo-Indian, was educated in Calcutta by Jesuits. 'He had a strict upbringing, and a very strong work ethic that was passed through to us children.'

In her primary school in London she revelled in the variety of music and drama on offer. She became a prefect and looked after the Reception class children during wet playtimes.

> *This was one of my happiest memories of school. I used to play the piano and have them dancing round the room to my accompaniment. It was this experience that made me determined to do teaching one day.*

Her first post was in a Roman Catholic primary school, working for 'a wonderful head teacher, who was very traditional, quite old-fashioned, but good with people, and who strongly supported me at that early stage of my career'. From her, Suzanne learned how important it is to value staff.

She was the only young teacher in a long-established, traditionally-minded staff who conveyed an impression, however understated, that displays of enthusiasm or inventiveness on the part of newly-arrived colleagues were not particularly welcome, especially, in Suzanne's case, by the music coordinator.

This was her first encounter with group antipathies, a closed-shop mentality, entrenched attitudes, and resistance to change – not uncommon in primary schools in those days. So from the beginning she realised she had to work sympathetically and sensitively with people.

Promoted to the post of music coordinator in another Catholic school in an even more socially deprived area, she was determined to speak up and take a lead when appropriate. But in this school – twice the size, and with complicated group dynamics – she sensed once more a resistance to any innovation that might threaten the settled routine of the school in any serious way. However, she realised that there are always colleagues who do respond positively and supportively to the work of others, and willingly contribute to it from their own expertise. Nevertheless, she witnessed, in more than one school, colleagues who encountered resentment and discouragement from dominant groupings when trying to promote initiatives that might challenge a prevailing orthodoxy. Such regimes were disabling to individuals, damaging to the harmony and effective working of the institution, and a matter of serious consequence for headship and leadership in general. It seemed that it was often easier to pretend it did not exist.

Primary schools, like all institutions, are run by people diverse in terms of experience, personality, outlook, and life circumstances, each with a personal agenda. Head teachers, for all the enhanced powers invested in them by education reforms, are not always guaranteed general compliance with their wishes (indeed, such unquestioning conformity from staff might well inhibit creativity). Many schools still harbour the possibility of negative interactions and responses, and this remains a concern that head teachers and leaders have to address. If heads are to achieve some form of amicable consensus they need access to effective levers of control or sanctions, otherwise they may do little more than hold the ring between competing groups.

THE BENEFITS AND LESSONS OF THE REFORMS FOR HEAD TEACHERS

With the revolutionary changes wrought by the National Curriculum, what was being taught in classrooms was no longer a secret to colleagues.

Despite their undoubted flaws, it was clear that these major developments were to transform schools and the quality of education they were providing. Teachers could no longer operate as free agents, able to do things as they wished with no great concern for how it would affect their colleagues. Suddenly, all were accountable to each other.

At the same time, there was important research into the ways in which children learned most effectively, the importance of formative assessment and the implications of that for teaching. Attention was focused on pedagogy, on the ways in which individual teachers taught and managed their pupils' learning.

The role, responsibilities and powers of head teachers were being clearly defined and mandated by central government; governing bodies were charged with making supportive partnerships with their heads. The large changes in staffing size and structure (underpinned by the transforming impact of LMS) gave head teachers undreamt-of opportunities for the recruitment and creative deployment and management of staff, giving them the chance to form teams, eventually leading to distributed leadership. Head teachers found themselves with unprecedented control over considerably enlarged school finances.

Heads no longer had to tolerate those for whom dissention and even disruption was a way of life, or to cope with those who would not act corporately; nor would they put up with the professionally incompetent or uncommitted. Heads were no longer expected to be solely and wholly responsible and accountable for all that happened in their schools. They were able to share the burden of leadership.

Now for Suzanne and others like her, experienced in middle management, these were the developments and opportunities they needed; they were going to change the course of their professional lives.

For the greater part of my career I had not aspired to headship, but the experience of senior management, and the opportunity I had to contribute to worthwhile change and development eventually convinced me that it was a career step I should take. I was impelled not by the idea of promotion but by the realisation that headship could change things, could make things better.

The best preparation for headship came in active involvement as a deputy head teacher in all aspects of leadership and management. She found the most challenging aspect of her work was in managing people. Having had many past encounters with colleagues who were resistant to change, insecure about their practice and understandably reluctant to reveal or acknowledge areas of uncertainty, she now took on the responsibility for enabling staff to be more effective in their practice. This was more demanding than she had experienced as a music coordinator, where most colleagues were willing to learn in a subject area where they felt uninformed and unskilled. Here, where leadership related to the whole range of teaching capacity, curriculum knowledge and competence, she found staff were not so easily persuaded, especially where such interventions were new or largely untried.

She had limited opportunity for playing a meaningful part in the financial management aspect of primary headship. She realised that this skill would have to be learned in conjunction with other areas of responsibility once in the position of headship itself. To newly appointed head teachers she would say fervently:

> *Learn fast, and secure the assistance and advice – pay for it where necessary – of skilled and informed people. Use them not as crutches that would keep you in thrall to them, but as tutors whose role is to liberate you as soon as possible by enabling and informing you. And for matters such as finance and data – its collection, organisation and interpretation – select senior staff for those specific roles, and have them trained and exposed to first-hand experience so they become your skilled and informed collaborators.*

HER VISION AND EDUCATIONAL VALUES

Appointed as head in a large, new primary school, Suzanne drew courage from the fact that she had learned much that was truly valuable in her varied experience as a teacher and a senior member of staff.

She says her vision is a simple one, based on deeply-rooted values that are shared by, and impel, the best of schools. It rests on the guiding principle that each and every individual is precious, unique and significant, and on the determination that each and every one must be treated as such. Believe that and act on it, and the way and the work are mapped out for you.

That commits head teachers/educators to developing and enhancing each individual's confidence and self-belief, and with that, their abilities, skills, talents and competences.

They are committed to making comprehensive provision and an environment wholly secure in every sense so that children – and the adults who work with them – feel free and safe to be themselves, and have a strong sense of their own personal, spiritual, social and intellectual development. They will encourage them to explore, experiment and take reasonable risks in the way that true learners do, so they will become the best they can be.

At the same time, there will be a strong, constant focus on high expectations, shared by all staff and communicated to the children.

Suzanne believes a glass ceiling exists where children are concerned. Educators must strive to break that ceiling, to have a clear sense of what children can achieve, and have high expectations of children's potential and achievement.

> Over the years we have talked about smashing the glass ceiling; too often I had seen teachers taking children so far and then pausing, almost spoon-feeding them. This was not the way to help them reach their potential. I was committed to high expectations, to the achievement of high standards, to a continuous drive upwards.

Part of that is the acceptance that people learn from mistakes and recognise it as a vital part of learning and maturing. This applies to the whole school community, to children and adults.

> Staff know that when things go wrong, when they have made mistakes, have fallen short, that it is all right, in all circumstances, to admit it, to be open about it. And children know it too. They know that it is safe to make mistakes, good to learn from mistakes, safe to own up, knowing they will be expected and helped to get things right the next time and the time after that, with the right levels of support and challenge.

THE LEADERSHIP AND MANAGEMENT OF STAFF

Once staff share the vision and the underpinning values, then they can build the school they want. This was a key criterion in appointing staff. Suzanne sought primary practitioners rather than year group teachers or those with specialisms. She wanted teachers who were flexible, adaptable, creative in their thinking, who would think outside the box; teachers passionate and enthusiastic in all they do. She would help them acquire leadership skills through working together.

From the beginning, at the new school, she was dealing with issues that her experience had prepared her for. She spent much of her time in classrooms, supporting teachers – especially newly qualified staff – helping them develop strategies for effective behaviour management, for classroom organisation, for the teaching of the core subjects and their complex and essential skills, and for good presentation. They learned with her alongside the children. In all of the classes she did a great deal of work in music, teaching teachers to teach and children to learn. She spent time in the Early Years Foundation Stage, especially during the first year, working with teachers to implement programmes for the development of thinking skills which were eventually disseminated through the Key Stages. Such a focus was central to children's learning.

She became interested in accelerated learning techniques and felt this was an approach which could greatly enhance their teaching and the children's learning.

> We studied the approach as a staff and I secured their commitment to it, partly because of the time and effort I devoted to it, in practical demonstration and in working alongside and supporting teachers. I was concerned that they would feel deskilled rather than empowered by it.
>
> I wanted to ensure that they would have the confidence, the opportunity and the resources to take ownership of it for themselves.
>
> The only way we improve is to see ourselves always as learners, and recognise that we are experiencing what our pupils experience when we require them to learn, and to have the same sort of determination and response that we ask of them.

A central role of the head teacher as leader – and integral to Suzanne's vision for the school – is empowering staff to feel capable of taking on new challenges and to benefit professionally from every experience so they are constantly learning, growing and developing.

She discovered something cyclical in the nature of leadership. If leaders do not feel confident about their work, if they do not have a strong and positive sense of their own professionalism and a well-founded belief in their capacity to do the job, it is unlikely they will be able to enable staff in the ways suggested above.

In the early days of her headship she was encouraged by formal comments from the local authority following official visits: the staff were empowered and developed through distributed leadership in a non-hierarchical context. All teachers, at appropriate times, were enabled and supported in developing the skills and competences of leadership, including deputy headship. The school's levels of consultation and information-sharing were assessed as very high. There were multiple opportunities for staff to develop and grow.

Suzanne describes the practical measures and strategies that support teachers' professional development and their capacity for leadership:

1. Teachers and teaching assistants undertake areas of leadership – subject leadership or intervention programme leadership – and assume responsibilities on an evolving basis in different year groups.

2. In this way, staff gain a clearer and broader understanding of children's learning needs across the entire primary spectrum.

3. They come to learn and understand the learning experiences of pupils before they come into their particular care, and can be updated about their learning in years and phases after that.

4. Staff gradually form a comprehensive insight into, and understanding of, the process of primary education, the pattern of children's learning, the nature of developing teaching and pedagogy.

This helps to demystify things for teachers: they realise there is no aspect of primary teaching, learning and curriculum that is beyond them, no job that is too formidable to undertake, no skill that cannot be mastered.

> In holding such high expectations of teachers' potential, it is important that, in terms of leadership, I, as Head Teacher, can 'walk the talk'. I have to show that I am flexible, open to change, willing to learn what is new and to remain a learner, able and willing to demonstrate what I know and to enable others to learn what is new and master what is unfamiliar. I must show myself willing to learn from other staff in areas in which I do not possess expertise. For example, our ICT leader has been greatly encouraged by my vision of the importance of ICT in the pupils' education and its potential as a powerful learning agent. In openly professing my lack of expertise in the subject, I demonstrate my determination to learn to keep up to date.

A critical part of management is putting people in situations that will enlarge their experience, taking them out of their comfort zones, adding to their repertoire of professional skills, making them conscious of their potential and making them reflective and analytical about their success and how this can be built on.

The opportunities and assignments afforded staff must contribute to the whole school vision and plan. Individual development must add to and enrich institutional development. Their development and progress, and the outcomes of their responsibilities and assignments, must be monitored and evaluated. They themselves must be involved in the processes of reflection and evaluation, just as the children are supported in evaluating the quality, outcomes and effectiveness of their learning and work, and identifying the strategies that make it successful. Finally, they must receive strong and consistent support in their teaching and pedagogy, and in carrying out the particular responsibilities allocated to them.

CPD is central to this and has to be carefully planned and provided for. Head teachers and senior management need to organise training and development that meets the specific needs of individual staff at different stages of their careers. The coordination and provision of such support is a major part of Suzanne's role. She does not believe that head teachers can stand apart from this, even in large schools. Although she has built up a network of learning team leaders, with all staff contributing to such teams at various times with their particular expertise, she plays a key part in the process herself.

Every member of staff is encouraged to take on particular responsibilities for the day-to-day management of the school. These could be relatively simple tasks such as maintenance, care of accommodation and resources, and liaison, or they could be more substantial matters, such as fiscal management, staff and pupil welfare, large-scale provision and purchasing, or external links and relationships. The latter call for greater experience and expertise on the part of those responsible. Such business, graded in terms of importance and complexity and allocated to staff in line with their professional readiness and capacity, provides a kind of staircase of responsibility which teachers can rise up naturally and appropriately.

> In preparing them for leadership we take account of teachers' particular strengths and predilections. Not all staff may be attracted to the management side of school business. Their centre of interest and responsibility will be found in the areas of curriculum, teaching and learning, assessment and evaluation. And, of course, 'management' and 'leadership' are not always so neatly or simplistically compartmentalised.

> The efficient coordination of a curriculum area necessarily calls for management processes. In recent years we have seen a move towards senior staff being offered what appears to be a choice of career advancement along management or education paths: one leading to leadership/senior teacher status, the other to a permanent role as a 'master' teacher, operating in classrooms,

engaging in practice-based research and acting as a model practitioner for colleagues in their own school and beyond.

Being a medium-sized school, most teachers have a subject-coordinating role. These are leadership roles as the post-holders must form teams for their particular areas of responsibility. The teams comprise other teachers on a transient, advisory or need-to-be-involved basis. They include teaching assistants who have relevant experience or a specific contribution to make or who are judged likely to benefit from involvement in a team at that time. Teams, usually with a cross-phase representation, may vary in size, according to the importance of the subject or area of learning.

Teachers who lead on management areas are less likely to form teams, but turn to colleagues for consultation, advice and input. It is important that staff are trained and supported in their leadership by the head teacher and senior colleagues. Suzanne wants them to aspire to the expectations she has for herself as a leader; she offers a model for them of how that can be achieved.

STAFF DEVELOPMENT

Staff development is a shared enterprise. Staff observe each other's practice, share their plans and teaching approaches with colleagues, and base their thinking, reflection and discussion on practical, common experiences. It is particularly important to develop teachers' subject knowledge. Suzanne maintains the importance of enabling subject specialists to develop teachers' subject mastery and knowledge, Subject leaders can develop their colleagues' capacity by demonstrating and talking about good practice in their area of responsibility.

> *It's all very well to talk about effective teaching and successful learning, and the practical strategies that make them effective but there is no escaping the fact that it has to be about the substance of subjects, the areas of learning. Without a main focus on subject content, on skills, ideas, concepts and knowledge, there simply cannot be attainment and progression, understanding and learning. 'Scholarship' may seem an old-fashioned word, but it is what we are after.*

As an example of such subject specialist coaching, she cites a choral lesson she shared with a young colleague. There was a focus on technique and strategies, such as deep breathing, projection and reading notation, but the central activity was making and interpreting a complex piece of music. To be able to do that, over a number of sessions the children had to be taught a sequence and progression of skills, competencies and insights, which called for highly informed and skilled subject mastery.

SELF-EVALUATION

Every year the school sends out a School Improvement Survey to all stakeholders, asking parents, staff and governors to list six successes achieved by the school, along with three ideas for further improvement and development.

Suzanne also discusses with the children what the school provides for them and asks them to say what works for them, what makes learning a reality, what sets their learning 'on fire', and, additionally, what they perceive to be impediments to their understanding and progress. She feeds back their suggestions to staff – who are sometimes surprised at the children's insights – and these findings become part of staff discussions about teaching and learning.

She refers to staff interest in the theories around accelerated learning (Smith et al., 2003) and the practical strategies and teaching approaches underpinning it. It has helped them to understand that schools 'cannot have irresistible learning without irresistible teaching. It is not the pieces of paper that make things happen, but the thinking behind it and the practice that comes from it that moves teaching and learning forward'.

The staff have reached a stage in their development where reflection on their practice has become consistent and systematic.

DISSIDENT STAFF

Suzanne says that the real business of leading a school – creating vision and policies, defining and implementing effective teaching and learning, modelling and managing performance, monitoring achievement and progress, and dealing with all the challenges to creativity, invention and effective management – is not the truly hard part of headship. Any discussion about staff management would be inadequate without reference to an issue seldom written about or widely discussed: the matter of dissident staff. Often there may be only one or two who have a strong agenda of their own but they threaten the unity and the mission of a school, because they are not merely out of sympathy with the head teacher's guiding vision but actively oppose it. They resist attempts to bring them on board. This is where your beliefs and values, your personal and professional convictions, are really challenged. This is the hard side of headship, the part that training does not always prepare you for.

According to Suzanne, 'The truly hard part is recognising destructive dissent, negative behaviour and what is, in effect, unprofessional conduct, and then dealing with it.' This aspect of the job can make headship an isolated and lonely occupation. It is something that requires, on the one hand, the courage to face conflict, to stand by one's beliefs and convictions, to be resolute and steadfast, and, on the other, a readiness to examine rigorously and reflect on one's own behaviour, dispositions and prejudices.

She stresses the value of head teachers seeking the counsel of a fellow head who is sagacious and experienced, able to take a detached view of such matters. The fatal element is prevarication, common when head teachers wish to sidestep conflict or delay taking action in the hope that the conflict will abate. Any hint of uncertainty and irresolution on the part of a head teacher may shake staff confidence and assurance, and damage the unity of purpose about the work of the school.

Nowadays there are formal processes and systems in place that enable head teachers to take action more easily and effectively. But such systems can never be a water-tight guarantee against truly disruptive action, and head teachers need to be prepared for that, in both practical and emotional terms.

RESOURCING THE CURRICULUM

The school strives to provide the fullest curriculum possible, but given the constraints of time, expenditure and resources common to primary schools, some of the subjects on offer will vary, if only temporarily.

The school is committed to the creative and expressive arts; to art and design, dance and music. Music is particularly important, because it is one of the most powerful means by which children can be creative and learn to express themselves. In teaching children to make music, as they do throughout their time there, they are giving them a skill that will enrich and sustain them in later years.

> It is obvious that all children have a right to an education, and an underpinning curriculum that can match what the best and most lavishly endowed independent school provides. I refer to the independent sector because whilst we can match the quality of their teaching, we can seldom compare with the staffing ratios, range of resources and level of facilities they have.

All children should have the fullest and richest possible curriculum available to them. I reject absolutely the argument that such a curriculum might be beyond them. What we too often lack is the expertise and the resources to provide it.

Therefore, for Suzanne, managing resources is key to the whole process of teaching and learning. The most important resource is the teachers themselves, and her most important responsibility is to get the best from them, and deploy them most effectively. For example, support staff are allocated to classes and given specific responsibilities, determined and driven by pupil need. It is not about giving so many hours to each teacher, but about serving particular needs.

Everything possible is done to reduce the burden of bureaucracy on teachers: paperwork is kept to a minimum and their time in the classroom is safeguarded. They are able to concentrate on the business of teaching, the work they are qualified and trained to do.

The school wants to cultivate in children a sense of awe and wonder, of aesthetic awareness and sensibility. Displays throughout the school are there to stimulate curiosity, enquiry and fascination, promoting an eagerness to explore, learn and discover. They are a source of information and knowledge, they provide models of achievement (exemplars of what is possible in terms of excellence) and celebrate children's work and effort. Every classroom in the school should be an arresting and engaging place, with numerous starting points for dialogue and discussion with the children.

Careful thought has gone into making the external environment a place where children enjoy being; where they are invigorated, exercised, refreshed and secure; where their senses and curiosity continue to be stimulated; where their learning continues. There they can grow and harvest flowers, fruit and vegetables; they can enjoy recreation, rest and tranquillity; they can be boisterous, energetic and exploratory; they can be accustomed to encountering all around them that which is beautiful and inspiring. They have a flourishing outdoor classroom which can accommodate a full class of children and a prayer garden that is used both by groups and privately by individuals.

Twice a week, before the formal start of the school day, staff and children dance and exercise together by the water fountain in the garden. The dance routines and exercises and the accompanying music are designed and led by Year 6 pupils, who set up the technology, the voice-over and the amplification. They are wholly competent, efficient and self-sufficient because they have been trained in the process. This event is a good example of children and adults working, learning, exercising, dancing and singing together in harmony, with the roles of teacher and learner almost indivisible.

The school places a particular emphasis on ICT provision and spends on ICT 'far in excess of recommended government spending, embedding it throughout teaching and learning in the school. This provision, so close to the strong interests and experience of children, is probably the most powerful tool in bringing learning alive in the classroom.'

Learning team leaders and subject leaders have always been given their own resource budgets and are expected to manage and organise these effectively. Recently they have moved to a different approach in this regard, putting curriculum money in one pot and encouraging people and teams of people to ask for funding to meet particular needs, initiatives and innovations, rather than allocating fixed sums that will be lost to them if not used. Whilst this limits subject leaders' experience in terms of financial management, they find that it makes the purchasing and use of resources more effective and relevant.

The children themselves have given valuable advice and suggestions in relation to resources and environmental enrichment, especially through the active and influential school council. Every class, together with their teacher and teaching assistant, has become involved in reviewing and planning their classroom environment. Consequently, new and much more suitable and comfortable seating has been provided for Year 6 children, who grow physically at a pace difficult to keep up with. Year 5 children claim that cushions on hard chairs have made teaching and learning more irresistible!

The challenge of funding resources raises the issue of how far headship requires the skills and involvement of a business manager.

Suzanne sees herself as an entrepreneur in that she devotes serious time to finding ways of securing money to fund the many projects that flower in a creative school, as well as taking extreme care in acquiring every penny of all the grants and funds to which they are entitled or have possible access to. What she does not see as part of her role is spending time making links with businesses in order to get sponsorship and funding. The school has links with business, but these are about children's education and learning, not about hunting money. Getting involved in that would take her away from where she is most effective: leading and managing her school. She believes she would be failing her duty if she did not ensure that they were tapping into every available fund and grant, but that is as far as she is prepared to take it.

THE SCHOOL AND EXTERNAL RELATIONS

Suzanne does not place parents in the category of 'external relations'. Although they are not in school observing the teaching and learning, they are the main stakeholders, so it is essential they are brought on board and are able to see the inside picture.

The school arranges seminars where children demonstrate to parents, through practical work, what it is they are being taught and, more importantly, what they are learning and achieving. This has been a notable success, arousing great interest and helping tremendously in building strong relationships with parents to secure their trust and support.

Similarly, where governors are concerned, it is a matter of bringing them in, keeping them fully informed, raising their awareness, getting them actively involved, giving them responsibilities and painting a vivid picture of the school in action. Every governor has an 'adopted' class and the school encourages their active involvement with them.

Suzanne is careful how she spends her time and does not attend many external meetings. She sees herself primarily as the leader of teaching and learning in her school, as the trainer and nurturer of staff so that they develop as leaders themselves. Therefore she will only attend meetings and events that contribute to that, and to anything that relates specifically to her school, legislation, local authority initiatives, central advice and directives. She is not remotely interested in 'local politics and manoeuvring, in internecine competition, tensions and gossip, and all those extraneous things that get in the way of effective leadership'.

Suzanne finds that it is always beneficial to engage in worthwhile external projects. 'At the moment our older children are involved in a project with ICI (Imperial Chemical Industries), working with their scientists and gaining an insight into an important aspect of industry that is very much linked to education. The children are finding this a fascinating and quite challenging experience.'

As a school, they also take an active interest in their local area. They do a range of charity work, putting on entertainment, singing carols at Christmas at the local nursing home, and so on. The charities have been grateful for their level of commitment, interest and generosity in supporting local asylum-seekers, and in responding to disasters arising from famine and poverty worldwide. Every year the school works hard to raise as much money as they can for the vulnerable and disadvantaged.

ACCOUNTABILITY

Suzanne is accountable to a number of agencies and people, including parents, governors and the local authority, but most vitally, she is accountable to the staff and the children. 'I'm fortunate to have a very good relationship with my chair of governors: the critical friend, the person that I can confide in and trust implicitly. I think in that respect, the relationship between the head teacher and the chair is absolutely paramount to the success of the leadership of the school.'

Her leadership team give her regular feedback on her management. Although they are not managing her, they are certainly monitoring her leadership and management in a vocal way that helps her consider the quality of her work.

She is accountable to herself above all, for the charge invested in her by the privilege of headship, for the vision she holds for the school and for the children entrusted to her.

> *I believe our greatest accountability and challenge as educators – and it must be the same for those in the caring professions – is to enable every individual in our charge to understand themselves, to find themselves, to learn to love themselves, so that they can do the same to others. When that is missing, or when that seems too great a challenge, then we really see how important our work is, how vital it is, and how absolutely determined and courageous we must be to see it continue and to see the vision come to fruition.*

CHAPTER NINE

ANDREW CARTER

South Farnham Primary School, Surrey

State school for boys and girls aged from 4 to 11
Pupils: 750

> South Farnham Primary School has topped the SATs league tables every year since their introduction, making it, according to those criteria, one of the country's most successful schools. In every inspection Ofsted has graded the school 'Outstanding' in all aspects of primary practice.
>
> What these impressive facts may not convey is the consistently remarkable quality of education the school offers. This is largely due to the visionary nature and irresistible drive of Andrew's leadership team and his capacity to inspire those who work and study there.

Andrew was brought up on a Shropshire farm. After his schooling he was not sure what to do. 'In farming communities it is a tradition that the eldest son does the farming and they persuade everyone else in the family to reject it as a vocation; to do otherwise would bankrupt the family.'

He decided to go into teaching, 'where there was a boom in the sixties'. He went to Bishop Otter College in Chichester, 'a very interesting institution because it was quite revolutionary for its time. The principal, Kate Murray, believed that everybody should study everything and not become prematurely stuck in specialisms, such as maths, English or science.' This experience was a great awakening for him. 'I didn't go there to be a teacher. I went there to carry on just being young and having fun and then I really got hooked on the business of teaching. I studied maths and left inspired to be a teacher. I could do it reasonably well; the thing was that I quite enjoyed it.'

He began his career in 1971 at Kempshott Junior School. Since then, apart from three days of unavoidable absence, he has 'not had a moment free of school and teaching'.

There were forty children in the first class. The head teacher told teachers they were free to do what they liked, so long as good discipline was maintained. Andrew attended courses whenever and wherever he could because, from the very outset of his career, he wanted to find out about things.

Early on I realised there were clever people around me who were doing the job better than I was. I would go into their classrooms and interrogate them, saying, 'How do you do this, and how do you do that, and why do you do these things in that particular way?' and then I would try them out and adapt them for myself. At the beginning of my career there was little risk of censure if something did go hopelessly wrong, so long, of course, as the discipline was maintained! We were learning from our mistakes and our experiments.

When a colleague who was responsible for coordinating physical education unexpectedly left the school, the head teacher, desperate to preserve football, asked Andrew to take on the responsibility. He accepted without hesitation. 'I hadn't realised how powerful a person could be in a primary school if they played football and knew how to organise and manage it.' Similarly, he became involved in the Parent Teacher Association. His commitment to parental involvement has continued to be a notable feature of his subsequent career.

He became deputy head teacher in a 'very tough' school in Farnborough. The school was on a Greater London council estate that took the overspill population from Elephant and Castle in South London. Andrew learned to deal firmly with some very tough families, and did so constructively and creatively.

His head teacher, in common with other heads for whom he had worked, trusted him to get on with things. He set up a television and video studio in the school, went out and filmed locally and produced daily television broadcasts with news bulletins and features of general interest.

The school was visited by inspectors and advisers and by heads and teachers who were curious about his work. At the same time, he visited other schools to learn from and be inspired by their innovation. He also attended the growing number of courses and the expanding INSET available.

Teachers realised their horizons were broadening and they became aware of creative teaching possibilities. Most importantly, they saw that children's potential was much greater than previously imagined, and that the more you challenge children, the more they rise to the occasion.

Having become deputy head in a large and demanding primary school, teaching classes of around forty older children and getting involved in a variety of school activities, including PTA work, Andrew began to think about headship. He had a head teacher 'who kindly let me go'. Reflecting on dealing with the loss of outstanding teachers in a school, he has learned that the best way of dealing with such situations is to let them go with grace and gratitude: 'Shake them by the hand, thank them for all they have done, say goodbye and send them on their way with one's blessing. When your new teacher arrives, look them straight in the eye and say, "Lovely to see you; we were expecting you." '

In his early thirties Andrew was appointed head of a 200-pupil junior school in the village of Hartley Wintney in Hampshire, a community very different from that of his previous job in Farnborough. The school was five years old, purpose-built, open-plan and the staff, many of them long-serving, had moved to it from the former, very traditional building nearby. The governors were looking for enthusiasm and vitality, an awareness of new developments and a commitment to necessary change.

Andrew says: 'I came, fresh-faced and full of enthusiasm, and for the first time I realised that not everybody likes you.' He was asking teachers who had been trained in the 1950s, who were nearing the end of their careers, to move into different areas of thinking and managing, to adopt new and different approaches. Some staff made it clear, sometimes belligerently, that they didn't want to do what he required of them. But there could be no vacillation – as a head teacher, having made a decision, it had to be seen through. He learned that if people are treated fairly and professionally and their views and opinions are listened to, it is possible to overcome their resistance.

The staff had been accustomed to traditional methods of working. They had fixed expectations as to what children could attain at specific ages, and consequently, the children were limited in their achievement and progress.

> *Times were changing. The government and the nation at large were engaged in a debate about education and the need for major reform. This was the early eighties, before the advent of the National Curriculum, but some of us realised that the large-scale government and political involvement in education was going to change our rather cosy world.*

Many in the profession welcomed the change, however uncomfortable it might be. A new generation of head teachers emerged during this time of intensive debate. They had access to CPD, INSET and a flood of educational publications. They were inspired and challenged to explore the work of innovative colleagues practising elsewhere. In addition, there was practical input from the growing number of educational advisers employed by local education authorities.

The process of change is often painful and challenging and calls for hard re-appraisal. When people move to a place where they feel uncomfortable, they have to be certain the leader who brought them there is not going to walk away and leave them. 'You never give up on them.' The leader has to convince them that he/she is with them, by practical involvement and an absolute readiness to do anything to help them. They should be confident that the head teacher is a leader who walks their talk, who never asks staff to do what they won't do themselves. 'You are trying things out together, reflecting on and discussing their practice, asking why things aren't working, whether they could do things differently and better, being ready to listen to each other whatever the respective status and experience. In this way, staff are being given ownership of the process.'

However, not everything went smoothly. Some people found the journey hard and struggled to go the whole way. But in time the school moved forward, and became respected and popular for all the things you hope for in a school. Andrew's school went from being the traditional village school that catered for the community, to a school that was vibrant and exciting, a place that drew people to the village. In the past, people in the village went to the school; now they are moving to the village for the school.

They were very successful in getting the community involved in the school, not just in raising money, but in getting large numbers of parents (including fathers, many of whom were working full-time) to come in and provide practical help in a variety of ways. Strong links were made with local communities and businesses. Members of a community are often willing to be involved in their neighbourhood school but simply don't know how to be. Everyone has something to offer, so what the school, the head teacher, and the school leadership have to do is to explain to them how they can help, why it is important, and how it might impinge on the lives of the children. The most important part is to get them in, involved and contributing. Schools must avoid potential barriers that inhibit or even prevent them from coming in. They have to convince people and communities that they are genuinely interested in their lives. Andrew says, 'Tell the business person, for example, "We are forming and shaping young people whom you will employ and work with one day, young adults on whom the success of your business will depend." '

Schools must talk to the community about its future and about a shared responsibility for the children who will be its future. Then, when head teachers and staff move on, as they do, the community continues with its ownership of the school, and the school continues with its sense of purpose.

CURRICULUM

At that time the curriculum was project-centred. It was based on themes the staff believed were closely related to children's interests and concerns that would engage their curiosity and interest, promote learning and enlarge their horizons. It was an attempt to make learning exciting and attractive. Because the themes were cross-curricular, it seemed that the project approach would avoid unhelpful compartmentalisation of subjects and would enable children to see the important connections between subjects and to understand the wholeness of knowledge.

The project approach did go some way to achieving these objectives and some memorable work resulted. However, the approach encouraged a superficial focus on learning, with insufficient depth or scholarship. Because of that, subjects central to children's learning, such as Mathematics, suffered from a lack of rigour and inadequate attention to progression and attainment. This could lead to an unbalanced curriculum provision because of individual teachers' preoccupations and expertise.

Over time the staff learned to evaluate the work and to be rigorous about balance and subject focus. A great deal of thought was given to pedagogy and to the organisation and management of teaching. They were seeking to organise things so they could solve the perennial problem of finding enough time for the teacher to engage with individual children for as long as possible, for as long as was needed, to attend to their personal and special needs. In short, they were trying to provide personalised learning.

Various ways of organising time, space, assignments and resources were tried. For example, they worked the so-called 'integrated day model', where clusters of subjects were combined under the umbrella of broad themes or topics, intended to reduce what were seen as unhelpful divisions between subjects. This more holistic approach to curriculum content was regarded by many people at the time as a more sensible approach to young children's learning. However, they found that no system is without its flaws and weaknesses, and subjects were sometimes being taught at too superficial a level. In the end, Andrew and his staff realised that it wasn't systems or timetable strategies that were effective.

The real solution was staring us in the face: it was to put as many informed and effective adults in front of a class as possible, so there could be more sustained and intensive interaction with individual children.

Put two good teachers rather than one with a class and you halve the challenge – or put another way, you double the opportunity – of managing their learning.

But Andrew did not have that resource, though his frequent partnership with teachers in classrooms showed what could be done (which is why good classroom support is now provided by TAs). Staff were learning a great deal in the process of finding what these innovations had to offer; they were sharpening their understanding, sharing their practical experience, and helping each other make important connections.

Andrew also learned a key lesson that he did not fully grasp until he came to his present school:

I learned that you must talk through, write down, record and document what you are doing, learning and finding out. You must make it the intellectual property of the school; give the school the intellectual ownership of the ideas it has created. It is only by talking it through and formulating it in writing that you can refine it so that everyone understands it. Then you can pass it on. A new head, a new regime comes in, and they can take the perceived wisdom of that organisation and build on it, not try to capture something elusive and hope they get it right. Often when heads leave schools, even today when things are documented through SEFs and so on, those who are left behind pass on the essential perceived wisdom, the things that are at the heart of school, but they leave out the bits they didn't like, bits that might be notable and critical.

That is why the community has to have ownership of what a school is doing, so that when a new head comes, the community says: This is what we believe in and stand for and this is what we are doing.

CHANGING THE LEARNING CULTURE

Andrew made the school a place that supported and fostered children's learning, in such a way that the children were neither overawed nor intimidated by it, but became involved with it.

When I went to the school, children were over-reverential and respectful, diffident about taking initiative, about entering into a real dialogue with colleagues. The environment was not conducive to that kind of interaction or communication.

Arising from their efforts to transform the learning environment, they created a school council, 'something quite pioneering in those days'. Children were involved in improving the art area. They were asked for their ideas, what they would like or felt would be useful and stimulating. At first these were little changes; the notion of asking seven-year-olds what they would like or thought might be a good idea was very challenging to traditional teachers.

> *I was not saying that seven-year-olds would get just what they wanted, but I did want to know what they were thinking. If it was worthwhile and practicable to make it part of what we were doing, then we would do it. Once the staff realised that you could canvass children's ideas and opinions without undermining teachers' authority in the process, that it was a positive and productive thing to do, then they accepted it.*

In a similar way they explored their working relationship with parents. There was a great debate about whether parents helping in classrooms – a major advance in itself – should be invited into the staffroom to share coffee with staff. Andrew persuaded staff to accept that if parents were generous enough to give their time and learn to work with them in classrooms – and they did have to learn how to do that – then the least the staff could do was offer them the brief shared hospitality. In the process, teachers learned more about them and their families and how to communicate with them; the parents learned about staff professionalism and of their commitment to their children. However, Andrew made one proviso:

> *Teachers cannot become personal friends of the parents of the children they teach. Relationships with them can be warm and friendly but cannot go beyond that. Teachers cannot allow themselves to be in positions where a personal friendship could allow them to be used or exploited. Teachers have to retain the distance that allows them to say the hard things when necessary.*

During his first headship, he had always sought advice and guidance from very good older heads; he did not feel embarrassed about admitting there were things he did not know.

> *I would go to heads who weren't good at everything, but were good at bits. I wanted to assemble those bits into a coherent whole. Sometimes I went to*

*schools because their heads had spoken confidently and eloquently in meet-
ings, and then found the school in a shambles. But even then there were some
things they were doing pretty well, that I could learn from.*

Andrew took over the headship of a 7–12 middle school located in the former girls' grammar school in Farnham, Surrey. The school had a chequered history. After Surrey reor-
ganised into a first and middle school system in 1971, a majority of the staff comprised
teachers who had experienced difficulty in finding positions in schools of their choice. The
previous head teacher had been the president of the union to which the staff had been
affiliated and, as a result, the school had become a focal point for the extensive industrial
action and strikes of 1987, with frequent closures and what seemed, to a highly critical
and resentful local community, to be constant disruption to their children's education.
The reputation of the school was at a low ebb, with a staff regarded as disaffected and
malingering.

*When I arrived there was a room for smokers and a room for non-smokers –
symptomatic of the disunity in the school. What they were united on was that
they wouldn't do this and they wouldn't do that. The staff had gone to seed,
unchecked in terms of professional discipline.*

The school had remained unchanged since its grammar school days. No structural altera-
tions had been attempted; the building was dilapidated and run-down, undecorated
for years. The 200 children rattled about in it. Andrew was confident that he arrived at
the best time ever to be a head teacher. It was 1988: the National Curriculum had been
introduced, change was coming and head teachers had a mandate to deliver it.

All he could see around him was potential: a large building and a community from where
children, rich in promise, could be drawn. Here was a chance to create a great school.

He describes the reality he faced: corridors where mob rule went unchecked, a secondary timetable he found difficult to unravel, and a so-called 'carousel' which operated in
the afternoons, allowing staff to teach their specialism, to which children moved in
rotation. This carousel system had deskilled everyone – the so-called specialisms (art,
RE, history and so on) were allocated on an arbitrary basis to staff, regardless of how
qualified they were. It was the worst possible amalgam of so-called primary and secondary practice, arising from a misconception of the middle school ethic. It had failed to
create an infrastructure and organisation that would provide the education the children
needed.

A fortnight after his arrival Andrew painted the staffroom over a weekend, took down the timetable, informed the staff that it was gone forever and that forthwith all staff would teach the whole coherent curriculum to their designated classes. There would be no more carousels. They would all learn together to teach subjects as well as they could possibly be taught. The staff replied that they couldn't and wouldn't do it. They regarded his proposal as a revolution they would not entertain.

A few staff began to canvass parents, convincing some that they were being asked to do the impossible, and fomented a campaign of denigration and opposition, culminating in a letter demanding the head teacher's dismissal or resignation. Through all of this, Andrew persevered with establishing the new system of whole-class teaching. He trained teachers, working alongside them in classrooms, going with them to visit and observe teaching in other schools, talking things through with them, getting them to articulate their difficulties and giving them the help they needed, helping them to recognise the progress they were making.

He emphasised that he wasn't trying to dictate to them what to do, but trying to show them how things could be better, and how their work and lives would be better in the process. He told them that the old world had gone. He promised them that if they came onto his side they, the whole school, would prosper. But he made it equally clear that if they persisted 'in going down the old route and doing the old discredited things, then in a few years they would find themselves dealing with and accountable to very much harder people than me'.

Even the most obstinate staff came to acknowledge the strength of his determination to have his way. The decisive confrontation was contested on the occasion of the Annual Parents' Meeting, an event that normally attracted a couple of dozen people. The staff, who were irrevocably opposed to him, had worked hard on parents, organising the meeting to create a situation untenable for him.

What Andrew wanted was an opportunity to talk directly to parents, to explain what he wanted for their children and how he intended to go about achieving it. He personally invited parents – a practice uncommon at the time – to come and hear his plans for the following academic year, and to raise any questions they might have. He also did something else unheard of: he sent a letter to the parents of every infant school in the area, inviting them to find out what their children would experience if they came to the school to be educated.

He had already gained a decisive advantage: he had swayed a timid and ill-informed chair of governors. A previous parents' meeting for new admissions to the school had generated over a hundred applications for places, compared to less than sixty the previous year. This definitely suggested that the developments he was putting in place in the school were attracting a positive and favourable response from significant parts of the community.

The annual parents' meeting was climactic and decisive. The hall was packed with over 300 parents in attendance. Andrew had insisted that all the staff should be present too. They came and sat at the back, excited and expectant, some still convinced that this was where he would 'get the missile'.

From the beginning, he says, it was obvious that opposition had been orchestrated, with a sequence of clearly prepared hostile questions and comments from a group of parents.

> Then I had my chance to speak directly to the parents, to tell them what I believed in and stood for as an educationist, the educator of their/our children. I laid bare my philosophy of education. I talked for an hour and a quarter without notes, going through all the things we were going to do. The staff saw me perform in this context for the first time. At the end I received a standing ovation. Afterwards, one parent came up to me and said: 'I don't know whether you can do all this, but you must believe it because you did it without notes. It must have come from your heart and we're willing to give it a punt.'

That occasion was the turning point. The majority of staff accepted the opportunity for professional dialogue and partnership. Andrew says, 'I never got cross, never lost my cool in our debates.' But he made it clear that there were certain things that were not negotiable: that children were at the heart of their teaching and learning, that the declared ambition and intention for all staff was 'to be a great teacher', and the ultimate development and destiny of the school. There was some residual resistance, but eventually those at the heart of it left.

Andrew then set out to cultivate the staff who would secure his vision for the school. He found a handful of bright young teachers willing to learn, who realised that a worthwhile future resided with him. Whenever someone was replaced he sought teachers who had the enthusiasm, the idealism and the capacity for hard work that would enable them to rise to his challenge 'to be the best of their generation'. He did not want clones. He wanted people who would challenge his thinking, his ways of doing things; inventive, creative people with different qualities, abilities, skills, dispositions and enthusiasms who would continue to revitalise him and push him further, who would add further dimensions to the school. They would be a variety of talented, knowledgeable people: salespersons, innovators, people who work beneath the surface bonding and developing – not a preponderance of one type.

Andrew sees the building of teams as a long and subtle process. He does not just rely on advertising, shortlisting and interviewing, but is constantly looking for 'high quality, driven, committed teachers'. He persuaded governors that when such people happen along that everything should be done to secure them for the school, even if there is no vacancy at that time. He assures them that they will be paid for simply by attracting another twenty children to the school.

In a culture of change, people who want to stay and commit themselves will stay, and those for whom the commitment is too daunting will move on. The school helps leavers make good, generous and kind transitions, either to early retirement or to schools where they will be happier and more at home. When teams break up as people move on, particular skills and specialisms – such as expertise in music – are lost. This is why it is essential to capture what a team has done, record it and share it with everyone, including the governors.

The great changes – the National Curriculum, the new assessment regime, inspection – provided a glittering opportunity to make things better for the children. If parents could see the school was confident about what it was doing at a time of highly publicised concern and worry, then they were more likely to send their children there. As a result, parents in increasing numbers began to enrol their children because there was richness on offer to them, and a commitment to providing excellence for their children.

Andrew encouraged his senior leaders to make themselves available to parents. He greeted parents every morning at the school gate, spoke to parents and children, knew all their names and was in the school 'deliberately and conspicuously' on Saturdays. He gave his home phone number to every parent, inviting them to ring him if they needed to. There have been times when parents have phoned in the middle of the night, but over twenty years no one has abused the privilege.

A policy was made that if a parent came in without an appointment, they had to be dealt with that day, without fail. Sometimes he would phone a parent during the evening and work to find a solution to their problem. Such things became regular practice, not merely to resolve difficulties, but to send a message to the community: 'This school, your children, and our work for them, matters so deeply to us that there is nothing we will not do, and no trouble is too great for us to ensure what is best for them.'

All teachers go into the playground at the end of the day, talk with parents individually, gleaning information, constantly implanting the school's message. Once parents are convinced about the school's intentions, they are invited to become involved. Thus the cycle goes on – they reciprocate and become the school's strongest allies.

The school has never done any marketing. The school brochure is a paper version of their website. Everything parents need to know is accurately and attractively presented there; the money that would have been wasted 'on glossy stuff' is available for the good of the children. For parents, the way to know everything about the school is to come and see it, and join in its life.

THE LEARNING ENVIRONMENT

Andrew believes that the school environment should be an irresistible stimulus to curiosity, exploration, experimentation and constant learning. Displays around the school should reflect 'extraordinary' teaching, and celebrate high quality. He ensures that the curriculum puts an emphasis on the creative and aesthetic arts, and performance, and photographs from school productions adorn the corridor walls, reflecting how much these aspects of learning are valued.

> *Education isn't simply about English, maths and science; it's about the whole child. You have to stimulate them intellectually, physically, emotionally and aesthetically, and if you miss out any of these then the other areas will eventually become deprived too.*

The run-down building Andrew inherited contributed to the teachers' low morale and general sense of depression. A question he puts to staff at the beginning of each academic year is: 'What can we do for the building?' He wants them to be practical, creative and inventive. If they need doors moved and walls knocked down then he would do it. As a result, they have created a drama studio, a dance studio, a fully equipped gymnasium and a professional development centre, where teachers can hold year group meetings, do PPA work, prepare learning materials and meet parents in private.

People ask where the money comes from. Andrew says that the world is 'full of money, but devoid of ideas. Get your ideas, then go out and ask for the money. You'll find the money is there.' They have proved that, by raising 3.5 million pounds from various sources.

> *The more you turn your ideas into practice, the bolder you become. If you want something to happen, you have to make it happen. If you can't make it happen, then you have to move over and let someone else have a go. You are not paid to run a commentary on the disasters and tribulations visited on your school; you are paid to change it.*

He and his staff give constant thought to what makes them unique as an institution, to the contribution it makes to society and to the dilemmas that confront it.

Their unique role and contribution is to make children into social beings who will recognise and realise their potential, who will be enabled to develop their best qualities and personal gifts to the utmost, who will succeed in acquiring all the skills they will need in a changing world, who will have a social conscience and be active, caring, positive members of their communities.

The school understands only too well what a tall order that is. Schools are still not clever enough at it, as can be seen not only from the often fragmented nature of society, but sometimes within schools themselves. 'Schools must have a social conscience, and be organisations that are able and ready to contribute to the wider community beyond their catchment area.'

He offers a practical example of this: his offer to the social authority to take over a failing school, bereft of a head teacher and deputy, and run it in tandem with South Farnham School. In such circumstances, he says, professional, moral and social conscience dictates that one goes not only to the aid of colleagues, but seeks to intervene positively in the interests of children who are not receiving the education to which they are entitled. There can be no question of standing by and seeing another school struggle on at risk. Although in the past there had been a general climate of, at best, indifference, or at worst, helplessness and resignation on the part of the education authority, times had changed. Hence Andrew's proposal that South Farnham would become a partner school in every important sense.

The following proposal is a good example of social conscience in action, outlining the steps the head teacher has to take to turn round a failing school – a blueprint for recovery.

As head teacher, Andrew proposed that he would:

- For two or three years, take responsibility for the leadership and direction of the school, with the aim of revising its fortunes and making it an institution that guarantees a high quality education.

- Give parents a detailed timetable for change and for the presentation of evidence on development and progress.

- Transfer two Year 6 teachers to the partner school in exchange for their opposite numbers, who would then join the staff of South Farnham. This would ensure significantly raised SATs results at the receiving school and provide the parents with evidence of progress.

- After a period, reverse the transfer so that the two re-invigorated and retrained teachers return to the partner school to provide a lead and inspiration to colleagues.

- Continue this transfer process with teachers from another year group.

- Together with senior staff and subject leaders, provide occasional but regular practical support, working alongside teachers in classrooms and providing an INSET programme geared to the needs of the school.

- Merge the finances of the schools and take over complete management. Since the partner school had run itself hugely into debt, he would guarantee to clear the deficit, provided the local authority was flexible in terms of time scale for recovery.

- Aggregate the school's SATs results as a tactical measure to regain the confidence of parents.

- Do this for no financial or material return.

With such a plan – essentially renewing the staff's faith in their abilities, giving a boost to their morale and revitalising the environment and resources – within three years the school should be able to move forward confidently and successfully on its own once more.

However, Andrew's proposal was not accepted, being deemed 'too far ahead of its time'. Now such developments are the fashion, not merely encouraged, but driven by the educational establishment.

We made the offer for one reason only: because we believed and continue to believe that, as a school, we are part, not of just our immediate community but of the wider society, and that we have a moral and social responsibility to its welfare, to contribute in the way that we are professionally equipped to do.

STAFF DEVELOPMENT

The recruitment and professional development of staff are high priorities in the school. 'It's about getting the right person on the bus, and only later putting them in the right seat.' They look for 'bright, alert people' about whom they feel an affinity and a sense of warmth. They seek to breed leaders at a younger and younger stage. New recruits go through training programmes, a carefully graduated series of developmental stages which give them increasing responsibilities while ensuring they are never overwhelmed.

When the school identifies people who are in danger of not succeeding as teachers, they give them the same attention as successful counterparts but pay greater attention to detail on what needs to be changed or developed, the problems that need to be overcome, and the strategies and practical steps for doing so. It is about how to make things better.

Senior and experienced staff have been trained to guide and advise, to correct where necessary, and to tailor their guidance according to their colleague's contexts, personality, potential and disposition.

The school places a strong emphasis on the training and development of teaching assistants. Every class has a full-time teaching assistant. There are two full-time professionals teaching every class of children: one a fully qualified teacher and the other in the process of being trained so that they will one day reach the stage when, if they wish, they can become fully-fledged teachers.

The school implemented a City and Guilds NVQ programme for assistants who had often started as 'helping mums'; now the school is a training centre for classroom assistants from other institutions.

Team building is very important. Teachers and teaching assistants need to work together and feel part of a unified force. Teaching assistants are trained to take and manage year assemblies, developing their ability to tell stories effectively and to engage children in the creative and expressive arts.

MOTIVATING AND DEVELOPING A LARGE STAFF

Every morning Andrew makes it his business to talk to every member of staff.

We have sixteen classes, twenty-five teachers and fifty-two staff in total. I talk to everyone, continuing the story we had the day before. I want to make sure that people self-actualise. The NQTs don't want my job, but they do want to be acknowledged for what they are doing. So I might well be saying to some younger staff, 'When I took our visitor into your room yesterday, I was so proud to have them see the environment you have created and the work you are doing.' I might thank a senior teacher for dealing unobtrusively and without fuss with an issue they realised I had not picked up because I had been diverted elsewhere.

Teachers are given responsibilities and opportunities to lead from an early stage in their career. On the part of the school, that calls for observation, light-touch monitoring and coaching in classrooms where there is a sense of partnership and mutual evaluation. Teachers are encouraged to view such practice not as judgemental but as opportunities to venture things, to show their paces, to be enquiring and demanding in a sympathetic professional context. When one of his two deputies gained a headship, he took this opportunity to restructure the upper senior management team. Two assistant head teacher posts were created to be filled by younger members of staff who have already proved themselves in a variety of roles and responsibilities. He asked the remaining deputy to be their mentor, to nurture and guide them, to be in charge of them. 'I have asked her, "Turn them into deputies for us, for the school".'

With this strategy he has created a more effective senior infrastructure with further distributed leadership. Two excellent young teachers have been acknowledged and rewarded for their work and set on the next upward stage of their career. Andrew has indicated to staff that he is looking to reinforce the structure by appointing a third assistant head teacher from within. His deputy regained her status, which was very important to her, and had her sense of professional esteem enhanced.

MANAGING TEACHING AND LEARNING

There is an ongoing professional debate about teaching and learning. The staff are constantly reviewing their teaching and its impact on the children's learning. There is a curriculum committee comprising staff and governors who keep a monitoring brief over the school's total curriculum. These are people for whom education is a consuming interest. They are there to keep staff accountable, to ensure they keep abreast of things and are constantly striving to be better. They are there to ask hard, uncomfortable questions – and to offer advice and suggestion.

Every teacher is observed each week by a senior teacher or another member of staff qualified to evaluate that particular lesson. This is followed soon after by a discussion/review of what took place and thereafter a note from the observer which highlights effectiveness and possible areas for development.

Every new appointee, whatever their experience or status, has a compatible mentor/coach allocated to them. The mentor's task is to induct the newcomer into the routines of the school, to help them assume the new role, and to monitor, advise and coach them until they are settled and assured. This process, with its careful matching of tutor and tutee – a significant management task in itself – yields a double return for staff and the school: the newcomer is happily and positively inducted in professional and personal terms, whilst the mentor further develops leadership and management skills.

There is a system of 'health checks': teachers observe other teachers, and in turn, are observed themselves. Such visits are followed by discussion and/or a written note, depending on what needs to be conveyed. Often this is no more than warm words of commendation, accompanied by a formative suggestion or two.

Sometimes the health checks are directed at specific issues: the effectiveness of teaching for children with special educational needs; the degree to which children are involved and on task; aspects of teaching and learning that have recently been raised in staff debate as something calling for revision and analysis and possible reshaping.

He says, 'The health check business may sound daunting, but it is part of the fabric of the school, something to which they are accustomed. Over time, all staff are engaged in this from both perspectives: observed and observer.'

Lessons are planned in cyclical fashion; the planning for next summer term is done this present summer term, and continues to be evaluated and changed where necessary. In this way banks of lessons are built up, to which teachers have constant access, thereby keeping them relatively free of the drudgery of elaborate, time-consuming planning. 'I want them to be able to focus on doing it as well, as inventively and as excitingly as possible, rather than on labouring endlessly over its construction. Teachers can draw from the banks of tried and tested lessons on our network, and adapt and vary as they think best.'

New teachers are provided with all their lessons for the first term planned in detail, simply because they could not be expected to plan satisfactorily for children of whom they have little or no knowledge.

A long-established practice is for teachers to be invited by Andrew, senior team members, or colleagues, to bring examples of pupils' work to appointed staff meetings. Coming from across the curriculum, it can be that of an individual, a group or the whole class, as long as it shows notable achievement and excellence. The teacher describes the work in detail: its original purpose, what motivated and inspired it, the resources that underpinned it, the children's perception and evaluation of it, the input from any other staff, the pedagogy required to manage it, the formative assessment involved, any areas that, in retrospect, might have been further developed and any possible future work arising from it.

Similarly, staff also present to their colleagues from time to time. The 'presenters' are tasked to identify things that did not go quite right or things that, with hindsight, they would have done differently. Because it takes place in a pleasant and laid-back atmosphere, with tea and buns, everyone is relaxed. People feel free to ask questions and to refer to similar things they have done. Other approaches, options and possibilities suggest themselves in the course of discussion. What they get are little master classes in teaching and learning; feasts of ideas and stimuli and natural opportunities for reflection, debate and analysis. And, valuably, teachers have the chance to hear colleagues describe their work from other areas of the school (upper school staff listen to Early Years practitioners, for example) where they themselves have not worked, and are not likely to, but for which they may well have subject leadership or monitoring responsibility. It can be a learning experience for all, but for some, a genuine revelation, an illuminating insight into unfamiliar practice. The practice provides one other very important benefit: it shows teachers a picture of continuity and progression in children's learning across the primary spectrum, demonstrating where the children have been and what they have done when they arrive in their class, and what they do in learning terms after they have left.

Every teacher receives a statistical analysis of their class and is trained to recognise what it is telling them about individuals. They are helped to devise courses of action that will meet individuals' particular learning needs. It becomes the focus of one of the head teacher's health checks.

> *I choose occasions to go into class and ask teachers about the progress being made by a specific child, and not just those with learning difficulties or those who are underachieving. If a teacher cannot respond in some detail, then I would doubt whether that child was receiving that day the treatment and experience that his/her needs and development required.*

MANAGING RESOURCES

The school is renowned for the extraordinary range and richness of its resources, for the physical transformation of the building over ten years and for the opulent extensions dedicated to learning. Teachers are seen as the prime resource – the salary bill for staff is over a million pounds. The school's recruitment policy is to find the finance, the ways and the means to identify and appoint staff of high calibre, even if there is no position immediately available, because for them there is manifestly a role and a valuable contribution to be made.

> *To get value for money, if you are going to make that million pounds work for you, you need to provide staff with all the resources for doing their business. You can't have high expectations of teachers unless you provide them*

with the means to realise those expectations. When I sit down with teams or year groups to consider what will best serve the children's learning needs, I say to them, 'I want you to dream dreams. Don't think about money; don't let money enter your head because it will change your thinking and your vision. Explore everything, investigate every source, and then just tell me what you need.' When teachers aired their dream of children being able to dance, we realised we needed a dance studio. So we built one. We needed half a million pounds for that.

Andrew tells people that they need a system for raising money and suggests some of the less obvious ways in which it can work.

He does not pay outside companies to run after-school clubs. At South Farnham the after-school clubs are run by South Farnham Services Ltd, a company wholly owned by the school. It makes a profit, pays corporation tax and covenants all profits to the school trust, which pays back its corporation tax. The school is currently working in a consultancy and advisory capacity to twenty-seven other schools, all of which pay for those services. That might mean a group of heads and senior staff spending a day at South Farnham to learn about raising SATs levels from 4 to 5. The school runs other courses and INSET, which are advertised on their website and bought into by a wide range of schools.

The school is paid a consultancy fee by the Surrey Graduate Training Programme; further revenue-earning courses are run for teaching assistants and NVQ students. School lettings currently earn £16,000 annually; that will rise to £25,000 with the leasing of the new suite. The school shop, in its early days at present, raises £6,000 a year. The entire school uniform can be bought online from a company that pays the school 15% of the revenue.

The school has a link on its website called Find a Home, which capitalises on the fact that it is sought-after by parents who want to live in the vicinity. The estate agent pays the school an annual five-figure sum for the privilege.

The school also raises money from parents. Andrew treats that as a complex matter to be handled thoughtfully and delicately. To all parents he explains that all the money raised is fed back into the school for their children, as is evident from all that has been provided by the school for the benefit of the children.

Although they could significantly cut back on the very large resources expenditure without apparently diminishing the learning and curriculum on offer, Andrew says, 'I'd know what was lost, and the staff would know, and it would be the children's loss. Remember, if your staff are valued at a million pounds, then the resources you allow them must do them justice.'

ACCOUNTABILITY

Andrew makes no important decision about the running of the school without discussing it in detail with the governing body. He liaises closely with individual governors in relation to aspects of management of the school in which they have a special interest or expertise. He is wholly transparent and accountable to his governors, and the school is always open to their evaluation. For example, curriculum coordinators regularly make a presentation to governors about plans and work in their subject areas. In the term following specific presentations, nominated governors visit classrooms to evaluate implementation in subject areas and report back, with recommendations, to the main body. A genuine partnership has been forged with this very able and informed group of people.

He is also accountable to the local authority for the satisfactory discharge of a range of legal responsibilities that they are mandated to monitor.

Andrew is accountable to the staff through giving them genuine ownership of the management and leadership of the school. They are formally consulted in a variety of ways, including through their membership of planning and special assignment groups. He believes his accountability is most effectively expressed through his relationship with individual members of staff and through constant contact that involves them not merely in professional dialogue, but in exchanges that are genuinely about mutual welfare and concern for each other.

Pupils always have an opportunity to express their opinion of things, to make their voices heard in formal ways through class and school councils, and through the teachers' openness to pupils' individual opinions. 'It is often through the innumerable, apparently casual comments and unsolicited remarks that we learn most tellingly about what they think of us as their educators.'

Most potent in terms of accountability is Andrew's own sense of self-management, expressed in his relationship with parents, children and staff. He wants parents to like him, not for himself, but because of what he does for their children; for his good stewardship of the school and leadership of the staff. He imposes accountability on himself by the need to achieve the demanding standards, open to rigorous public audit, that he and his staff have set for the school.

CHAPTER TEN

HELEN O'DONOGHUE

CET Primary Schools, Tower Hamlets and Westminster, London
Free school for boys and girls aged 4 to 11
Pupils: 208

To use Helen's musical metaphor: the establishment, leadership and management of any new school demands not merely high quality musicianship and performance, but the composing of a score which has not previously existed. The Free School staff players are simultaneously playing and composing.

For Helen O'Donoghue, the challenges of leadership are complicated by the fact that Free Schools are relatively new in a changing education landscape and are, in some quarters, mistrusted. What encourages Helen is the commitment and involvement of the parents and the community and their enthusiasm for what she and her staff are doing to create as effective and international a school as possible. The curriculum planning benefits from internationally-inspired principles from Helen's previous international school experience.

She regards developments to date as work in progress. The substantial advances made so far – the commissioning of new premises, the cultivation of an international ethos, highly motivated pupils and strong parental support, to name but a few – suggest that these two Free Schools have a notable contribution to make to their communities.

Helen is the daughter of working-class parents. Her childhood and adolescence were happy and secure. She was protected within her family, free to mix and play with the other children in her neighbourhood, able to explore the world in the streets outside. Her parents had no deep awareness or understanding of her schooling; they just accepted it as necessary and worthwhile for their children.

Still at the core of education is children's perennial need for the care, concern, profound interest and support of parents, family and the adults who are involved in, or are responsible for their welfare.

The end of her primary schooling marked the beginning of her fascination with knowledge and scholarship generally – history in particular, inspired by one of her secondary teachers, who was 'in love with his subject'.

Another delight was playing hockey, simply because it provided her first impression of a truly collective activity, where people strove together and supported and encouraged each other in a shared enterprise.

This concern with scholarship, with the cerebral and intellectual, with the cultivation of the mind and the spirit, runs through her discourse. Apart from nurturing the intellect, her particular academic pursuits and the subjects she read sharpened her critical faculty; she developed a political interest, a moral and social awareness, and a deep conscience about the lives of others.

Still with no thought of teaching, during one university vacation she worked at a summer camp for primary-age children from disadvantaged urban communities. At first, this was simply an enjoyable experience with children who responded to enthusiasm, affection and inventiveness. By the end of the period, it was instrumental in refining and reinforcing that moral consciousness. It motivated her to endeavour, as far as she could, to make a difference in the world. She decided to teach primary children in the 'politically and economically battered' city of Liverpool, to which she felt she owed a debt.

She worked in schools in socially disadvantaged areas, teaching children from dysfunctional families for whom deprivation was almost constant. It was 'either feast or famine'.

Helen's teaching career started before the Education Reform Act and the National Curriculum. In those days, teachers were left largely unsupported. She survived from lesson to lesson and from day to day, learning on the job, through challenge and adversity and from her mistakes. Even though the curriculum lacked shape, coherence and continuity, Helen and her colleagues were able to do things for and with the children that were educationally worthwhile, offering ventures and initiatives that enriched their experience, enlarged their constrained lives, and were exhilarating, inspiring and memorable for them.

> In that bleak urban environment we were deeply into natural history, field trips and educational outings. We baked and cooked with them; we celebrated in flamboyant and glorious style the great feasts and festivals; we seized every opportunity to transform the environment in ways that would invest the children with a sense of awe and wonder. That was not a fashionable phrase at the

time, but I believe we made things better in practical, educational and, if you like, in spiritual and cultural ways, for these undernourished, sleep-deprived children, from fractured relationships and dysfunctional families.

Personal circumstances led Helen to take up a teaching position at the British Primary School in The Hague in the Netherlands. The school was international in terms of its intake of pupils from over fifty nationalities and languages.

The school, in common with most British and some international schools, taught the National Curriculum. There were, however, some major differences from the primary mainstream in England in terms of curriculum provision: the teaching of a second language for all pupils from five onwards and extensive provision for the teaching of English as a Second Language.

For Helen the most notable difference from her previous professional experience lay in the staffroom, in the new colleagues with whom she was working. 'There was a real spirit of collegiality, a common mindset, not merely about children and their education but about life in general.' There was an open-mindedness; a receptiveness to new ideas, cultures and lifestyles; an eagerness for exploration and discovery, for wider experiences, which characterises a majority of people who teach abroad.

Such qualities were also evident in the colleagues with whom she subsequently worked in a number of international schools abroad. It made for good team players, for teachers who interacted readily and creatively with others and whose wider world, diversity and richness of experience combined to make staffrooms vibrant and stimulating places, not merely educationally, but in the broadest sense.

Helen returned to England to be close to her elderly parents. After some time working with international schools through Fieldwork Education, she was appointed to the executive leadership of Constable Education Trust Primary Schools, in London's Tower Hamlets and Westminster. These two schools were set up in response to a shortage of places in those boroughs.

The CET Primary Schools Trust has, for a number of years, run the Moat School, an independent secondary school for children with special and additional learning needs.

This partnership with the Moat School has confirmed Helen's long-held belief in the importance of early identification of learning needs, of immediate and effective intervention, targeted to overcome individual barriers to progress. Too many eleven-year-old children are unable to read competently. Many run the risk of being labelled as being troublesome or disruptive, when often theirs is merely a different way of learning. Failure on the part of schools to recognise this can prevent such children from achieving their potential.

Helen had the challenge of establishing these two Free Schools from scratch. A Free School is an all-ability state-funded school, set up, sometimes controversially, in response to what local people say they want and need for their children. The Tower Hamlets CET School started with seventy-four children in temporary accommodation and had to be resourced and staffed in a relatively constrained timescale. The Westminster CET School started with fifty-six pupils; it took over a year to find a permanent home.

Being Executive Head Teacher, running two schools on separate and temporary sites, is a formidable set of challenges. She has established compatible and sustainable systems and structures for both schools. These include an ICT infrastructure and 'iCloud' that facilitates planning, moderation and evaluation, and curriculum management and delivery.

As with all schools, recruiting high quality staff is a priority. Helen looks for people with a strong commitment to the Free School ideal and determination to succeed. The role of the deputy head teachers is crucially important to ensure honest and trusted communication. Helen has managed to appoint colleagues who consistently communicate the shared, core message and keep her in the loop. Her senior management on both sites know that she is always available for them.

At the end of their first year of operation, the CET schools shared four training days; similar shared CPD is planned for the future. The staff have the opportunity to visit each campus to observe and have dialogue with colleagues who perform similar roles and bear common responsibilities. This makes demands on organisation and planning, and on the stamina and resilience of her staff, but it affords opportunities for developing skills and expertise.

Executive leadership means always keeping to the core mission of improving and enlarging children's learning – there can be no compromise on that. It means being disciplined and motivated to 'a fanatical extent' to the task of imbuing children with a passion for learning and life.

Newly established institutions such as Free Schools have no history. 'The leader and the staff of the school must create their own history, culture, climate and vibe, and this is extremely hard and challenging work. There is no place for the faint-hearted.'

Helen warns there are 'many predators out there', closely and critically watching the Free School movement. It is therefore important – while remaining mindful of the needs of neighbouring schools and being genuinely ready to offer them whatever support may be possible – to provide the best possible education for the children who have been entrusted to your care in this new venture. Parents have made a bold choice. They are consumers and therefore the most powerful advocates for the school.

CHALLENGES OF HEADSHIP

Helen uses the symphony orchestra metaphor to convey her concept of school leadership. Her position as Executive Head equates to the role of the conductor. The successful conductor has to be a practising musician, an expert comprehensively informed and authoritative on the complex theology of music, having a profound understanding of its intricacies and a passion for expressing and communicating it as a medium of human enrichment. Similarly, the head/leader of a school will be steeped in and comprehensively informed about education, and wholly committed to it as a transforming and enriching element in the human condition.

Effective head teachers will already have been successful practitioners. They will know teaching and learning thoroughly, both in theoretical and practical terms. But, as with conductors, there will be areas of practice and subjects where they are unable to match the expertise and knowledge of individual members of their team. That expertise will have been incrementally enlarged, honed and enhanced through regular practical engagement, especially as the primary curriculum grows in volume and complexity and demands specialist teaching. The role and genius of the effective head teacher lies therefore in their ability to draw together staff in the creative enterprise of providing effective education.

One of the great challenges of headship is identifying, training, nurturing and developing staff who will take on the responsibility of leading colleagues in the management of essential business, the maintenance of everyday but essential routine, high quality teaching and learning, effective assessment, self-evaluation, the provision of training and CPD, and the fostering of sound relationships with parents and the wider community.

As with all the sections that comprise the orchestra, the school needs systems and processes for enhancing professional skills and for promoting awareness and knowledge. There must be a common recognition of the need for unremitting learning and renewal; for rigorous review and evaluation involving all staff, at levels appropriate to their professional development.

TEACHING AND LEARNING

As a school leader, Helen's prime responsibility is to provide quality teaching and learning for every individual pupil. This defines the worth, value and effectiveness of a school on a daily basis.

It begins with efficient administration and organisation. If these are not right, then people's ability to do their work is seriously impaired and the corporate effort is slowed up, diverted or even halted, perhaps not irreparably, but inevitably at a cost to the children.

She has created a designated team to manage the school's organisation and routine business. She assumes overall responsibility for the process, which she handles almost entirely 'out of school time', when the children and staff cannot distract her. She is 'the first to arrive and the last to leave', arriving at seven in the morning and often leaving twelve or more hours later. Any administration that cannot be completed in school, she takes home and does in the evenings or at weekends.

> It varies in urgency, volume and intensity, but it all has to be done efficiently and punctiliously, since the smooth working of the school and the provision of the right conditions for the children depend on it. At the same time it must not distract me from the essential business of education throughout the school.

Helen sees herself as 'the gatekeeper of the children's learning', the main guarantor that the children will receive education of the highest quality possible. For this reason she spends a significant amount of time in classrooms, observing and monitoring teaching and learning and being involved in it in a variety of ways.

Initially she taught in every classroom, the staff having provided her with their plans. She used those plans, but not exclusively. Plans are springboards from which she sometimes takes off in directions other than those predicted, which results in interesting and worthwhile outcomes relevant to the children's needs and interests.

Helen wants to get a sense of the different learning environments in her school and their worth and potential as centres of learning. She also wants to learn what it is like for the children, and what their classrooms and lessons mean to them. She tries 'to see all sides of the story, as far as I possibly can. I pay particular attention to what I call "the children's voice".' The school encourages the children to be articulate, to talk about their work and what they think and feel. Their learning projects, research and investigations are structured to generate dialogue, discussion and debate. It enables the children to make a worthwhile contribution to staff insight, thinking and planning. For example, the school council plays a valuable and active part in the life of the school. In addition, children are invited into discourse and dialogue with staff and with each other, to express their views, opinions, hopes and aspirations. 'I talk with them and listen to what they say. They in turn engage with me on a range of issues. Very occasionally I am seen as a final court of appeal. Such encounters will sometimes provide me with illuminating insights.'

Helen continues to teach across the school, though necessarily on a restricted basis, and provides an extra pair of hands on educational visits and outings.

Helen has established, in the administration and education teams, occasional sessions for colleagues to discuss and reflect on relevant and significant educational issues. They refer to articles, essays, commentaries and news items circulated in advance of meetings. These sessions are designed to broaden and sharpen their thinking about education, to encourage reflection and analysis, and to help develop the concept and ethos of a 'thinking and learning' school.

While anxious not to sound patronising or elitist, Helen maintains that staff development is partly about helping colleagues to become rounded, cultivated people who read widely, who keep themselves informed of developments and movements worldwide, and who readily engage and communicate with others and share ideas.

DEVELOPING COLLEGIALITY

Implementing collegiality is a complex and unpredictable matter. It takes time and effort and calls for trust on all sides. Everyone must opt in; in a collegial community there is no place for domineering egos or prima donnas. Everyone and everything must be committed to a common vision and endeavour. Helen tells her staff that she would, in a professional context, lay down her life for them. But they have to be very clear on what is expected in return: dedication, openness and honesty, a total commitment to the purposes and aims of the school.

In a truly collegial context, teams can live with setbacks, failures and mistakes and work together to eventually overcome them. Head teachers and leaders must make it clear that there has to be total openness about issues. Attempting to conceal things, hiding the true state of things or deciding not to raise something in the hope that it will go away or be forgotten, are completely unacceptable.

Helen meets regularly with staff on an individual basis. Many of their dialogues, always conducted in a sympathetic and creative way, are about teaching and learning, pedagogy and their class management. Teachers are asked to talk through and explain samples of their lesson plans and clarify how these are intended to enhance the children's learning, how they relate to the work, policies and intentions of the school and, at times, how the plans might be improved and enhanced.

She says, 'I constantly impress upon them: if they need more resources they can have them. If they want more time, I'll make it available. If anything extra is needed for field trips and educational expeditions it will be provided. The quid pro quo is that every effort is made to ensure that teaching and learning and outcomes are as good as they can be.'

EVALUATION AND ASSESSMENT

From the outset of her leadership at the Free School, she and her staff have improved their evaluation systems. These are now evidence-based and are rigorously analytical rather than merely descriptive.

Evaluation based on purely narrative accounts of observed lessons – usually positively biased – are unfit for purpose. Their evaluation systems focus on the quality and effectiveness of teaching and its impact on work and outcomes, taking into account attainment and achievement.

Helen and her teachers have introduced an appraisal system for assessing and evaluating how effectively performance in teaching and learning realises the aims of the school. A predominant feature of staff meetings is a rigorous engagement with issues of attainment, performance and achievement. Teachers have had to refine their skills of observation, monitoring and moderation regarding children's learning and written work. They are now obliged to identify, interpret and act on intelligence relating to the value added to pupils' education and achievement.

In starting a school from scratch, staff have had to deal with new structures, different modes of working, specific expectations about performance and demands for accountability. Many teachers have willingly assumed responsibility beyond the demands of their immediate classrooms. They have had to accept the sophisticated concept of the school as a learning community and all the implications inherent in that for their teaching and distributed leadership roles. To help them with this, teachers visited and observed other year groups, occasionally teaching them, thus informing themselves about teaching and curriculum throughout the school.

DISTRIBUTED LEADERSHIP

The Executive Head Teacher role provides an example of distributed leadership. Helen supports her deputies at their campus, encouraging them to develop their leadership qualities and potential, whilst allowing them a large measure of independence in managing their separate institutions. She believes a head teacher needs to be friendly, warm, positive and encouraging, but cannot become the teachers' friend: 'My life outside of school, my personal life, is not a concern of theirs and they do not need to know about it.' But as head teacher, Helen maintains an open-door policy, acknowledging that she must give staff the time they need and listen to the 'bad stuff' as well.

> What I promise **to** them, and **for** them, I will deliver. I will ask nothing of them I would not do myself. I will work without reserve for them and, through them, for the school.

Good leaders are fascinated by people: by their attitudes, the way they react to and engage with others, the things that motivate and influence them, and their worldview. Leaders need to develop a sense of humility, and an ability to listen to other people's truths, stories and viewpoints, however irrelevant they may be. The danger with leadership is the temptation to be beguiled by the undoubted power and importance it confers, forgetting that we remain learners forever.

Helen is convinced that many of her colleagues, who are wholly occupied with meeting the demands of the National Curriculum, seem to have had the creative insight and imaginative flair for teaching and learning squeezed out of them; she believes this is due, to a considerable extent, to the fact that they are overly concerned with teaching content.

The 'baby boomer' generation of teachers still want to question, to challenge things, to be venturesome, to think about how children learn and develop. She wonders if the younger generation of teachers are the product of a restrictive curriculum, the product of training colleges that were committed to content before concept.

She suggests that school leaders need to take account of the age their teachers were born in, because that will have had a significant effect on their attitudes, dispositions and worldviews. It may significantly shape their relationship with children, the ways in which they teach them, and the ideas and values they convey to them.

STAFF DEVELOPMENT

One of the great responsibilities of leaders is the professional development of staff. In some senses, endowing them with and cultivating the skills of teaching, classroom management and curriculum mastery may well be the easiest part of the task. Developing their sensibilities and awareness in relation to people and children, especially broadening their view and understanding of the world, is probably more complex. It is naïve to think that all staff yearn for continuous and challenging professional development and aspire to collegiality with equal avidity.

Helen feels it is necessary for staff to broaden their awareness of the world, to acquire and develop an international cast of mind and to cultivate a sympathetic and informed understanding of other cultures. One of the great strengths of the international school system is that, by its very nature, it provides a rich mixture of experience, formed by an uncommon diversity of people, contexts and encounters. The same international-mindedness is evident in her London schools, where between them the children speak nearly fifty different languages and represent a similar number of cultures.

THE MAKING OF A CONTEMPORARY SCHOOL

Helen's mission statement, 'All pupils have the potential to succeed,' commits the school to developing students so that they become independent and enthusiastic about life and learning.

She aims to create an open and inclusive community that treats everyone with fairness, listens to and respects those with different points of view, seeks consensus, establishes community spirit through responsibility and accountability, empowers its members to be proactive, and encourages parents, students and teachers to work together.

With their largely urban and multicultural demographic, the CET free schools recall the international schools with which she has worked in the UK and overseas. Helen is well-qualified to identify what makes a school international in the truest sense of the word – it is certainly more than having a large number of nationalities or mother tongue languages.

The key factor is a passionate commitment to providing an education system that empowers pupils to be genuinely international in outlook and true citizens of the world. She wants to imbue children with an international sense: a genuine and profound empathy with other cultures, beliefs, value systems and models of living, and the willingness and eagerness to reach out to them in the most positive and receptive of ways.

Any urban or international school's intake will be diverse in terms of experience, culture, language, expectation and need. Diverse religions, faiths and cultures and nationalist allegiance will sometimes make for particular tensions among parent groups and, indeed, within the community of schoolchildren itself. This will necessitate improving the staff's proficiency in language teaching and in enabling pupils to master English as an additional language.

RELATIONSHIPS WITH PARENTS

Any good school must establish effective working partnerships with parents. Many families face the challenge of adjusting, acclimatising and settling into a new and unfamiliar cultural environment. Conventions, attitudes and social norms may well be significantly different from what they had expected.

Helen explains to all new parents that the school will welcome what their culture adds, and they in turn will be enriched by the diversity of the school.

> *I make it clear to all parents that when they come to the school they buy into our school's way of life and our values. Our children here are drawn from multi-faiths, multi-cultures.*

Parents see evidence of this in the course of the children's education and in frequent opportunities to listen to them describe and showcase their work. This is a predominant feature of Helen's school: the range of international nights, the weekly evening events, the weekly information morning, the number of occasions when parents are welcomed into the school to see what their children are doing and achieving, and to reciprocate with their opinions, suggestions and wishes.

Parents also benefit from Helen being an 'untiring communicator' to the world outside and to all who have a stake in the school. She does this through information days, school publications and newsletters, the children's detailed report cards, and countless conversations and dialogues with parents.

Helen wants a school without walls that is open to the outside world and uses London as its classroom; a school that encourages and supports innovation, gives free rein to the creativity and imagination of its members, and is a community in which all its members see themselves as learners.

CHAPTER ELEVEN

PAT HOLLISTER

Fleet Primary School, Camden, London
Non-denominational school for boys and girls aged 3 to 11
Pupils: 240

At Fleet School, in a racially and socially diverse community that is marked in places by material deprivation, Pat and her staff established a school that is genuinely comprehensive, united by a common vision and purpose. Pat put particular emphasis on the professional development of staff and nurtured their capacity for leadership. She and her staff implemented a broad and project-driven curriculum and made rich provision in the creative arts central to the children's educational experience.

Pat Hollister's career and her development through ascending phases of responsibility and leadership took place through a period of unprecedented change, challenge and progression in the world of education. Her notable achievements, hard won, in different schools and in extraordinarily complex urban contexts were underpinned by a profound conviction about the transforming potential of good education, and a belief that only collegial action by skilled teachers would enable schools to provide the best for its children.

Pat Hollister came from a working-class family, where her paternal grandfather was involved in the leadership of a Scottish mining community. This legacy generated a strong belief in the family that it was important to be clever, to learn, read and understand all you could and to be quick on the uptake, but was less concerned with worldly achievement.

For Pat, teacher training was an introduction to a world of debate and critical thinking. It broadened her intellectual and social horizons immensely. When qualified, she and her friends were snapped up by the Inner London Education Authority (ILEA), where there was a massive shortfall of teachers. She opted to teach junior-age children, feeling more at ease with children of that age. She has never seen herself as possessing the qualities essential to the good Early Years practitioner. She is probably better equipped now, but believes she is not 'a natural' at it. Nevertheless, the ILEA, desperate for teachers, placed her in the infant department of an all-ages school, located in a disused secondary build-ing. Pat says she was 'very unhappy for that first year'.

The school population consisted mainly of Afro-Caribbean children, who had arrived in London from the Caribbean in large numbers. There was a huge mismatch between the Plowden ideals that teachers were striving to take on board and the experience and needs of these children. The children had come from countries with schools where there were classes of fifty or more and where corporal punishment was standard. In addition, there were issues of culture, assimilation and parental expectations that needed to be brought into the open and discussed; issues, about which some administrators, college tutors and educationists remained in denial, reluctant to accept that there was a need for debate and action.

Many of the schools in Brixton, and indeed in some other areas of London, were at times little better than battlegrounds. The children weren't told what to do but were expected to decide for themselves what they wanted to do; the head teacher seemed to be in retreat and was seldom, if ever, present in classrooms. The teachers struggled, often in isolation, to create some sort of learning environment and maintain some control.

Pat found the challenge exhausting, and sometimes intimidating. She dealt with things as best she could by adopting a social worker approach. She visited the families at home, in her own time. On Saturdays she took groups of children, at her expense, to places of interest. She was, with a few other young colleagues who were in a similar situation, attempting to establish a relationship with the children so that she could cope with them in the classroom.

As to curriculum, we were left to do what we could; in fact to do exactly as we wanted. Sometimes, I despaired whether the children were learning anything.

The major movements in curriculum development were still to come, as were the debates about practice and methodology and teaching and learning. As young teachers together, they generated ideas about teaching and learning and the curriculum, devising lessons, classroom assignments, activities, materials and ways of working, reflecting together afterwards on their effectiveness.

I shared a house in Wandsworth with five other teachers. There was a kind of camaraderie, educational as well as social, through which we supported, stimulated, enriched and enabled each other professionally.

What that period and experiences later in her career reinforced in Pat was a determination that wherever she taught children, and from whatever background they came, they should all have an equal opportunity that provided them with optimum educational advantage and value. It seemed incontrovertible to her that no child from a socially disadvantaged or alternative background should have less opportunity than those of advantaged children.

For example, when she became a head teacher, at Fleet School, instrumental tuition was available. However, it was wholly taken up by children from middle-class backgrounds, so she stopped it altogether and was immediately berated by a parent, who was then head of Radio 3, who saw what she had done as philistine. She replied, 'Well, you find a way of making it genuinely accessible to every child in the school and I will reinstate the provision.' As a result, they started a charitable music fund which was completely subsidised so that the tuition was available to all.

When middle-class parents, again at Fleet, complained that there wasn't after-school French tuition, she told them that the school would have it if everyone could have access to it, which would mean producing a subsidy for those children whose families were on benefits. 'Unfortunately, in many cases, that was the end of that. Parents' enthusiasm didn't quite extend to paying a little extra for a privilege to be shared by all.'

These examples reinforced what her early days in Brixton had brought home to her: Pat reflects that incidents of that nature reflected the fragmented and disparate composition of the ILEA. Some districts of London were characterised by want and disadvantage while others were wealthy and affluent. In important ways, the primary schools, and the educational sections or divisions in which they were located, reflected these disparities. Schools in socially and economically disadvantaged locations were faced with formidable challenges: mobile, ever-changing intakes; pupils with pronounced special needs, often exacerbated by their particular circumstances; the need to provide for high proportions of children with English as an additional language; and broken families often traumatised by life experiences. Here were the ingredients of dysfunction and chaos.

These circumstances were to some extent counterbalanced by the action of a wealthy and interventionist authority, driven by a belief that an education service could be a transforming influence in the lives of not only children and students, but of communities as a whole. Initiatives and developments were fostered that foreshadowed the education revolution of the 1980s and 1990s. Predominant among these were:

- A commitment to high-level resourcing for the entire school system

- Growing access for teachers to INSET and CPD

- The wide availability of curriculum materials, resources and authoritative guidelines

- Quality assurance through regular school inspections (preceding Ofsted by a number of years), underpinned by the formulation of embryonic modes of school self-evaluation.

Above all, there was a passionate commitment to the provision of equal opportunity, through policies, targeted funding, specialist centres, language and literacy programmes and a drive against racism and sexism.

But for all the progressive intentions and provision, the City remained an intensely challenging and demanding place in which to be a teacher. A significant proportion of schools fell short of what was required. Important issues of pupil attainment and of their curriculum requirement were glossed over. Consequently, the education experience of some children remained what one senior authority official described as a lottery.

Pat's second career move, prompted by domestic circumstances led her to move from her school in Brixton. She was appointed to a Scale 3 post with responsibility for English in Northbury Junior School in Division 4 of the ILEA, a notably disadvantaged borough. Her new post was in a large junior school located in one of the many three-storey Victorian buildings, with tarmac play areas.

This was not a posting for the diffident or the faint of heart, nor was it for the uncommitted. Many of the children she taught had special needs and were demanding in various respects. But they also possessed resilience and fortitude, along with an awareness and capacity to respond to experience and opportunity. Like many young teachers, Pat brought a strong sense of purpose and mission, underpinned by optimism, curiosity and energy.

She found herself part of a cohort of supportive and enthusiastic young teachers, imbued with a common belief in their vocation and their capacity to be a transforming influence in the lives of the children they taught. Over the next few years they grew together in professional awareness, skill and proficiency.

HEADSHIP AND LEADERSHIP

Her head teacher provided her first insight into the role of leadership. Perceptions of headship varied; some heads saw leadership invested in themselves alone, often conveyed, not always explicitly or easily comprehended, through the deputy head.

The head teacher in her new school was more concerned with the work of the teachers. He was often in the staffroom – unusual at that time. He stimulated discussion about education issues and encouraged teachers to keep abreast of current developments. He nurtured their commitment, encouraged them to express and cultivate their particular interests and skills, and gave them responsibility for curriculum areas and for aspects of school business and management. He needed them to help manage the children's behaviour. His expectations of them were high and he made occasional unreasonable demands, expecting them to work beyond what was normal and to take on responsibility that should have been the preserve of more experienced teachers (but whose enthusiasm and sense of dedication had been eroded over time). He anticipated that they would, in time, come to positions of leadership, and was preparing them for it.

These young staff were anxious to advance their careers. They stimulated and fed off each other's efforts and contributions, learning from each other and from their joint enterprises. They provided a wide range of extra-curricular activities for the children. Much of what they did called for liaison with parents and, in some cases, for their active involvement and participation.

At that time schools did not often see a need for CPD to meet the needs of individual staff, but Pat came to realise that the creation and maintenance of a continuing process of staff development was an important function of enlightened headship. Schools needed to find ways of providing these services for themselves, ideally in conjunction with partner schools. There were pressing reasons for this: the strong possibility that these services would not continue to be available from education authorities, the need for schools themselves to identify and address their whole professional and educational needs, and to become what was fashionably described as 'thinking schools'. She saw, with other colleagues, the importance of collegial institutions which grow together, guided by shared aims and purposes, whilst making tailored provision for individual development. Such notions, she says, are held as precepts now, but it was not so then.

MAKING PRODUCTIVE PARTNERSHIPS

When she was appointed Deputy Head of Berger Junior School, also in Division 4, she had the opportunity to work on establishing partnerships. The head teacher himself had not long been in the post, and until then had been obliged to work without a deputy head. They shared a broad philosophy of education and a conviction that the school could be a positive influence on the whole life of a community.

The head teacher and Pat set out to shape a partnership of leadership and management. They maintained a dialogue concerning the direction and work of the school, and formulated an action plan on a range of objectives which they saw as the building blocks of the school they wished to fashion. While such objectives are now seen as non-negotiable, at that stage in her career – prior to the Education Reform Acts of the 1980s, 1990s and afterwards – they had to be fought for.

The main objective was to create a genuine working partnership between the junior and infant schools located on the same site. While recognising the unique qualities and values of good infant schools, they concluded that the separation of the phases too often led to a serious break in continuity in terms of children's learning and attainment.

Such a partnership was an attractive ideal, but in practice extremely difficult to achieve, particularly at a time when heads cherished their autonomy and many infant school heads were apprehensive about the possible subordination of Early Years practice to an unpalatable model of junior education. However, the infant school head was a deeply committed colleague, imaginative and forward looking, and as anxious as they were for a partnership that would amalgamate the schools in continuous and enhanced provision for the children.

Pat's involvement in a transforming partnership was a significant period in terms of her professional development. She had had to grapple with fresh perceptions of the role of deputy (and of leadership in general), a whole new experience of teaching and learning with very young children, and the challenge of forming a practical and meaningful partnership. It meant that the head teacher himself and the majority of staff had to become informed and as competent as possible in the intricacies of Early Years practice.

As a trio they conducted an exhaustive review of issues central to continuity and progression across the primary spectrum. Some of these were acquiring a new prominence in educational debate: the effective measurement of attainment, the evaluation of learning, and the extent and nature of curriculum entitlement. They organised teacher exchanges and the sharing of resources, and explored ways of providing professionally qualified classroom support. The role of post holders was enhanced to enable them to manage, in practical and evaluative terms, the development of their curriculum area through the school.

This process cemented Pat's partnership with the head teacher. Together with the infant head teacher they advanced professionally, through exchanges that called for constant debate and reflection, flexibility of thinking, and a willingness to explore and test a range of points of view, including some that were not always readily acceptable to each of them.

PROVIDING A MODEL OF TEACHING AND LEARNING

By choice, Pat taught the upper junior class almost full-time. She was adamant about the need for this. It put her in a position to evaluate the effectiveness of their whole school policies, the quality of progression and continuity in pupils' learning, and their levels of attainment. Just as important was the fact that she provided a model of high quality practice for less experienced colleagues. In particular, she wanted to show the value of a broad curriculum, the viability of the thematic approach and the critical importance, in her opinion, of the place of literature in the development of language and literacy.

To this end, they built up an extensive whole school library and class libraries. They encouraged regular borrowing by pupils, the majority of whom would not have been accustomed to books in the home. She regarded literature as a key to rich curriculum experience for children. She recalls a term-long study with Year 6 on Leon Garfield's novel *Smith*, a work now set as a GCSE text and one that many would have judged too complex and advanced for pupils of their age, experience and background.

Their shared reading of the work was underpinned by an ambitious itinerary of visits to the different areas of London where major aspects of the plot were located. To their delight, in many cases they found that most of the architectural and topographical features of the period in which the novel was set were preserved, largely unchanged.

The effort, planning, resources and expenditure of this initiative (and others like it across the school), were amply rewarded by the enrichment they brought to the lives of the children; alluring horizons were revealed to them and they were given insight into generosity and heroism in human nature. Above all, such experiences awakened an eagerness for more in the children, something that would survive into their adult life.

Pat once overheard a conversation between two boys passing each other outside the school library. One examined the book just borrowed by the other and then said earnestly, 'It's very good, but when you've read it, you should read ...' and he named another book. 'It's like this in some ways, but it's even better.' Both boys, she said, were tough, streetwise, engaged in combative sport, and came from backgrounds bereft of books, where such a conversation would be unknown. It struck her with renewed force what the children might gain from the school's emphasis – and expenditure – on story and literature, and the range of texts involved. It confirmed for her that literacy was the area of learning paramount in terms of importance to the children's education; she acknowledged the critical importance of mathematics and science, but literature could provide an important way of extending and enhancing children's learning.

RELATIONSHIPS AND LINKS WITH PARENTS

Finally, Pat and the head teacher created a partnership with parents, going far beyond merely keeping them informed, in the belief that parents had the potential for making invaluable contributions to aspects of their children's education. The infant school, accustomed to making substantial contact with parents, was already establishing a forum for shared activity: setting up mother and toddler groups and providing seminars about children's learning experience, giving relevant guidelines, materials and resources, especially in relation to initial literacy and numeracy, and in making the home a learning environment. However, both they and the infant head teacher were aware that as soon as children transferred to the junior stage there was a significant decline in the partnership; this was due to factors such as the demands of rearing younger children, the pressures on time, and above all, the parents' belief that they were not competent to offer any further valuable support to their children.

Fortunately, the partnership with the infant school did much to encourage many of the parents to maintain their involvement in their children's learning well into the junior stage. This was aided by the literacy initiative and a strongly developing music tradition, fostered and led by the head (himself an accomplished musician).

At that time, many of these developments seemed innovatory. But in areas such as assessment, evaluation and pupil monitoring, staff thinking was being changed and enlarged by external forces, and sometimes in ways to which they were not wholly sympathetic, and which seemed more likely to separate the schools rather than bring them together.

Perhaps unsurprisingly, the progress they made in terms of forging a learning partnership with parents was partial. But the positive outcomes far outweighed the setbacks and the whole experience was an immense development for Pat. 'I flourished in the climate of aspiration and ambition, of ongoing professional and intellectual debate, of opportunity to build with the head teacher a shared vision and the procedures to bring it to fruition.'

COLLEGIALITY

Of great importance was the attempt to create an ethos of collegiality in the school. At the time, the term 'collegiality' was not in vogue, nor were staff familiar with it, so the first task was to define it. This would involve staff helping to make policies, systematically developing them from early stages in their career, fostering their continuing professional development and affording them opportunity for leadership responsibility.

Collegiality is easy to talk about; making it happen is rather more difficult. It is a complex matter involving finely balanced networks of relationships and inter-actions. At its best it is at the heart of successful institutions; where it is limited, their development will be circumscribed.

People have to be convinced and inspired to buy into collegiality. Heads have to be prepared to share aspects of their leadership and power. But in a sense, it has to remain hierarchical, a kind of paradox.

Collegiality does not mean government by committee. Ultimate responsibility lies with the head, and senior management groups to whom it is delegated. Collegiality, above all, is about accountability.

A REFLECTION ON HEADSHIP

The next stage of Pat's career was unpredicted and in some ways harrowing, but gave her an enduring learning experience. Her head teacher took a year's secondment, on an exchange basis, to a small school in rural Australia. His enthusiastic and hard-working replacement found life in an inner-city school beyond him, and soon relinquished the position. Pat's difficulty in finding an adequate replacement coincided with a period of volatile and implacable industrial action, extending over a year. Teachers refused to cover for absent colleagues, and with supply cover almost non-existent, as acting head she had not only to teach full-time, but on occasions teach, unassisted, as many as three classes in the hall. She alone was responsible for all lunchtime supervision, and was obliged to support uncertain welfare assistants in their playground duties.

In the process she learned much about the business of headship, as distinct from leadership: in a crisis, headship is about total responsibility, difficult if not impossible to share with others. Such challenges call for exceptional qualities of courage and resilience, and in the face of adversity, a determination to resolutely stand by your principles and values.

It also brought home to her the possibility that institutions, however firmly grounded, could be blown off course by unexpected events or emergencies; in such circumstances a school needs to remain faithful to and be guided by its philosophy, principles and values. She also found that a school's record of caring and achievement – its prime concern for the pupils and its carefully nurtured relationships with parents and the community – builds up a bank of credit that can be called on in difficult and straitened circumstances.

Shortly after the resolution of the industrial action, Pat was appointed to the headship of Fleet, a one-form entry primary school in Camden, a school very different from Berger School. Fleet was regarded as an elite school, led by a charismatic and high-profile head teacher, and was much sought after by parents. It claimed high academic achievement, with a reputation for music-making and performance. Yet Pat soon discovered that attainment, though ostensibly high, was below what should be achieved by children coming from advantaged and supported families. (However, it was difficult to elicit the criteria by which that achievement was being judged.) Music showed a striking example of a failure to reach its potential, especially since there was a full-time music specialist and rich provision of equipment and materials.

Although the school administration was managed efficiently, it seemed to Pat from the outset that there were major issues that she could not leave untouched. The first was the nature of the school intake. The school was exclusive in terms of its pupil admission policy, and operated a selective process which was determined, perhaps unwittingly, by social nuances. In short, families from neighbouring council estates, especially children drawn from the Afro-Caribbean community, found the admission process complicated and difficult. As a result, the school intake came predominantly from socially advantaged backgrounds, backed by supportive, ambitious and professional parents.

Any head teacher would rejoice in the presence of so capable and aspirant a community in the school, but what Pat could not accept was the notion that such a state should be engineered by policies of exclusion, particularly in such a socially diverse neighbourhood. Not only did this seem to her unjust and morally unacceptable, it deprived the school of an intake that would help build and enrich it in ways that would more faithfully reflect the wider community.

She continued to warmly welcome professional families as they brought with them assets, qualities, expectations and a commitment to excellence that would underpin the education they sought to provide. However, she was determined to change an institution that was restricted and artificial, that neither reflected the nature of the whole community, nor represented for pupils the larger world in which they would grow up and in which they must learn to live.

The change, when it came, caused disquiet for many parents. It was not universally accepted within the school itself. Some retained a hope that eventually it would all go away; that the status quo would be restored and the school would go on as it always had. But once parents became aware that genuine opportunity for admission was being offered, they took the chance. An anticipated 'walk-out' on the part of some parents was minimal.

The transition was neither comfortable nor easy. A section of their new population brought to the school their own predispositions, expectations, aspirations and modes of behaviour that were not always easily accommodated or integrated into a strongly entrenched culture. Some parents were challenging, difficult and combative in a way that was new to the majority of staff. Pat expected that it would take time, effort and unrelenting determination to achieve what she had hoped for: a diverse body of learners, contributing fully, positively and enthusiastically to the school community. However, the transition actually happened more quickly than she had anticipated because from the outset she trained staff and worked with them to convey their vision for the school to all parents – in unequivocal terms – and their high expectations, both of themselves as staff and of them as parents.

The education would be broad, rich and relevant, designed to expand every good horizon possible. As a staff they were pledged to ensure that no child would ever receive less than the best they could offer. In return, they required of them a willingness to respond in ways compatible with the aims of the school. Whilst parents were being offered a partnership, something new and unfamiliar to many of them, they were left in no doubt that it was Pat who was ultimately accountable and responsible for management, for the success and the welfare of the school. They were already accustomed to the strong leadership of her predecessor, but in a changed context it was all the more important that its uncompromising nature should be transparent.

It was crucial that the curriculum they offered was the practical exemplification of their educational vision. The model they had inherited had been acceptable, geared as it was to the academic requirements of a homogeneous school population, but it had not always been consistently delivered across the school or rigorously monitored and evaluated. Pat planned to maintain the best of it, the commitment to music especially, and to enlarge and shape it to the needs of all the pupils. They wanted to provide learning that would enable children at all academic levels to achieve their best.

The staff would own that curriculum and the learning it generated because every individual, whatever their experience or particular responsibility, would have contributed to and shaped its continuing development. They kept parents informed about their children's learning experience and their involvement in a range of notable activities, and gave them opportunities to witness aspects of that diverse programme.

The second change and development to which I was committed was to dispersed school leadership. I believed the need for change was urgent there.

179

Pat had inherited a school that had been strongly and effectively managed, but this leadership was invested almost exclusively in the head teacher alone. Delegation of specific tasks was left to a senior member of staff and to a deputy who acted as a kind of staffroom-based 'lightning conductor'. This egocentric leadership created a sense of security and certainty for staff, but the shortcomings of that style were large, however ostensibly impressive the style might be. It made the school dependent on a unique and possibly idiosyncratic vision, often isolated from current developments elsewhere. It seriously limited the professional development of staff; it inhibited their creativity and forfeited the immensity of what they could have offered to the school.

A SHARED VISION AND PURPOSE

Pat wanted a different kind of leadership, similar to that which had evolved in her time as Deputy at Berger School, to bring staff together in unity of action, a corporate endeavour to which all contributed.

> *That is a cliché easy to articulate, but the reality is infinitely more complicated. Get it right, and everything takes off from there. Without it, or having it only in part, an institution is going to struggle, whatever its aspirations and no matter how heroic its endeavour.*

Staff unity means that everyone knows what the school is about, what it stands for, what it regards as its mission, what makes it special. Within that, each individual knows clearly what his/her job entails. There is an understanding common to all staff about what they believe about education and what that means in terms of teaching and learning. Each member of staff has the confidence and concern to challenge what they regard as not good enough, to suggest what might be improved and how.

Pat sees the professional development of staff as vitally important, including their readiness to share everything about their work. Staff must be unafraid to talk about difficulties and setbacks, in the belief that what affects any one of them affects everyone in the end. She insisted that no one would be heard to say in the staffroom, 'Well I never have any trouble with them; they're always fine with me,' and that no part of the school, or school life, would be treated as someone else's responsibility.

That kind of unity or shared purpose is not achieved by merely wishing for it. There is always the issue of inherited staff, who have been shaped by different, even antipathetic philosophies and ways of working. Pat found, 'One of the most critical challenges to leadership is persuading staff to embrace your vision, especially where there is a need for substantial change or where staff are resolutely resistant or, in some cases, ill-equipped to manage new directions'.

Winning the support of staff for a shared vision may seem easier now, in an age when school effectiveness is described minutely and the vital factors that make it so – leadership, management, teaching, learning, assessment, self-evaluation, the nature of the curriculum – are clearly delineated.

Achieving staff unity, even on such complex issues, is now a matter of form. There is no room for the endless debate or debilitating staffroom divisions of the past. In that respect leadership is easier.

However, Pat believes that staff will be most sympathetic to a vision, and a way of working, if the value for children is manifest and practicable, and relates well to the teachers' experience, practice and current circumstances.

As a new head, Pat set out to assist staff to develop their leadership skills, in stages, by taking responsibility for particular areas of the curriculum, by leading small teams in particular initiatives, and by recognising that all this was to build together an institution that enhanced the education they provided.

Acquiring curriculum expertise was relatively easy – the real challenge lay in mastering a role that required them to be creatively authoritative; to work alongside colleagues, giving practical support; and to monitor, evaluate and set goals and targets. Inevitably, some readily assumed the role and the responsibility; others were more tentative. It developed, perhaps most naturally, in the creative and expressive arts, where an individual's expertise was more readily accepted, indeed sought after, by colleagues.

Pat was convinced from her own experience that the deputy head had to fill a full-time teaching role, involved with one class group, especially in a one-form entry school. She was seeking an outstanding teacher who would be a reference point for all staff, someone demonstrating notable expertise and insight. The deputy's intervention and contribution on all issues relating to teaching and learning would be critical, informing, supporting, inspiring and enlarging the practice of others. They would be the centre around which the 'leaders in waiting' would be gathered.

CURRICULUM

Another major issue that had to be tackled was the curriculum. The one Pat had inherited reflected the interests, preoccupations, inclinations and skills of individual teachers, but lacked substance and coherence. It was difficult to determine the true nature, or indeed the value, of the learning that children had experienced in their time at the school.

The introduction of the National Curriculum, external assessment and, later, Ofsted inspections, necessitated a significant reappraisal of teaching and learning at Fleet and indeed every primary school. The national Numeracy and Literacy Strategies included an unprecedented degree of curriculum prescription.

In spite of these radical shifts – which occurred nationally over a ten-year period – with specific amendments to the content and delivery of the primary school curriculum, at Fleet they maintained a curriculum planned around termly topics throughout the school.

The majority of the curriculum at Fleet is planned and taught through cross-curricular integrated topic work. While teachers avoid making tortuous links to include all subject areas in their centre of interest, they maximise subject links appropriately to make teaching and learning meaningful. The topic work gives priority to children learning through first-hand experience, whether this comes from outings, visits, visitors or practical engagement through art, design and technology. She emphasises particularly what she calls the 'unforced' coverage of subject areas.

> *The Plowden Report, so influential for so long, embodied the child-centred approach to education. I prefer to describe our practice as curriculum-centred. Of course, children are the centre of school life, but the quality of their learning and achievement is primarily determined by the richness of the curriculum, and the creative expertise of those delivering it on a daily basis. My experience as a teacher since 1970 leaves me in no doubt that an integrated curriculum, planned around termly centres of interest is, at its best, the most effective way of maximising children's active involvement in their own learning, helping them to become interested and interesting citizens of the future.*

LINKS TO THE WIDER EDUCATIONAL COMMUNITY

After nine years as the head teacher at Fleet School, Pat accepted an invitation from Camden Local Education Authority to accept secondment for a year into their inspectorate.

This was a memorable and invaluable experience that greatly enlarged her understanding and insight as an educator and enhanced her capacity for leadership. Pat spent an intellectually stimulating year in the company of highly qualified colleagues, drawn from a broad range of specialisms and expertise, who brought with them informed, enlightened and challenging views about education.

She saw at first hand the work of a wide range of schools and differing styles of leadership, observed and analysed what made for effectiveness and high quality, identified the factors that inhibited success and development, and ascertained the means, approaches and strategies that would bring about positive change and advance.

Above all, this experience strengthened her conviction of the critical need for schools to work together in partnership, to pool their corporate wisdom and expertise, to work together to solve the problems that beset them, to be creatively involved with and genuinely supportive of each other. Nevertheless, at the end of the year she declined the invitation of the authority to join the inspectorate on a permanent basis.

For all the experience had brought her, and for all her gratitude for the opportunity, she knew with heartfelt certainty that her place and destiny were in school, undertaking again the challenge and privilege of leadership. She believes, 'Whatever else we may do and achieve, whatever status we might eventually aspire to and fill, it is in schools that education is at its most valuable and enduring, and is truly shaped by those who are privileged to lead their fellow professionals and the children they teach. Nothing can quite match that, for fulfilment.'

CHAPTER TWELVE

CHRIS WHEATLEY

Cotgrave Candleby Lane School, Nottingham

State school for boys and girls aged from 4 to 11
Pupils: 535

Since its genesis lies to a large extent in the setting up of Cotgrave Candleby Lane School, it may be appropriate here to remember the determination that Chris and his colleagues had that the school would transform the lives and prospects of children, families and their community.

One gains the unmistakable impression of a whole community that believes the school is something remarkable, which is their own: a kind of lighthouse to the area. Members of that community are uplifted and empowered by that awareness.

One parent, now actively and creatively involved in the management of the after-school life of Cotgrave Candleby Lane School, said that as an illiterate parent he had been ashamed to bring his children beyond the entrance to the drive to the school. There, one day, he got into conversation with the head teacher, who coaxed from him the cause of his reluctance to become involved with the place where his children were being educated. He said:

> *Mr Wheatley himself taught me to read and write, alongside my child, but he made me think I was teaching her, when in fact I was learning like her and with her. It changed my life, made me see myself as a different and better person, someone my children could be proud of.*

As much as anything, his experience is evocative of what the school had set out to do and is continuing to achieve.

The notable qualities and achievements that distinguish the work of the head teachers and schools described in the preceding chapters are to be found in comparable fashion in Cotgrave Candleby Lane School. However, there is another reason for Chris Wheatley's inclusion in this book.

He represents an emerging group of head teachers who might be described, however fancifully, as 'new wave'. To a large extent they are the product of the National College of Leadership; informed, shaped and motivated by the beliefs and particular vision of headship/leadership that it advocates. Furthermore, they are empowered and enfranchised by central government policies, not just in relation to school improvement, but for nothing less than a re-ordering of important areas of the education system.

Their advent to headship at this time, and the autonomy and freedom it confers on them to pursue radical new ways, marks the dawn of a new era.

This has been summed up by Anthony Seldon (Master of Wellington College, biographer and historian) as:

> A revolution in schools which happens only once every twenty-five years in Britain ... The grip of the old education establishment – local authorities, trade unions, bureaucrats, education departments in universities – has been forever broken. Academic aspiration for all pupils, driven by the relentless focus on GCSE, and enforced by Ofsted's laser emphasis on teaching and learning, has been embedded; it will not be undone. Individual schools and chains are the new powerhouses in British education ... There can be no turning back now that heads have tasted the benefits of independence.

Chris Wheatley is a National School Leader, the head teacher of a Teaching and National Support School, commissioned by central government through the National College. What differentiates Chris's form of headship is his involvement in the oversight of a federation of schools: his particular mission and commitment to work with, support and enhance the practice of individual, clusters and federations of schools. It is, however, the boundaries that he and others of similar persuasion are ready to cross that implies a seminal change in education, and suggests an approach to headship that is crucially different, in at least one respect, from the broad model represented in most of the previous chapters.

In the main, those head teachers readily accept the desirability, proposed and encouraged by government, of individual institutions reaching out to a wider community of schools to form a commonwealth of expertise and successful practice, dedicated to shared support and enrichment. Some of the head teachers we have already encountered have become practically involved in the process in various ways: Lois Crane in her role as National

Leader, and Claire Robinson, Maxine Evans and Andrew Carter, who operate as agents providing guidance and a range of services on a commercial basis. Their intervention, however, is confined to a limited number of schools, usually for short periods of time, with income used exclusively to enlarge their own school resources.

Chris Wheatley, on the other hand, has built a radically more ambitious and far-reaching model of partnership across a community of schools. He stands apart from the majority of the head teachers here in terms of the unusually accelerated nature of his career development – from SENCO and Deputy Head in the school to which he was first appointed, to the position of Head Teacher of Cotgrave Candleby Lane in less than seven years, before the eventual amalgamation with the other institutions on the site.

Such fast-tracking is likely to become more common in a climate of changing conventions and perceptions about the configuration and nature of effective school leadership and the particular abilities it demands. Perhaps most contentious in this evolving view of headship/leadership is the argument that the organisational and managerial aspect of the position is substantially the most important. It includes responsibility for direction and oversight of teaching and learning, while effectively relinquishing practical involvement in the process, especially when schools are becoming a driving force in institutional partnerships.

The majority of the head teachers here largely reject such a viewpoint. For them, the 'instructional leadership' of teaching and learning remains the main responsibility of their headship. Maxine Evans is an exception. She argues that high quality teaching resides in, and arises from, the expertise and experience of teachers, practising and honing their professional craft day by day, sharing, analysing and elaborating on it, supported by the structures and resources organised by the head teacher.

In other important respects, however, Chris's beliefs, values and practice align with those of the other head teachers. Like them, he did not come from a privileged background, nor did he benefit from unearned advantage; he, too, believes that aspects of his early childhood, his school years, his professional experience and those who supported and motivated him in these different phases, have been decisive in his development as a person and an educator.

From a broken home and deprived circumstances, Chris talks of:

- Loving grandparents, with little available to them in terms of material possession, who cherished him and assured him of his worth; particularly his grandfather, who encouraged him to aspire and achieve.

- A teacher in the fifth year of his primary school – the first to help him recognise his intelligence and convince him that he possessed academic ability.

- A PE teacher in his huge secondary school who encouraged his sporting prowess and revived his flagging belief in himself. This led to university and a teaching career, an outcome inconceivable to his grandparents who had rescued him and brought him up.

- The head teacher of the school where he began his teaching career, 'who recognised in me gifts and capacities I'd never dreamed of; who guided and tutored me, from the outset, through increasingly challenging roles of responsibility, eventually to senior management and deputy headship and, when she judged it the right time, convinced me I was capable of headship'.

Some of his work in his first headship at Cotgrave Candleby Lane, and the developments he initiated, may serve as a source of some inspiration to colleagues working in similar contexts. He believed that if his vision of what a school might achieve were to be realised, then the nature and circumstances of the headship made it imperative to secure a partnership with parents.

The Cotgrave coalmine – large in terms of size and importance – finally closed shortly after the industrial conflict of the seventies. It left the village bereft and, in many senses, devastated. Cotgrave workers had been involved in the bitter disputes that divided the National Union of Miners, and incurred animosity that almost extinguished the scant sense of esteem in which the traditionally inward-looking and beleaguered community held itself. Time and circumstances had accustomed its people to think poorly of themselves, to shrink from aspiration, to be resigned to limited horizons and prospects. They were not hostile to education, but had little reason to think that it was a force for good or improvement in the lives of their children.

Chris believed that until that mindset changed, until they came to share his view of what the school could do, not only for the children but for the wider community in which they lived, then his vision and work, and the dedicated commitment and labour of his colleagues would prove largely unavailing.

To nurture a new optimism and secure the parents' practical involvement, he believed they must witness development happening in the lives and learning of their children. This could only happen in the context of an enriched education and a radically changed and improved school environment.

Two major developments transformed the existing situation and provided a powerful practical impetus to his intentions.

Unusually, the junior school, of which he was head teacher, shared the same site as an infant school and a primary school. Although separated narrowly in physical terms, in educational outlook and practice the schools were far apart, almost to the point of alienation. It was clear that in the best interests of the children and the community at large, this situation could not be allowed to continue. The solution lay in amalgamating all three schools into a single institution.

Chris persuaded his colleagues in the three schools to work towards realising that vision. Having secured the local authority's commitment to the proposal, they planned meticulously for its implementation, organising activities in ways that developed team building and instilled a sense of shared identity and purpose. 'Forming a positive culture was at the forefront of all our planning. We recruited those who bought into the vision and ethos of the school, determined to add to it and carry it through.'

That the new staff was formed without redundancies (including some teachers with old loyalties and styles of working inherited from other schools) says much for their rigorous preparation, and for the professional commitment and aspiration of those involved.

Appointed as the head teacher, he shared his vision of a school that would not only be a transforming influence in the children's education, but a force that might change the fractured life of the community for the better.

The local authority was responsible for the second decisive development: the provision of a completely new building to accommodate the combined schools. Chris and his staff were invited to contribute to the design and planning of the new school, and to influence the nature of the whole construction. They worked closely with the architects and planners, and with educationists – experts in the design and organisation of space for teaching and learning. Out of this came a flexible building designed for diverse forms of teaching and learning, adaptable to the educational aptitudes, development and needs of a range of learners. It was organised for the accommodation and effective use of state-of-the-art technology and resources and it would remain accessible to families at the end of the normal school day, and to the whole community in the evenings, at weekends and holidays.

As envisaged, the school is open every day from eight o'clock in the morning until nine o'clock at night, offering a huge array of activities for pupils that enhance their overall development and progress in the classroom.

The school, in an area once derided and dismissed as of little worth – is, at the end of the working day, a beehive of activity.

Inside, the schoolchildren engage in a wide range of extra-curricular activities. Former pupils, now at the secondary school, return to make programmes in the recording studio; the full-time manager of the studio is editing the weekend broadcast of school and community life, which will be heard by an audience of thousands. Everywhere are parents, pupils, governors and members of the community, drawn voluntarily to help with the teeming life of the place.

Notable among the activities are a radio club, a science and engineering studio/workshop, a small farm, a gospel choir, gardening and cookery clubs, and generous provision for music education. These activities are an integral part of the targeted support provided for children and the school goes to great lengths to ensure that they reach those children who need them most: those who give cause for concern due to issues related to attendance, behaviour, academic progress and attainment, or the nature of parental involvement.

Funding is directed to support children whose economic circumstances are likely to prevent them from participating in after- and out-of-school activities. With half the children above the national average for deprivation, it is vital that they can participate fully in extra-curricular activities that supplement the normal learning programmes.

> *Through our nurture coordinator, all free-school-meals children, and those identified by teaching staff, are personally consulted; we identify the clubs and activities most likely to motivate them and address particular identified needs.*

From the outset it was essential to secure parental engagement in their children's education – the single biggest determinant in the children's educational outcomes and attainment. In a community where achievement was low, where parental perceptions of schooling were very negative, the task of empowering them to genuine partnership was a challenge. The school devised programmes for securing their initial involvement, including social events such as film nights, family breakfasts, open classrooms and family lunches. These have continued, alongside the vital support/educational provision, including family learning, targeted parenting skills sessions, curriculum workshops and basic skills lessons. Further practical support is available through the Citizens Advice Bureau and the Jobcentre Plus, which are both located on the school site.

Parental voice is provided for through a parents' forum, The Friends of Candleby Lane Association, parent suggestion boxes, and the ongoing open-door policy, making it possible for a parent to engage with a teacher at any time.

Evidence-based parenting programmes have been a success with some of the hardest-to-reach parents. They have targeted these people and worked with an external provider to develop and deliver 'The incredible years parenting programme', which helps the parents to support their children most effectively. Evidence to date, collected by the school, suggests the initiative has had a demonstrable, positive impact on the parents and the children.

One of the most powerful influences in securing effective partnership with parents has been engagement with the national charity, Achievement for All 3As. This was created and financially subsidised by the DfE to ensure that their whole school improvement educational programme reaches as many schools as possible. The programme's mission is 'to transform the lives of vulnerable children, young people and their families, including those with special educational needs and disabilities, by raising their educational aspirations, access and achievement'.

Chris says that three factors have contributed to the impact of the Achievement for All programme in their particular case, resulting in the 'extraordinary progress, attainment and achievement made by very large cohorts of children who, in other circumstances, might have been thought to have reached their limit, even by those most committed to their cause'.

These three factors are:

- An effective, realistic, hard-nosed strategy that refuses to accept underachievement as a pre-condition of any child's fate.

- The critical place of whole school leadership, with all staff involved at varying and appropriate levels, and a collaborative ethos within the school, based on an assumption of shared professional concern and aspiration.

- Finally, and perhaps most notably, the place of parents and carers in the programme. Their engagement and commitment is central to the programme and a driving force in its success. The Achievement for All programme features regular structured conversations between parents and class teachers (thirty to sixty minutes on a one-to-one basis), with teachers trained in techniques that encourage deeper understanding and greater engagement. These Structured Conversations have had a significant impact on parents and children. In all, the school believes the programme continues to enhance the lives and opportunities of many families.

CREATING AN ENVIRONMENT FOR LEARNING

Because many of the children come from 'very chaotic' homes, it is vital that in school they encounter learning environments and circumstances that enrich the imagination, civilise and nurture the spirit, and develop and sustain their confidence and self-esteem. The school strives to help the children be receptive to a broad curriculum and the rich learning that flows from it.

Considerable energy has been invested in the physical environment. Classrooms and corridors are vibrant, with stimulating displays; photographs celebrate students' work and videos show new developments, good work and the celebration of school events.

The staff have also put in place a range of rigorously evaluated systems, measures and processes:

- A group of multi-skilled professionals – including pupil counsellors, a nurture coordinator, a behaviour specialist and a parent supporter – are all trained in child support. Their principal task is to remove barriers to learning through individual or group support, through working with a family to resolve issues, by building self-esteem and by nurturing in the pupils a clear understanding of right and wrong. This is achieved by focusing on children's emotional development through a range of activities requiring social skills.

- Newly arrived students are meticulously supported and carefully integrated into the school community. EAL (English as an Additional Language) students enjoy a closely supported programme working with other EAL students, and systematically develop their social understanding, relationships and communication skills. They continue to receive support until they are able to cope independently in all of their classes.

- Supporting pupils' emotional needs is central to the ethos of the school. Support systems are facilitated by staff. These include PALS groups: small, carefully selected conflict resolution groups where the children can directly challenge others who treat them inappropriately; they may gain the necessary support to master strategies for dealing with particular situations or simply have their feelings recognised. PALS groups have clear guidelines and roles and all staff have received training to support the PALS system.

The full-time nurture coordinator in the school is tasked with supporting all children, including those in vulnerable groups. She gives one-to-one support, small group pastoral care or parental support. The school strongly believes that a child has to be emotionally secure and well-prepared for learning and that the best learning takes place when a child feels safe and focused. A trained counsellor works directly with the most vulnerable children.

Children who require extra emotional support are put on an individual programme. Many of the children who were at risk of exclusion elsewhere thrive at Cotgrave Candleby Lane. Help for vulnerable pupils in both Key Stages includes highly individualised pathways, planned for developing social and academic skills. This has had a positive impact on attendance and progress. The aspirations have been raised for a group of young people who might previously have become disengaged.

The school puts special emphasis on the development of pupils' emotional intelligence. All staff are trained in the use of SEAL (Social, Emotional Aspects of Learning) strategies. The use of SEAL techniques in the classroom has aided the development of learning. Staff working with the nurture groups also use Circle Time training as part of the Achievement for All programme. PALS groups, class council and whole school council also enhance this. Teachers are confident that these classroom strategies have enabled individual children to develop empathy and respect for their peers, to raise their achievement and to enhance their relationships.

The school values and promotes the pupil voice and ensures that all children have the opportunity to be school leaders and have a say in the direction the school takes.

Our school council oversees all school procedures and makes many decisions at their weekly meetings and assemblies. Every week they facilitate a whole school debate and discussion with very little input from staff. This shows their level of confidence and the trust we have in them to take whole school decisions. A large group of Year 6 children have particular roles and responsibilities within the council, from leaders to 'reflection-taker' or scribe. The two council leaders also join full governors for their termly meetings. Class councils are weekly. These groups also follow set structures and rules; any issues can be taken to full council to feed into the whole school. These class councils develop in pupils the skills and confidence that prepare them to participate in the whole school council on entering Year 6. Members of the school council are voted in by all children in the school, following a week of electioneering and presentations.

We also have a learning committee, a group of children who are tasked with overall school improvement. This year the committee has assessed effective classroom environments, observed lessons and fed back findings directly to staff during staff meetings. This has had a real impact for pupil voice as the children see changes made directly because of their observations and ideas.

THE CURRICULUM

Chris stresses that spiritual, moral, social and cultural development are at the heart of the life of the school and central to the journey of improvement teachers and pupils have taken together since its establishment six years earlier. Such development depends on a broad and rich curriculum; on the inspiration, insights and stimulus inherent in the creative and expressive arts; in music, literature and poetry; and in the story of human struggle and achievement to be discovered in the humanities and science.

We have a curriculum designed to stimulate the children's imagination and curiosity by engaging them in programmes of practical, relevant and challenging activities. We seek to cultivate their individual self-reliance and independence as learners, their capacity to research using computer technology, and their ability to organise and present evidence and conclusions.

The school curriculum is underpinned by programmes of enrichment activities, by educational visits and by visitors who bring into the school evidence of, and insights into, the world of work, enterprise, creativity and service in the community and the wider world.

We pay equal attention to getting the basic curriculum right and to ensuring its relevance and value to the needs of learners of all abilities, hence our commitment to Achievement for All. Teachers work zealously at personalising the curriculum to the needs of the individual learner.

A vital component in the children's learning is a cross-school curriculum initiative, called Candleby Life. This project helps develop pupils' life skills and provides opportunities for making a positive contribution to their local and wider community, as well as developing an understanding of enterprise. The core aim of Candleby Life is to teach life skills in a meaningful context. Children engage in activities where they become the decision-makers and work towards an outcome. They begin by selecting an activity based on the skills they feel they need to develop. Before being placed in an activity, pupils are interviewed by school staff and partners from business. Underpinning each activity is a core set of skills which is made explicit to the children through their work. These skills include effective communication, teamwork, initiative, creativity, reflective thinking, empathy and independence. Children reflect on their progress in the core skills throughout the process. Their progress is monitored through their 'reflection books' and through teacher assessment.

Finally, the Children's University offers all pupils from Years 3–6 the opportunity to participate in all of the after-school activities which have very clear, validated learning outcomes. Pupils are awarded a 'passport to learning', and receive credits for their participation in validated activities. These credits enable pupils to work towards awards at different levels. Through a partnership with Nottingham Trent University the school offers an end-of-year graduation ceremony hosted by the university. 'This programme has increased the participation of pupils in after- and out-of-school activities, the value they place on this participation, and their aspirations and understanding of the opportunities that university could bring.'

WORKING WITH A WIDER COMMUNITY OF SCHOOLS: THE FLYING HIGH TRUST

It is Chris's innovative work with the wider community that gives us an insight into a new and radical dimension in headship/leadership at the heart of a changing education. Defining it, he quotes the National College of Leadership:

> If all children are to have an entitlement to high quality education, then it seems that successful schools and their leaders have a responsibility to work with, and alongside, other schools to support their improvement. This is leadership with moral purpose – school leaders accepting collective responsibility for improving the whole system and working together to mutual benefit.

This led him to set up the Flying High Trust, currently comprising a group of twelve schools. The sole aim of this trust is to enable its member schools to work collaboratively and support each other to reach and maintain a consistent standard of excellence in the education they provide, and the attainment and achievement they foster in their pupils.

The partnership is funded by individual schools on a sliding scale of three to five per cent of full budget, based on the amount each school can give back to the trust, with Government Capacity Grant as an additional funding source.

Partners in the enterprise include the National College for School Leadership and the Teaching School Alliance, of which Cotgrave Candleby Lane School is a member, having gained Teaching School Status in 2011. Trust schools have access to the expertise of the Alliance schools. Chris holds the position of Chief Executive on the Board of Directors.

This organisation is complex in structure, but committed to a simply expressed ambition: the provision of outstanding education over an expanded community. It is, in effect, filling the void left by a diminished and declining local authority. Its powers are exclusively invested in the hands of educators. Whether this is a forerunner of similar developments, it is not possible to say. What is clear, however, is that where educators are assuming ever-increasing autonomy and independence in the management of their schools, and government is promoting the concept of communities of schools working corporately, the nature and style of leadership may well be entering a new phase.

Chris offers a powerful model of such development. For successive years his headship of the school has been, manifestly, a textbook example of progressive and effective practice. He has provided classic instructional leadership, modelling exemplary practice and pedagogy, coaching colleagues, and shaping their professional competence and development.

At the same time, he has provided for leadership succession, preparing colleagues, in sequenced and ordered fashion, to assume leadership and managerial responsibility, and to provide CPD for colleagues in the areas where they lead. By training staff in the leadership and management of teaching and learning, curriculum, human resources and financial resources, he can now take on a greatly different role, while retaining final responsibility for the direction of the school.

The practice is not unique. Some of the other head teachers whose work is described here are engaged in innovation that takes them beyond their own school, and promote the kind of succession planning that Chris advocates. But the Flying High Trust is possibly more far-reaching than anything similar to date. Should its ambitions be achieved, it may serve as a model for development on a far wider scale.

CHAPTER THIRTEEN

OVERVIEW

This chapter summarises how the work and performance of the head teachers relate to the criteria defining the nature of headship and leadership in outstanding primary schools. The head teachers' personal accounts, perspectives and convictions are cited in relation to the management of areas and aspects identified in Chapter One.

HEADSHIP AND LEADERSHIP

The head teachers, without exception, see headship – and the leadership inseparable from it – as the most important factor in the life, well-being and success of schools:

As a head you are the master of your own destiny. If you want something to happen, you have to make it happen. If you can't make it happen then you have to move over and let someone else have a go. Because that is what you are paid to do; you are not paid to run a commentary on the disasters and tribulations visited on your school. You are paid to change it.

The role has changed out of recognition. It used to be very much about the cult of personality. But that won't do the job anymore; it's too subtle and complex for that. It requires us to be inventive, at the cutting edge of things, leading a team to search for, evaluate and try out the new.

The head teachers hold that schools can be a transforming force in the lives of children and are committed to developing children into assured, accomplished and positive social beings, constantly learning and achieving at levels that reflect their potential. They nurture pupils' spiritual, moral, social and cultural development and foster values that will sustain them throughout their lives. They envisage schools standing at the heart of their communities, interacting with the external agencies engaged in the education and welfare of children, and creating partnerships with parents, designed to support children's learning and development.

Although their visions vary in emphasis and degree, the head teachers see them as binding staff together in a shared purpose, and regard their calling and work as a form of sacred trust and charge. They insist:

Children will be assured of memorable experience, and be richly equipped in terms of learning competences and skills.

They will leave school with spirits and senses attuned to awe and wonder; responsible, caring, with a strong desire to learn.

The school's unique role is to enable children to be assured social beings who will recognise and realise their potential ... who will be enabled to develop to the utmost their best qualities, personal gifts and attributes; who will succeed in acquiring the skills they need in a changing world; who will do the best for themselves, but have, too, a social conscience, a commitment to being active, caring, positive members of their community.

Central to this is the issue of pupils' progress and achievement. As effective learners, they will master the skills and strategies that will enable them, over time, to do successfully what they had not previously been capable of, to recognise the nature and extent of their learning, to identify the progress they make, and to understand how they can build on that.

The head teachers distinguish between attainment and achievement. Attainment shows that a child has reached a certain learning level – a point on a standardised scale. Achievement is a measure of how much progress the individual child has made – the 'distance travelled'.

To ensure that children can maximise their achievement, the head teachers provide:

- A relevant, appropriate, broad and generous curriculum, accessible and geared to individual needs and personal learning, adapting to changing times and circumstances.

- High quality teaching, without exception, throughout the school.

- Detailed tracking using standardised testing and teacher assessment to create a comprehensive profile of individual pupil attainment and progress against specified targets, and to provide data that records progress at whole class and school level. This informs the school of the educational value gained by pupils, individually and collectively, indicating to what extent achievement is matching priorities.

- Effective evaluation and formative assessment throughout the school, informing and improving the quality of teaching and learning.

- Inclusive education, with targeted support for children from ethnic or marginalised minorities, for pupils with pronounced special needs or for particular medical or physical conditions.

- Total accountability of all staff in relation to the achievement of the school mission and priorities; the attainment and progress of pupils; collaboration with, support and leadership for colleagues; and the effective implementation of personal curricular and other responsibilities.

- Training programmes for the professional development of all staff and for increasing responsibility for aspects of leadership and management within the school framework.

- Creative, effective and efficient management of finances to secure high quality provision in every area of school life.

- Inventive use of the opportunity provided by workforce reform, combined with greater control over finances, to secure an extended and diverse range of staff and enhanced curricular expertise.

- Strategies and procedures for the effective management of change, crises and the unpredictable.

- Wide-ranging strategies for involving parents in their children's education.

- Sensitive, positive and effective modes of discipline and codes of behaviour, understood and entered into by the children, contributing to consistently high standards of behaviour.

The head teachers describe the importance of these elements in the life of their schools:

> *Leadership is about identifying what it is you need to get done, identifying the best people to get it done, putting in resources that will help them get all the systems in place to enable them to achieve the targets, empowering them to get on and do it, but coming back to make sure they are still on focus. Asking critical questions: are they the outcomes we had hoped for, are they as good as they could be, how can we be sure of that, or why have you chosen to do things in that particular way?*

Leaders must have conviction and determination to do what has to be done, based on hard, strenuous, mature reflection and judgement, for the good of the institution and the betterment of the children. Heads who struggle and flounder do so because they lack the courage to see and acknowledge things as they are, the vision to realise what they might be, and the resolution to take the action that will make it so.

The development and training of teachers is inescapably one of the most important functions of headship and must be carried out, to a large extent, by the modelling of good example. They need to see me doing what I am talking about.

Instil in staff the notion of accountability, and make it a central tenet of the work and life of the school.

Assessment is at the heart of good teaching and successful learning. Pupils must be equipped with the strategies that will help them personally identify the skills they must cultivate to take that learning further.

In their biographies, the head teachers provide accounts of their approach to what are generally accepted as the most crucial of these issues.

Below is a summary, as far as it is valid, of a collective viewpoint of the head teachers in relation to what we identified together as the critical areas of their work.

TEACHING AND LEARNING

The heads, with one exception, regard teaching and learning as the area of work and responsibility most important to them as leaders and endeavour to secure and maintain high-calibre teaching. They see the school as a place of learning for all, with teachers permanently involved in the learning process themselves.

The viewpoint was succinctly expressed by Gwen Lee (Chapter 6):

If people aren't competent teachers, they have no right to be in front of a group, particularly of inner-city children, who already face enough barriers to their learning ...

There is general agreement that the prerequisites of effective teaching include at least the following:

- Thorough subject knowledge informed by comprehensive schemes of work.

- Class management that ensures children are motivated, enthused, engaged and committed to their work.

- High expectations that provide for worthwhile, appropriate and differentiated challenge for learners.

- Effective and creative use of ICT to promote children's learning.

- Productive involvement of teaching assistants in paired planning and teaching.

- Facilities for shared and team teaching.

- An emphasis on meta-learning, which enables pupils to make sense of their experience of learning and to take increasing control over its planning, monitoring and regulation.

It is commonly recognised that skills cannot be taught in the abstract or in isolation, but, as the *National Curriculum Handbook* insists, are essentially located across the broad curriculum.

Teachers in a number of the schools are encouraged, in their planning and practice, to take account of Gardner's theory of multiple intelligences, and of predominant learning styles: visual, auditory and kinaesthetic. (It is important to note that this theory is regarded as contentious in some quarters.) Many teachers committed to this approach devote a great deal of effort to organising learning activities intended to enhance multiple intelligences and encourage pupils to exploit their favoured learning style and develop those less preferred.

We find examples of the implementation of learning styles in the work of two head teachers, Lois Crane and Claire Robinson, who provide case studies that show the thought, care and energy they apply in achieving high quality teaching and learning.

CASE STUDY ONE (CHAPTER 4)

In this school, the strategy was driven by:

- The head teacher's belief that the nature and depth of children's learning depends largely on the quality of teaching they experience.

■ The need to promote children's meta-cognition: developing the ability to focus and reflect on what they are learning, understanding and mastering; recognising strategies and devices which best help them learn; and seeing where their learning should go next.

The head, Lois, realised that for her children the transformation did not come easily:

This is not easy; it is a highly sophisticated process whereby children are taught to be evaluators of the value and standard of what they do, to make sound judgements about the quality of their learning and what they can do to make it more effective.

We spent a year embedding the process, tutoring and coaching the children, helping them to understand what they were doing, providing them with enabling strategies.

It drew us as a staff into a powerful and common enterprise, with collaborative practice and exchange about the business of teaching and learning that is central to our professional lives … We were literally learning and growing together professionally. The outcomes by the end of a year were remarkable.

CASE STUDY TWO (CHAPTER 2)

Describing the training and pedagogy that her staff received, Claire says:

I knew what I wanted for my school. I travelled the country, visiting schools and talking to heads. I saw things I could use or adapt; things I rejected; things we were already doing. What I wanted was a teacher toolkit that they could dip in and out of, that equipped them to use a range of strategies for a range of purposes to meet all the needs of their children.

HEAD TEACHERS AS LEADERS OF TEACHING AND LEARNING

The majority of the head teachers were clear that it was essential that they should be leaders of teaching and learning in their schools, providing models of high quality practice for classroom teachers.

This viewpoint is persuasively argued by Helen O'Donoghue (Chapter 10):

In my first term I taught in every classroom to the teachers' plans because I believe it is essential to put myself in their shoes ... I wanted to know how the lesson plans that consume so much of their time work out in practice and to what extent they are likely to enthral and intrigue, to stimulate curiosity and fire the imagination, what it is like for the children.

The phrase 'being able to walk the talk' was used by several head teachers. It implies that teaching is not just theoretical pedagogical expertise, but effective practice, and an ethos which permeates all that they do in the classroom. Some indicated ways in which they did this, given the competing demands contingent on their leadership of the school. It was clear they regarded high quality teaching as the *raison d'être* of their schools, and the criterion by which their work was most surely judged.

There was one notable exception to this. The dissenting head teacher, Maxine Evans (Chapter 5), was clear, provocative and challenging on the matter. She argued that the real business of headship was the proficient management of crisis and challenge to ensure the school functions effectively and realises its vision.

A defining characteristic of her well-qualified colleagues, with whom she had shared NPQH training, was their comprehensive understanding of teaching and learning: Maxine said, 'They had spent their professional lives immersed in it!' But, to her, they were too easily content, too ready to treat teaching and learning as a dominant and almost wholly consuming aspect of their preparation for headship. They were happy to remain in a comfort zone of continued debate and discussion of the area where they felt most secure, rather than engage with the real and esoteric business of leadership and the profoundly complex issues which they were unfamiliar with and largely untried in.

For Maxine, the core role of headship and leadership is:

Facing down the constant challenges; overcoming the impediments and the crises; securing accurate insight into and analyses of the state, trends and developments of the school; identifying strengths and weaknesses; establishing and implementing purposeful agendas for progress and development; and clearing the way for staff to get on with the thing they are expert in, equipped for and most suited to: teaching and learning.

CURRICULUM

The heads are unanimous that all children are entitled to, and are more likely to do well with a comprehensive, enriching, relevant and generously resourced curriculum, which provides for personalised learning. Claire Robinson says:

> *A significant part of learning is dependent upon experience. A diminished curriculum, one mainly comprising basic or core subjects, is likely to provide diminished experience, unless that limited handful of subjects is taught with unusual inventiveness. A broad, enriching and inspiring curriculum is more likely to help them attain and achieve, particularly in those basic or core areas.*

Some heads are deeply committed to the provision of the creative and expressive arts lessons: dance, music, art and design. Suzanne Alexander-Sowa emphasises the value of the creative and expressive arts, and the development of diverse and high level skills acquired through individual subjects:

> *Music is particularly important to us, because it is one of the most powerful means by which children can be creative and express themselves. When we teach children to make music, as we do throughout their time here, we are giving them a skill that will enrich and sustain them long after they have left us.*

She maintains that the curriculum should be a powerful agent of spiritual and moral development. This is shown by a deep commitment to support children in embodying the life-enhancing values envisioned by the National Curriculum, so that they may live positively and meet life's challenges. These values include: honesty, personal responsibility, a sense of fairness and justice, respect and tolerance for others, and moral courage. For these values to grow, the child needs an ordered, beautiful and inspiring environment, opportunities for tranquil reflection, clear and positive codes of behaviour and discipline, cooperative working and supportive interdependence.

Some head teachers wish to preserve the integrity of individual subjects or areas of learning and focus on content, skills, ideas and knowledge. Neglect these, they claim, and progression and attainment in vital spheres of learning and understanding are unlikely. This raised the issue of teachers' subject mastery, necessary to teach certain subjects at the upper end of Key Stage 2 – in other words, specialist teaching. Music is a particular example of an area of learning, where children can develop valuable skills and participate with enjoyment, but meaningful progression and deeper competence are dependent on the mastery of a hierarchical repertoire of skills and competences which demand expert teaching.

Similarly, the effective teaching of Modern Foreign Languages also requires an in-depth competence. Some would argue that a 'traditional' subject such as Geography is now, at the upper primary level, so complex that it is increasingly neglected or discarded for want of specialist expertise.

The head teachers vary in their ideas of how the curriculum might be most effectively structured and delivered.

Andrew Carter (Chapter 9) reflects on the developments that have taken place in terms of curriculum since his early days in headship when schools were liberated from the restrictions imposed by 11+ selection.

> *The curriculum changed because we were working through a project-centred approach, around themes that we believed were related to children's interests and concerns, that would engage their curiosity and interest. In other words, would promote learning and would enlarge their horizons. It was an attempt to make learning exciting and attractive. Because the themes were cross-curricular, it seemed to us that the project approach would avoid unhelpful compartmentalisation of subjects and would enable children to see the important connections between subjects and to understand the wholeness of knowledge.*

> *There was no doubt that the project approach did go some way to achieving these objectives and some memorable work resulted. But we learned that the approach encouraged a superficial focus on learning, with insufficient attention to depth and scholarship. Because of that, subjects central to children's learning, such as Mathematics, suffered from a lack of rigour and inadequate attention to progression and attainment.*

Whilst it was relatively straightforward to design a curriculum that provided deep learning, it was concluded that such a curriculum could only be implemented where you had additional qualified and informed adults working with the children in the classroom. For him, constructing the curriculum was not the issue; delivering it was.

On the other hand, Gwen Lee (Chapter 6), who, with her staff, had spent a year reflecting on and exploring ways in which the curriculum might be most effectively presented, decided that a thematic approach would be the best option for securing deep learning. Despite the drawbacks of such an approach and the possible impediments to continuity and progression in attainment, they felt that a curriculum structured along individual subject lines was less likely to provide children with an insight and a developing understanding of key concepts and principles of knowledge.

Similarly, John Foley (Chapter 7) wanted a curriculum that was 'as extensive and deep as they could manage', placing special emphasis on the humanities and expressive arts, seeking with his staff to establish meaningful links between subjects and the creation of 'blocks of learning'.

He shares a concern about the depth and profundity of children's learning, and the complex issue of providing appropriate cognitive challenge for academically able children. Despite misgivings, especially about the possibility that over time staff would become deskilled in the teaching of particular subjects, they decided that aspects of the curriculum called for specialist teaching, especially at the upper end of Key Stage 2, where teachers struggled to deliver an extensive and increasingly complex curriculum to a sufficient degree. (One head pointed out that in most Year 6 groups there were likely to be some children capable of dealing comfortably with GCSE-level work in specific subjects.)

Pat Hollister, like Gwen Lee, remains ardently committed to promoting a curriculum founded on a thematic or project-based approach to teaching and learning. She says:

> The major part of the curriculum is planned and taught through cross-curricular integrated topic work. While teachers avoid making tortuous links to include all subject areas in their centre of interest, they maximise subject links appropriately, to make teaching and learning meaningful.

Pat expands at length on the educational and philosophical arguments that persuade her and her staff to locate the substance of the children's learning within a thematic structure.

Head teachers are divided by the subject-centred approach versus the thematic approach. The majority are prepared to take account of the argument that children learn in significant ways by making connections, and do not necessarily recognise 'artificial' categories of knowledge in the form of a set of curricular areas. However, not all are convinced that a thematic approach guarantees a coherent, progressive, logically ordered and cognitively challenging curriculum.

Lois Crane (Chapter 4), committed to providing a broad curriculum, attaches particular importance to ICT and its transforming impact on children's learning. Children, she says, are heavily influenced by the media revolution and that has implications for the way in which learning is delivered.

MONITORING, EVALUATION AND ASSESSMENT

The heads are clear that teaching and learning can no longer be considered separate from assessment, monitoring and evaluation, which, rigorously and effectively applied, have become essential elements, underpinning successful practice, enhancing pupil under-standing and raising pupil attainment. If teachers are to provide effectively for continuing progress and achievement they have to be minutely informed about the stages of pupils' learning. Data from systematic tracking and assessment is essential, as it provides critical feedback and commentary, for both teachers and pupils.

Gwen Lee, referring to her responsibility as a deputy for dealing with the assessment and pupil tracking systems, says:

> *This was commonplace for my generation, accepted as something that needed to be done and done properly, in a way that wasn't readily acknowledged by teachers who had flourished in the systems and approaches of the seventies. There was a definite need for rigour, for not allowing children to slip through the gaps.*

Claire Robinson sees assessment as an essential element in realising the school vision and mission.

> *I monitor regularly; coordinators monitor subject responsibilities; we do paired monitoring, matching and evaluating our judgements. I do 'learning walks' with coordinators and teacher leaders, taking a 'helicopter view' of aspects of teaching, learning, curriculum implementation, the learning environment and other aspects of our practice, and their particular responsibilities.*

Lois Crane regards the access, analysis and interpretation of data as a key leadership com-petence. The school runs intervention programmes for pupils who fall below expected levels. Teaching assistants, responsible for the management of the programmes, are trained to track progress, to analyse outcomes and to report developments to the head. In her work with struggling schools as a National Leader of Education, she inaugurates systems for monitoring and evaluation, for lesson observation and feedback and for effective pupil assessment and tracking.

Maxine Evans, describing a particular monitoring and assessment process in her school, argues that an essential part of headship is to implement and maintain monitoring and tracking systems, to gather data about children's attainment and progress.

Andrew Carter sees the school as 'a working machine, where we are constantly reviewing what we are doing in terms of our teaching, and its impact on the children's learning. We have a system in place to ensure that it is more than a pious aspiration ... Monitoring, evaluation (and celebration) of teachers' work forms part of the timetable for the head teacher, deputy, senior teachers and subject leaders.'

Every teacher is observed each week by a senior teacher or another member of staff qualified to evaluate that particular lesson. This is followed soon after by a discussion/ review of what took place, followed by a note from the observer highlighting effectiveness and areas for development. Occasionally the discussions are joined by colleagues such as the head or deputy, 'to raise the occasional helpful question, to clarify anything unclear or simply to listen and learn'.

> Each child's progress is meticulously tracked and monitored, and personalised provision ensures they achieve to the limit of their ability.

> Every teacher receives a statistical analysis of their class. We train them to understand what it is telling them about individuals, and we work with them to devise courses of action that will meet individuals' particular learning needs.

Suzanne Alexander-Sowa extends reflection and evaluation to a wider context.

> My experience of discussing and auditing teaching and learning has encouraged me to take the process further. I discuss with selected groups of children different aspects of our provision. So, for example, I have explored with children how we can improve provision for them and enlarge the learning challenge we provide.

CONTINUING PROFESSIONAL DEVELOPMENT

All heads insist that staff are the most important resource of all. Claire Robinson suggests that the head's visions and lofty dreams come to nothing without the staff to see them through. Lois Crane sees her major responsibility as 'getting the best from them and deploying them most effectively'. Maxine Evans says that investment in resources is likely to be negated unless the right people are appointed and their talents are identified and developed. Even though her school building was dilapidated, that was of less account. What really mattered was that the teaching in classrooms was 'vital, alive and exhilarating'.

The approaches and strategies for continuing professional development (CPD) advocated by the heads include:

- Training based on partnership teaching in the classroom for as long as necessary – underpinned by practical advice from skilled and experienced staff. Some argue that head teachers have to be able and willing to demonstrate expertise.

- Involving all staff, teachers and learning assistants, no matter how experienced and whatever their status, in collaborative practice and exchange about the business of teaching and learning.

- Maintaining a dialogue – professional conversation, questioning and enquiry – that keeps teachers reflective and self-critical.

- Being intolerant of what is manifestly not working or not good enough.

- Implementing processes for systematic lesson observation, evaluation and feedback.

- Constantly reviewing the impact of teaching on children's learning.

- Having a weekly observation of every teacher by a senior member of staff or a colleague qualified to evaluate the particular subject or area of learning involved, followed by a discussion of outcomes, effectiveness and areas for development.

This kind of teacher evaluation is not merely a radical departure from the laissez-faire approaches of yesteryear, but a highly professional process whereby teachers are steadily progressing in terms of awareness and competence. The evaluation systems vary in complexity from school to school, but every teacher has become accustomed to having their practice and planning regularly surveyed, analysed and evaluated against criteria which establish the degree to which pupils' learning is progressing. Evaluation also identifies strengths and potential areas for improvement, indicating factors that might impede advancement and how these might be dealt with.

All heads see training staff to assume positions of leadership as an increasingly important part of their CPD. In one school, all staff are trained to lead and manage from an early stage in their careers as part of teams charged with carrying out specific tasks. For Lois Crane, semantics are important; she deliberately refers to staff in charge of teams as the leader, as this implies status, responsibility, authority and trust. The experience of heading up tasks, however minor, leads to increasingly skilled and confident leaders.

Leaders throughout the school are bound together by a system of performance monitoring and observation that makes clear their interdependence and mutual accountability.

In Gwen Lee's school, leadership is developed through the work of curriculum coordinators, who are designated lead subject teachers for the local authority in core subjects. They produce supportive guidelines and materials for all staff, engage in team teaching with colleagues and implement training schedules for teaching assistants and support staff.

A school cannot afford to ignore expertise wherever it is to be found. Gwen tells how a parent who started helping voluntarily with ICT became a teaching assistant, and was then trained to become the specialist ICT teacher. Another non-professional, gifted in art and design, was trained and supported to lead on the subject throughout the school. The individuals in both of these cases represent a model of leadership in the senior management team, which they in turn replicate for colleagues.

Andrew Carter, head teacher in a large school where leadership and management responsibility is carefully distributed across a network, says that they seek 'to breed leaders at a younger and younger stage'. A first-year teacher, identified as a future leader, will have a purpose-built graduated training programme, supported by senior colleagues through regular observation, mentoring and coaching.

John Foley, describing the process of distributed leadership and management in his school, says that staff learn from an early stage about leadership and are trained in its practice. The senior management team spend much time in practical support, training and development of staff, including shared planning, monitoring and observation. They work alongside them in classrooms and evaluate achievement. The resource implication of this means that three senior staff are freed of all class responsibility to enable them to fulfil this particular leadership function across allocated year groups; practical support and backup are provided by the head teacher.

Maxine Evans, who inherited a flat leadership and management structure, sees this as a fatal deficiency for a school. An organisation lacking an assigned deputy head teacher role depends solely on the energy and wisdom of a single individual to keep everything going. This eventually results in a kind of paralysis and an inability to be self-reflective or to formulate a corporate vision or plan for the future. The irony of such situations is that invariably there are people within the organisation who are capable of exercising transforming leadership. If ignored, their qualities and inherent skills will atrophy and their enthusiasm will wane.

Maxine noted that, when she restructured the school, she found that it was younger staff who, shielded from the need for decision-making or independent action, chose to move school, rather than become involved in the challenge of leadership and management.

Her review identified highly capable established staff who had hitherto worked quietly and had managed to minimise the negative consequences of an inadequate organisational structure. Now they could contribute their talents to the new structure.

ENVIRONMENT AND RESOURCES

All the heads understand the need for having the best learning environment and resources available. They are at great pains to construct environments that stimulate intellect and imagination, encouraging enquiry, investigation and exploration. Resources are provided for the widest possible range of cognitive and sensory experiences, including state-of-the-art technology relevant to all the subjects and areas of learning.

Claire Robinson argues:

> *Some of the problems I inherited with the school were attributable to a down-at-heel and depressed environment. Create an environment that children and teachers can be proud of and they will take it, add to it and cherish it, and, in the process, enhance their teaching and learning.*

But she insists:

> *It would be a mistake to delude ourselves that the making of the environment is sufficient. It is using it creatively, as a kind of machine for learning, that matters.*

Suzanne Alexander-Sowa says that 'if children are to develop a sense of awe and wonder, it is vital they are surrounded by a beautiful, appealing environment.' Outside, there are attractive seating and planting areas, which encourage every class to grow vegetables, flowers and shrubs. There is an outdoor classroom which can accommodate a full class of children, and a prayer garden used by both groups and individuals.

> *We are seeking to extend the classroom, the teaching and learning, to the outside. In the process we have become accomplished at making creative use of every space, however small.*

For Maxine Evans, the resourcing of specific curriculum areas – music, ICT and modern languages – are a particular priority. 'We believe it is essential that children engage in the language and the culture of others in the contemporary world; the ability to talk another language is transformative.'

Music was a decisive influence in my personal development, so it would be natural for me to create a special place for it in the school. Music can be expensive, especially as children become more accomplished and need the often sophisticated resources to maintain progress. That is beyond the reach of many parents so we have to do what we can.

Given her background in a computer software company, she also places great importance on ICT and the children are highly competent in using it; this has made them independent learners.

Andrew Carter's school puts extraordinary emphasis on the learning environment. The school is renowned for the range and richness of its resources, for the physical transformation of the building over ten years, and for the opulent extensions dedicated to the children's learning.

For him, teachers are his prime resource (the annual salary bill for staff is over a million pounds). He says:

If you are going to get value for expenditure of that nature on staff, if you are going to make that million pounds work for you, then you need to provide staff with the resources to do their business to the absolute limit. You can't have high expectations of teachers unless you provide them with the means to realise those expectations.

Now the difference in financial expenditure between a well-equipped school and a poorly-equipped school is probably between ten and twenty thousand pounds, and if you're going to be mealy-mouthed and defeatist about that kind of money in the context of total expenditure, then you'd do better not to start.

He tells staff he wants them to dream dreams: 'When teachers talked about their dreams of people being able to dance and engage in the fitness business, we realised that we needed a dance studio. So we built one. We needed half a million pounds for that!'

They use a wide range of strategies to raise this level of finance and every penny is fed back into the school for the benefit of the children. Whilst Andrew Carter is an example of exceptional environmental enhancement and resource investment, the following forms of provision were commonplace in all the schools in the study:

- Interactive, informative and stimulating displays of children's work.

- A comprehensive range of EAL and EFL resources.

- Richly equipped ICT suites.

- Formal and regular engagement with external educational sources such as The Forest School.

- Rooms dedicated to the provision of a comprehensive range of teaching and learning resources.

- Purpose-built teacher workrooms/laboratories.

- Every classroom and teaching area furnished with state-of-the-art whiteboards, laptops and tablets.

- Minibuses for educational expeditions.

- External learning environment comprising outdoor classrooms, nature areas and a range of gardening activities.

- Strong support for teaching and learning in music.

- Extensive provision for the teaching of Modern Foreign Languages, including additional specialist teaching support secured, in some cases, through contact with embassies.

Despite all the sophisticated material resources they provide and the elegance and richness of the environments they create, heads state that their staff are the most important and potentially valuable resource available to them. As Andrew Carter insists:

Unless you get the people right and you make the right investment there, and you spot, nurture and develop their talents, you could waste a whole host of money, investing in other things and other resources.

LINKS WITH THE LARGER WORLD OUTSIDE SCHOOL

Heads are obliged to establish close links and maintain effective working partnerships with the growing network of agencies and groups external to the school. However, there is less of a consensus about which links and relationships are essential. Some are wary of outside engagements that would involve their absence from their own school and which might reduce the time and commitment that effective leadership demands. Others formally initiate external connections and attachments and engage in business and commercial enterprises.

Claire Robinson describes her formal external relationships as a mixture of entrepreneurial and purely educational. Like some of her fellow heads, she holds that schools increasingly need to add an entrepreneurial dimension to their life and work; that the business of schools must not be exclusively with children but involve the marketplace, even to the extent of advertising and promoting their schools.

All heads agreed that there is an urgent need to attract significant additional finances because any enhanced school environment will inevitably require extra funding.

Gwen Lee reluctantly agrees with the need to be entrepreneurial but does not think it is the best use of her time. She claims that if she had a secondary-type budget, she would be able to 'reduce the size of groups, take the children off and do all kinds of interesting and worthwhile things. There is such a rich environment nearby; just think of the museums alone that we could use if we had more resources in terms of personnel and money.'

Maxine Evans's school is a provider of high-level teacher assistant training for a group of local authorities. Her training team, comprising members of staff and outside specialists, provides the workforce-remodelling training programme for their own local authority. Through consultation and advisory work, she supports two schools in Special Measures. Such initiatives offer professional and material benefits to the school. While not disguising the associated difficulties and challenges, she sees a valid and productive sphere of professional operation being created in an 'open market' for schools, something that would be professionally valuable for all concerned.

Andrew Carter sees a key relationship between school, society and the wider world. He envisages the school at the centre of society, nationally and locally, as an organisation that serves and contributes to the wider community beyond its own catchment area. At one time he offered to take over a nearby failing school and run it in tandem with his own, as there was no question of standing by and seeing another school fail. His conscience dictates that one goes not only to the aid of colleagues, but seeks to intervene positively in the interests of children who are not receiving the education to which they are entitled.

Lois Crane is a National Leader of Education with an obligation to support struggling schools on a one-day-a-week basis. This includes working with heads and senior staff to provide guidance on the implementation of systems for monitoring and evaluation, lesson observation and feedback, and effective pupil assessment and tracking.

Consequently, some of her own staff have benefited from working in partner schools, bringing their own particular curricular expertise and experience of management and teaching to the improvement and development programmes. Her staff are also involved with other schools in 'needy circumstances', acting as role models for visiting teachers and providing learning materials for their use. Her curriculum leaders, especially in the core subjects, spend time in the schools helping colleagues in a hands-on way. Lois believes that such experience not only enhances teachers' leadership and management skills, but provides for 'succession planning'.

Claire Robinson works as a School Improvement Partner (SIP) with eight primary schools, with all the financial returns fed back into the school for educational extension and enrichment.

Beyond these commercial and outreach activities, she also extends the notion of service to a wider community. She once donated an outstanding teacher to a 'competitor' school confronted with a staffing crisis. She says:

> Only by a genuine coming together can we heal and improve society for the sake of our children. Our relationships with the world outside must have a spiritual dimension to them.

Suzanne Alexander-Sowa sees the benefits of having her children participate in worthwhile external projects. Currently the older children are involved in a project with ICI, working with their scientists and gaining insight into an industry closely linked to education. She involves herself with external matters, claiming it 'helps me keep my professional edge'. However, she is not interested in 'high status networks':

> That is a deliberate choice. I don't attend many meetings. I look very carefully at how I spend my time ... I am not remotely interested in local politics and manoeuvring ... in all those extraneous things that get in the way of effective leadership.

Gwen Lee and her staff have educational links with the outside world. Teachers are released to teach in a French school for a fortnight for immersion purposes, with their French counterparts returning to observe English teaching. Other members of staff, sponsored by the British Council, travel abroad to explore creative teaching.

RELATIONSHIPS WITH PARENTS

Heads rarely think of parents in the context of external relationships, and regard such a categorisation as inappropriate and impersonal. Without exception, they believe that the involvement, cooperation, understanding and goodwill of parents are essential to the success of their work.

The onus on schools is to facilitate the parents' involvement in their children's education. Generally, parental response is positive, but such complex relationships can raise challenges and difficulties, whatever the environment or the socio-economic circumstances. These head teachers have acquired deep insight and formidable expertise, refined through hard-earned and sometimes daunting and dispiriting experience. Whatever the circumstances, their commitment to the concept of partnership remains unshaken.

Maxine Evans believes it is imperative for schools to establish an unequivocal contract with parents about the nature of their mutual responsibility for the welfare of children and precisely how that should work in practice. Parents should be clear about how they should behave in their dealings with schools, and schools and parents should be united in modelling for children the behaviour expected of them.

Lois Crane believes strongly in the importance of partnership, and the necessity for effective communication with parents about the school's day-to-day education of their children. She sees an overarching need to have high expectations, an understanding of what can be achieved, and a determination to make it happen.

Suzanne Alexander-Sowa regards parents as the main stakeholders in the life, business and work of the school, who must be brought on board and enabled to see and understand the inside picture. However, her experience in dealing with the diversity of people encountered as the leader of a school taught her that heads have to relate to people 'burdened with their own particular frailties and flawed dispositions', including those rare parents who are intimidating or even violent. She sees the building of a successful partnership with parents as a constant endeavour and never an easy option. From a practical perspective, she invites parents to observe at first hand the children engaged in the daily routine of work, as this provides a vivid insight into what they are learning and achieving.

The inner-city head teacher Gwen Lee is convinced that parents have a much bigger impact on their children's progress than schools can have. Having worked with her predecessor to build a school that would be a centre of excellence at the heart of its community, it has become a haven for families, a high proportion of them severely disadvantaged in socio-economic terms. Many have escaped from oppressive regimes and are struggling to create new lives in an alien and challenging culture. For them the school is a meeting place; a source of advice, support and encouragement, where their identity is respected and valued and their culture celebrated.

Chris Wheatley also believes that parental engagement is the biggest determinant in children's development and education. He says, 'In a community where parental expectations of what schools can provide have been limited, it has been essential for us to alter their perceptions for the better, to empower parents in supporting their children and to give them a genuine voice in the life of the school.'

Andrew Carter goes to remarkable lengths to promote school-parent partnership. He makes this offer to parents: 'This school and your children and our work for them matters so deeply that there is nothing we will not do, and no trouble too great for us, to ensure what is best for them.' He trains his staff to practise 'drawing parents in' and to learn that 'the parents are our first allies'. For him and his staff, 'just as there are no problem children, so there are no problem parents!'

ACCOUNTABILITY

Accountability is a transforming force in the development of the contemporary primary school. It underpins collegiality – the notion of shared responsibility for the life and welfare of the whole school community, staff and pupils. It fosters mutual support; it means, as one head put it, an end to professional isolation, to concealment, to 'secret gardens and solo operations'. It creates the belief that shared corporate knowledge and skill, insight and imagination are irresistible forces for individual and collective professional development and, through that, for institutional effectiveness and achievement.

Accountability is multi-faceted; it involves teachers, pupils, parents, governors, the wider community, external agents officially involved in the work and business of the school, legitimate stakeholders in the welfare of the children and, not least, central government. Heads were largely agreed as to whom their personal accountability was owed and to what degree. They accepted, though not always uncritically, that there were bodies to whom they were formally answerable by virtue of legislation.

Gwen Lee sees accountability as far from straightforward. 'Being accountable is easily dealt with while a school is doing well.' Her school has a very high mobility rate and this inevitably affects the outcome of the Year 6 SATs, given that many of the children will have only been at the school for a few weeks before being tested.

Historically, the main line of accountability for head teachers for the proper management of their schools has been through their governing body to the local education authority. Head teachers would have regarded themselves, in a sense, as agents of the authority and therefore answerable to it.

Education reform changed that situation to a significant extent and, with it, head teachers' perceptions of that relationship. While they continue to be accountable in terms of school performance, achievement, quality of education and the general welfare of children, there is significantly less unequivocal response to local authority dictate or the perceived need for their intervention and advice.

Many head teachers are now invested with growing autonomy over the critical areas of financial management, curriculum, staff recruitment, management and development and INSET provision. As a result, they see themselves as significantly more suited to the total management of their schools rather than officers increasingly remote from the complexities and challenges of contemporary primary education.

In some cases local authorities are transferring many important powers and control of implicated finance to federations of schools. Even so, local authorities remain responsible to central government for the monitoring and evaluation of school performance, as measured by national standardised testing and the outcomes of inspection, and, so far as their resources allow, for intervention in the case of underachieving institutions. Therefore, in a technical sense, schools remain accountable for performance to the local authority, acting as agents of central government. It is perhaps here, in recent years, that the greatest shift has taken place, in the accountability of heads and their schools, with the radical shaping and extension of the role, responsibility and power of governing bodies.

Empowered by law 'as strategic leaders of schools',[1] their purpose, legally defined, is 'to conduct the school with a view to promoting high standards of educational achievement'.

Governing bodies are required to have a strong focus on three core strategic functions:

1. Ensuring clarity of vision, ethos and strategic direction;
2. Holding the head teacher to account for the educational performance of the school and its pupils; and
3. Overseeing the financial performance of the school and making sure its money is well-spent.

These functions resonate with Ofsted's criteria for the evaluation of effective governance of schools and academies. Inspections expect governors to know about the strengths and weaknesses of the school; to understand the school's performance data, in relation to local and national outcomes; and ensure that the head teacher and the staff are working to ensure that all children are achieving their best.

The contribution of governors to the school is evaluated as part of the judgement on leadership and management. It is possible to believe that, in some cases, head teachers

---

[1]   The Education Act 2002.

and indeed governing bodies themselves are still coming to an understanding of the extent and significance of these developments and the implications inherent in them for accountability.

Whilst stressing unquestioning acceptance of accountability to her governors, and her efforts to ensure they were constantly and fully informed, Claire Robinson made it clear that the process was very time-consuming and not always productive. She found her governors supportive at their best, but the relationship was not always as productive as it might have been, or easy to manage.

Gwen Lee did not see the point or purpose of governors, although admitted that hers were supportive. She felt that governors by and large had neither the knowledge nor the time to be really useful to heads, who, in turn, had to spend a disproportionate amount of time simply keeping them informed. She found that they tended to be 'a waste of energy'.

Suzanne Alexander-Sowa regards the relationship between head teacher and chair of governors as of high importance to the successful leadership of a school, with the chair in the role of critical friend and trusted confidante – a state of affairs she enjoys in her current situation. However, she made the caveat that it was purely fortuitous and some-thing that she knew from experience could change radically with the appointment of a new chair, sometimes with negative consequences. Few institutions, she said, could be expected to prosper and develop in an assured and confident way in such unpredictable circumstances.

A couple of heads gave the impression of having a carefully managed relationship with their governing body, scrupulously observing and discharging their statutory duty to be accountable, keeping the governors informed and punctiliously seeking approval for initiatives and developments. It seemed that the governors, satisfied as long as legis-lative requirements were discharged, then allowed them a measure of independence amounting to autonomy so far as decision-making and action were concerned. There was a sense of role reversal in such cases, with experienced, accomplished and successful heads managing compliant or less assured governors.

The most positive comment about the relationship came from Andrew Carter, who regarded his governing body as a very strong, able, informed and committed group of people, deeply involved in the direction and evaluation of the school. The school, he said, is constantly open to them; they are comprehensively informed about all its work and business and he regards himself as wholly accountable and transparent in all his dealings with them. They are meaningfully and creatively involved in the life of the school and in the making of policy. He believes that a genuine and powerful partnership has been forged between the school and the governing body in the best interests of the children, staff and the wider community.

In the final analysis, without exception, the head teachers declared themselves accountable, above everything, to and for the children for whom they are responsible.

Educational reform has transformed the nature of accountability demanded of schools today.

The following were instrumental in bringing about these changes:

- A greatly enlarged focus on special educational needs and the nature and extent of children's potential for learning and attainment.
- The drive for equal opportunities and the rights of individuals.
- The increased emphasis on inclusion.
- The creation of a national curriculum available to all children, backed by standardised testing that identifies individual attainment and progression.
- The schools' obligation to provide all parents with detailed and accurate information about the whole education and curriculum available to their child, their total welfare while in the care of the school and their attainment and progress at every major stage of their statutory schooling.

John Foley poignantly describes the transformation that has occurred over the period of his professional experience in relation to accountability. Recalling the despair he had felt as a young teacher at prevailing attitudes towards children 'who sat at the back and were perceived as probably uneducable', he reflects on the advances made in education and the fact that it would now be inconceivable for schools to regard any effort on behalf of children as futile or wasted or not to believe that 'every child matters and has within them the capacity to learn and do things that will delight us all'.

CHAPTER FOURTEEN

CONCLUSION

The purpose of this book has been to describe high quality headship and notable leadership in primary schools, largely by reference to, and in the words of, individual head teachers.

In their individual chapters, they have delineated the elements that characterise such leadership. Among them are:

- forward-looking and inspirational vision;

- innovative curricular design and provision;

- effective management of teaching and learning, which enriches and transforms the pupils' education in cognitive, spiritual, moral and physical terms;

- the creative professional development of staff; and

- the making of strong partnerships with parents, carers and the wider community.

The schools which these head teachers lead are places where children achieve and attain in accordance with their potential, and where their progress is meticulously evaluated and nurtured.

But there are further dimensions to the head teachers' work that go beyond these criteria, which we need to take account. These are qualities and abilities that are not easily encompassed in a body of quantifiable criteria, however concise, informative, comprehensive and eloquently articulated. They are rare human attributes that enable those possessed of them to turn vision into reality, sometimes in the face of the most adverse circumstances.

When teachers find themselves for the first time in sole control and with total responsibility for the leadership of a school, they are entering a domain that tests and challenges them in ways for which the most carefully ordered training cannot wholly prepare them. It is then that outstanding heads and leaders call various qualities and resources into play – mental, psychological, intellectual, physical and moral. Not least of these is the kind of courage, self-belief, determination and tenacity, amounting to doggedness, that enables outstanding heads to persevere, especially in the early days of their office, in circumstances which are not of their own making. The following qualities distinguished these heads in their work and practice:

- They are sharply aware of what they perceive to be the growing complexity and intractable nature of the role, one that demands mastery of a diverse range of knowledge, insight, understanding and competences.

- They recognise by reflecting on personal experience the extent to which education is changing and developing in line with educational reform, away from the cult of the charismatic hero head and personal agendas to infinitely more subtle and complex forms of leadership. Just as importantly, they understand the reasons for the change.

- They are, without exception, highly intelligent and sharply analytical, with the capacity to evaluate and understand the significance of information and data; they are able to weigh up an argument and separate what is important from what is less consequential. This is especially evident in their command of the inordinate quantity of written communication and directive to which they are subjected, and their ability to manage it and relate it to what they judge to be in the interests of their school and children.

- They are independent thinkers, wary of official dictat, sceptical of fashion and novelty but open-minded, seeking and receptive of good counsel, and flexible and adaptable to changing circumstances and developments.

- They learn from their experience; they are objective and dispassionate in identifying and recognising their mistakes and misjudgements, in determining cause and effect and in building safeguards against repetition.

- They are self-aware, thoughtful, reflective and introspective, conscious of their capabilities and their particular gifts and abilities. At the same time, they are clear about the areas of their work and activity that would be reinforced by authoritative support, informed guidance and professional partnership. This is reflected in their readiness to investigate and study innovation and development elsewhere, and to seek out and draw on the support and advice of others.

- They exhibit, without exception, notable strength of character, mental and physical resilience, moral courage and unflagging perseverance. They command deep inner resources that sustain them in their ultimately lonely and challenging position.

- All remain dedicated teachers at heart, regularly finding time from demanding schedules to work in classrooms alongside their staff. They do so to emphasise the centrality of teaching and learning, and to provide support, encouragement and inspiration to their teachers. This does the following:

- Offers a model of good practice
- Keeps them aware of what is happening in terms of the realisation of the school's purposes, goals and targets
- Adds to the range of qualified staff available to pupils
- Satisfies, to some extent, an unquenched yearning to be doing again what had first taken them into the profession. As one of them put it rather wistfully, 'Perhaps I shall finish up teaching in the end, after all.'

- They are people of high moral courage and integrity. Their leadership, their behaviour, the decisions they make, the policies they drive through, are unfalteringly determined by impeccable codes and principles that are explicit to all. They steadfastly adhere to the right way to do things and unfailingly reject the easy option.

- They are driven people with a consuming belief in the value and importance of their work. They are ready to sacrifice themselves without question or reservation in carrying through what they believe is a sacred trust. One head, when asked how she manages the extraordinary programme of activity over which she presides, replied, 'If necessary, I sometimes stay up until two o'clock in the morning.'

- Their humanity and optimism, their compassion and belief in others, their conviction that there is always a better state to strive for, and their readiness to sacrifice themselves for that, shines through everything they do.

In my interviews with the head teachers I was privileged to hear the unvarnished truth covering the range of issues that engage, often opaquely and turbulently, the profession today. However, it is clear from a reading of the viewpoints in their chapters that they would be equally forthright in public in expressing the truth of things, as they see them, affecting the profession and the children in their care, even where this is likely to conflict with political nicety and current conventional thinking.

An example of this is the readiness of some to challenge the belief that heads can easily become part of a collaboratively working team, while at the same time enacting a judgemental and corrective role that demands improved responses within the context of implied sanctions. Again, some question the widely propagated belief that all staff are willing, by nature and inclination, to respond positively to criticism, with the intent to improve poor performance. Such views seem to be expressed not out of disillusionment or rancour, but from long experience and a determination to tell things as they are.

Each head had particular experiences that were influential in their personal and professional development, and instrumental in establishing vital principles and beliefs that guide their practice.

For almost all of them, these were the most decisive factors in their later developments and adult lives: their homes; their early experiences; their relationship with their parents; the nature of the support and encouragement they received; the values, examples and role models to which they were exposed; and the aspirations and expectations that were entertained for them.

As a result, without exception, they believe that genuine and creative partnerships with parents and families are indispensable, if schools are to educate children effectively and successfully and enable them to achieve their potential. At the same time they have no illusions about the magnitude of the task.

They do not accept the notion that parents represent a homogeneous constituency, eagerly anticipating being in partnership. Whilst a majority fit that description and are supportive of schools' work on their children's behalf, in some cases head teachers strive against negative attitudes, ranging from apathy and indifference to adversarial stances and occasional incidents of hostility. Some head teachers were familiar with verbal abuse, and even threats of physical violence. One head teacher recalls being shocked by some parents' neglect of their children's welfare. Another regarded a major challenge, and one that schools could not ignore, as the need to support partnerless mothers struggling to bring up a family; mothers whose unrealistic and even threatening demands they felt obliged to accede to. But to these head teachers, so strongly committed to the challenge, such difficulties seem more an impetus than an impediment.

The head teachers see the part played by schools (and often by particular teachers) as vitally influencing the children's lives and development. They would argue that, for many children, having gifted teachers in an enriched school context, providing memorable learning experiences, is more likely to produce enduring and worthwhile consequences than having excessive testing, unremitting evaluation, and a narrowly focused curriculum. For one head teacher, the schools and her teachers were the transforming influence, 'the door to another world'. For another, the dedication, generosity and enthusiasm of a secondary school teacher who went to remarkable lengths to broaden the horizons of pupils remain a source of admiration and inspiration to this day.

Whilst their childhood and school experience remains a remarkably potent influence, what most powerfully shapes them as heads and influences the directions in which they lead their schools, is the entirety of their professional careers and the experience and models of practice and leadership they have encountered in the process. Such models are remarkably diverse in nature and conspicuously divergent in quality.

On one hand there are those progressive, informed and creative head teachers whose practice and outstanding work provided positive inspiration. Then there were those at the other extreme, from whom, as one head teacher put it, one learned largely from negative experience; from observation of the frailties, uncertainties and shortcomings of others.

Some speak of the complacent and unchallenging headship that allowed teachers to go their own way, bereft of evaluative, instructional or directive leadership; of staff left largely in isolation, their professional development neglected, their best work unseen and lost to the benefit of the wider school; of short-term headship and deputy-headship appointments, leading inevitably to flawed and incoherent leadership and crisis-driven management, a situation not uncommon in the laissez-faire and minimally regulated era prior to the major education reforms of recent decades.

Such disparities between forms of leadership, make even more remarkable the advances to excellence made in primary education, in the space of a couple of decades. The extent of these advances must be largely attributable to the quality of contemporary leaders. These accounts of outstanding leadership, in this book, are offered as a source of guidance, and hopefully an encouragement to those who seek to develop their own leadership qualities and their own unique leadership style.

There seems little doubt that their achievement has been made at considerable personal cost. One sensed that, for much of the time, their lives were consumed by their calling. Some talked of dimensions to their existence beyond work, and clearly some of the ideals that sustain them must come from an enriched life outside of school. But one is left at the end with a conviction that much may have gone by the board, or been sacrificed, in the interests of that vocation. It might not be too much to say that they give their lives to it and for it.

One of the head teachers provides us with a motif that reflects the inspiring influence of great teachers and leaders, remembered down the years. It is something she says to teachers, especially those new to the profession: 'The children you teach will make you immortal. They'll talk of you a generation hence.'

BIBLIOGRAPHY

Alexander, R. et al. (2010). *Children, their World, their Education: final report and recommendations of the Cambridge Primary Review.* London: Routledge.

Brighouse, T. and Woods, D. (2008). *What Makes a Good School Now?* London: Bloomsbury.

Coleman, M. and Earley, P. (2005). *Leadership and Management in Education: Cultures, Change and Context.* Oxford: Oxford University Press.

Davies, B. (ed.) (2009). *The Essentials of School Leadership.* London: Sage.

Davies, B. and Brighouse, T. (2008). *Passionate Leadership in Education.* London: Sage.

Department for Education and Skills (DfES) (2004). National Standards for Headteachers. Ref: DFES-0083-2004. Available at: https://www.education.gov.uk/publications/standard/ publicationDetail/Page1/DFES-0083-2004 (accessed 17 December 2013).

Earley, P., et al. (2012). *Review of the school leadership landscape.* Nottingham: National College for School Leadership.

Fink, D. (2004). 'Developing leaders for their future, not our past' in M. Coles and G. Southworth (eds), *Developing Leadership: Creating the Schools of Tomorrow.* Maidenhead: Open University Press.

Hargreaves, A. and Fullan, M. (2012) *Professional capital: transforming teaching in every school.* New York: Teachers' College.

Hayden, M. and Thompson, J. (2012) *Taking the IPC Forward: Engaging with the International Primary Curriculum.* Suffolk: John Catt.

Leithwood, K., Day, C., Sammons, P., Harris, A. and Hopkins, D. (2006). *Seven Strong Claims about Successful School Leadership.* London: DfES.

Lewis, P. and Murphy, R. (2008). New directions in school leadership. *School Leadership and Management* 28(2), 127–146. London: Routledge.

Mahoney, T. (2004). *Principled Headship: A Teacher's Guide to the Galaxy.* Carmarthen: Crown House Publishing.

Ofsted (2003). Leadership and Management: Managing the School Workforce. Ofsted Ref: 2048. Available at: http://www.ofsted.gov.uk/resources/leadership-and-management-managing-school-workforce (accessed 17 December 2013).

Ofsted (2014). Framework for School Inspection. Ref: 120100. Available at: http://www.ofsted.gov.uk/resources/framework-for-school-inspection www.ofsted.gov.uk/resources/framework-for-school-inspection (accessed 13 January 2014).

Penlington, C., Kington, A. and Day, C. (2008). 'Leadership in improving schools: a qualitative perspective'. School Leadership and Management 28(1), 65–82.

Rose, J. (2009). Independent Review of the Primary Curriculum: Final Report [Rose Review]. Ref: DCSF-00499-2009. Available at: https://www.education.gov.uk/publications/standard/AbouttheDepartment/Page3/DCSF-00499-2009 (accessed 17 December 2013).

Smith, A., Lovatt, M., Wise, D. and Baiton, J. (2003) *Accelerated Learning: A User's Guide*. UK: Network Educational Press.

Southworth, G. (2013) Primary School Leadership in Context: Leading Small, Medium and Large Sized Schools. London: Routledge.